"Anyone who has ever believed in meritocracy – that being good enough, working hard enough, and persevering long enough would be enough – should read *The Dark Side of Academia*. This powerful book exposes academia's underbelly and makes a compelling case for confronting toxic cultures head-on."

Dr Jennifer Leigh, *University of Kent*

"Like the dark side of the moon, academia hides shadows few dare to illuminate. Professor Brewer's *The Dark Side of Academia* bravely exposes the systemic barriers so many marginalised colleagues face daily. Honest, unsettling, and empowering, this book gives voice to the silenced and demands change within the ivory tower."

Dr Hamied Haroon, *Chair, National Association of Disabled Staff Networks (NADSN)*

"This is an essential read for anyone who wants to understand wellbeing in higher education. Professor Brewer's book provides important insights into the challenges of working in a university and the impact of the numerous policies, metrics, and economic factors we face as a sector."

Dr Sue Wilbraham, *University of Cumbria*

"Professor Brewer critically examines the dark side of academia through consideration of the challenges facing the profession. With particular emphasis on the experiences of marginalised staff and students and recommendations for positive change, this is a must-read for all in higher education."

Dr Faye Skelton, *Edinburgh Napier University*

The Dark Side of Academia

The Dark Side of Academia provides an insight into the prevalence, form, and impact of harmful practices within academia. By combining contemporary research, practice, and policy, it examines the experience and impact of issues such as precarity, burnout, and violence within higher education.

This key title synthesises expertise on a range of vitally important issues impacting higher education right now. Addressing the experiences of academic employees, it shines a light on the prevalent but often unspoken underbelly of academia. Structured into three main sections, it focuses on key topics such as performance and competition; health, wellbeing, and burnout; precarious contracts; inequality and discrimination; disability; gender and gender identity; race and ethnicity; and bullying and sexual misconduct.

Each chapter includes clear recommendations for policy and practice and is essential reading for all those working in higher education, but particularly those in positions of power. This book is designed to encourage greater attention to the experiences of all staff employed in the sector and to offer implementable strategies to provide better support for academics.

Gayle Brewer is Professor of Psychology and Education at the University of Liverpool, UK. Professor Brewer has worked in higher education for over 20 years, and she informs Equality, Diversity, and Inclusion practice and policy on a national level. Professor Brewer has published over 100 journal articles and holds doctorates in both Psychology and Education.

The Dark Side of Academia

Competition, Inequality, and Violence in the Ivory Tower

Gayle Brewer

LONDON AND NEW YORK

Designed cover image: Getty images

First published 2026
by Routledge
4 Park Square, Milton Park, Abingdon, Oxon OX14 4RN

and by Routledge
605 Third Avenue, New York, NY 10158

Routledge is an imprint of the Taylor & Francis Group, an informa business

British Library Cataloguing-in-Publication Data
A catalogue record for this book is available from the British Library

ISBN: 978-1-032-63931-4 (hbk)
ISBN: 978-1-032-63930-7 (pbk)
ISBN: 978-1-032-63932-1 (ebk)

DOI: 10.4324/9781032639321

Typeset in Galliard
by SPi Technologies India Pvt Ltd (Straive)

This book is dedicated to those who have been marginalized, discriminated against, and excluded from academia and to those working to make higher education safe, accessible, and inclusive. It is also dedicated to my parents, who gave me both a love of education and a will to make a difference.

Contents

Illustrations

Figures

Tables

Acknowledgements

This book provides an overview of the prevalence, experience, and impact of harmful behaviour and cultures in higher education. It could not have been written without the insights provided by those with lived experience and the work (both research and practice) of those striving to challenge structural inequality and violence across higher education. This book is for them.

Introduction

It may surprise readers – given the title of this book – to learn that I love academia. I write this book not because I have fallen out of love with higher education but because I care about the people who are part of it. In this book, I focus on those aspects of academia that negatively impact employee wellbeing and signal to them (either explicitly or implicitly) that they are not welcome; that they do not belong in the ivory tower.

Section 1 provides an overview of the academic environment and the impact of this on employees. First, there is an introduction to the monitoring, competition, and excessive workloads that characterise higher education (Chapter 1), followed by a review of health, wellbeing, and burnout issues across the sector (Chapter 2). The section closes with a discussion of precarious contracts and the experiences of doctoral students and postdoctoral researchers (Chapter 3). Section 2 focuses on representation and inequality with respect to disability, chronic illness, and neurodivergence (Chapter 4); gender, parenting, and sexual orientation (Chapter 5); and race, ethnicity, and culture (Chapter 6). Finally, Section 3 addresses the violence and aggression that exist in academia, outlining first the bullying and incivility that occur (Chapter 7) and, secondly, the prevalence and impact of sexual harassment and violence (Chapter 8). Each chapter includes recommendations for policy and practice, with additional resources provided in Chapter 9.

This book primarily addresses the experiences of academic employees, reflecting both the greater body of research focused on academic staff (compared to those on non-academic contracts) and my own familiarity with the academic role. It is essential to recognise that the issues discussed in this book (e.g., workload pressures, ableism, and sexual harassment) are not restricted to academic staff. Further, academic staff often have greater autonomy, opportunities, and power than their professional services colleagues. For example, academic staff have access to resources (e.g., external funding) to support professional development that are often closed to non-academic employees. The issues discussed in this book also directly or indirectly impact students. For example, students witnessing derogatory comments or discriminatory behaviour from faculty are more likely to exhibit bias (Burke et al., 2017) and

DOI: 10.4324/9781032639321-1

symptoms of mental ill health (Hardeman et al., 2016). In contrast, contact with marginalised academics is associated with engagement with the subject (Rask & Bailey, 2002) and lower student bias (Phelan et al., 2017). It is hoped that this book will encourage greater attention to the experiences of all staff employed in the higher education sector and to the relationship between staff and student experiences.

The Higher Education Sector

The higher education sector has undergone substantial change. In the 1990s, government policy increased the number of students and academic institutions across the United Kingdom. Though rapid expansion might suggest a "golden era" of academia, competition between institutions and scrutiny of higher education providers have also increased. As a consequence, academics can be ranked on many different measures of "quality" or "value" and are under significant pressure (Burrows, 2012). This change in academic practice, policy, and culture is not, of course, restricted to the United Kingdom. Neoliberalism and the negative impact of neoliberalism on staff and students have been discussed with reference to many countries and continents (e.g., Akala, 2021; Austin Henry & Beserra, 2022; Bal, Grassiani, & Kirk, 2014; Berg, Huijbens, & Larsen, 2016; Morgan, 2022; Roper, 2018).

Erickson, Hanna, and Walker (2021) report the results of one survey (n = 5,888) of academic staff, focused on satisfaction with senior managers and university governance. The survey covered a range of subjects, including senior management's impact on students and treatment of staff. Findings indicate widespread dissatisfaction, and the percentage of staff satisfied with how their institution was being managed ranged from 0% to 27% (mean satisfaction 11%). Qualitative responses highlighted areas of particular concern, including the use of metrics, excessive workloads, accountability, constant change, the silencing of academics, and mental health. Comments from survey respondents included, "*The University sector is not in good shape and senior management is never held accountable for this*" (p. 2142), and "*Frankly the context of constant rudderless change and endlessly growing bureaucracy in HE means that they end up exposing us to a process of continuous revolution which erodes staff well-being, rarely benefits students' learning, and undermines grassroots creativity*" (p. 2143). Summarising many concerns, one academic stated, "*The university is in the dark ages. It is a systemically mean spirited place, kept afloat by those dedicated admin and teaching staff who are conscientious*" (p. 2143) (Erickson, Hanna, & Walker, 2021).

Inequality

Though it is important to improve the academic role and environment for all employees, it is essential to recognise that some employees face additional barriers to inclusion and progression. Illustrating this inequality, Cech (2022) discusses the privilege of being a White, non-disabled, heterosexual man in

Science, Technology, Engineering, and Mathematics (STEM). Analysis of survey data from over 25,000 STEM professionals with over 30 intersectional gender, ethnicity, disability, and sexual identity categories indicates stark differences in experience. White, non-disabled, heterosexual men experience more social inclusion, professional respect, and career opportunities than all other groups and receive higher salaries. White, non-disabled, heterosexual men are also less likely to experience harassment at work than all other groups analysed.

Further, research suggests that the "Matthew effect" (Merton, 1968), whereby the "rich get richer", has a significant impact on academic staff progression, with initial status and prestige influencing a range of academic outcomes. For example, those with early career funding success secure twice as much funding in the subsequent eight years as researchers whose funding applications received similar review scores but were not funded (Bol, De Vaan, & Van De Rijt, 2018). Support for early-career academics is therefore required. The negative consequences of the "Matthew effect", disproportionately experienced by those with protected characteristics (e.g., female academics), have been termed the "Matilda effect" (Rossiter, 1993). Indeed, women, those with caring responsibilities, or physical or mental health conditions, may be deemed to contradict notions of the "ideal academic", i.e., staff who are able to dedicate themselves to their career (Bleijenbergh, van Engen, & Vinkenburg, 2013; Sang et al., 2015). This book highlights the extent to which inequality impacts academic experiences.

Structural and systemic inequalities are typically discussed (as occurs in this book) in relation to characteristics protected by legislation (e.g., gender, ethnicity, and disability). Inequality also applies to characteristics such as socioeconomic status that are often less well recognised. Similarly, inequalities can be examined in relation to the discriminatory historical practices that shaped the policies, practices, and institutions that continue to stigmatise, marginalise, and exclude these individuals. This book does not focus on the historical foundation of inequality and instead focuses on contemporary experiences of higher education. Indeed, recent challenges to equality, diversity, and inclusion work (highlighted later in the introduction) illustrate contemporary threats to marginalised academics and allies who support them.

Whilst this book (and the research more broadly) discusses issues of gender, ethnicity, disability, etc. in relative isolation, it is important to recognise the role of intersectionality. For example, Toren (2009) explores the intersection of gender, ethnicity, and social class and the experiences of Mizrachi women (of African or Asian heritage) employed in universities and colleges in Israel. As stated by one participant,

> It is impossible to separate gender, ethnicity and class…As a woman I am not appreciated by male colleagues and always have to prove that I am their professional equal; this is very tiring sometimes. Moreover, my ethnic origin and family background have a denigrating 'added value'.
>
> (Toren, 2009, p. 158)

It is also important to acknowledge that discussing the lived experience of higher education in relation to broad categories such as disability or ethnicity may mask important differences within such groups (Miles et al., 2022). It is hoped that this book will encourage further discussion of these issues and a more nuanced approach to research, policy, and practice.

Equality, Diversity, and Inclusion

Equality, diversity, and inclusion (typically referred to as diversity, equity, and inclusion in North American contexts) initiatives recognise the structural and systemic barriers experienced by particular groups and seek to address this inequality. The themes of identity, justice, empathy, and power are commonly associated with such initiatives. Educational practices intended to promote equality, diversity, and inclusion include unconscious bias training and the introduction of mentoring programmes to support marginalised and under-represented students and staff (Corsino & Fuller, 2021). A broad range of positive outcomes is associated with equality, diversity, and inclusion initiatives, including cognitive development and civic engagement (Bowman, 2010, 2011; Gurin et al., 2002), though such work can be tokenistic or superficial. Hence, Abrica and Andrew (2024) describe such an activity as "*a mechanism by which colleges and universities can appear antiracist or social justice-oriented while obfuscating any meaningful engagement with race, racism, or Whiteness*" (p. 4).

Despite greater academic interest in the diversity of higher education (e.g., Turner, González, & Wood, 2008), this book has been written in an environment increasingly hostile to equality, diversity, and inclusion activity, both in academia and broader society (McGowan et al., 2025). As noted by Schoorman (2024), "*inclusivity is now a dirty word*" (p. 404). Universities have attracted attention (and criticism), in part because academics are perceived to hold liberal beliefs and because of the influence they are believed to exert over their students. Particular criticism has been targeted at initiatives focused on decolonisation of the curriculum and attempts to diversify the recruitment of students and staff. Such subjects frequently form the basis of discussion in the mainstream press. See Shaw (2025) and Harper (2025) for reviews of anti-diversity, equity, and inclusion campaigns and misinformation, and Davies and MacRae (2023) for the British actors, campaign groups, and broadcasters that are especially hostile to equality, diversity, and inclusion movements. It is important to support those engaged in equality, diversity, and inclusion work (disproportionately impacted by such activity) who are often from historically marginalised and excluded groups themselves (Dhanani, Arena, & Bogart, 2024).

In North America, especially, the hostility targeted at equality, diversity, and inclusion activity has had a significant impact on the teaching, research, and wellbeing of marginalised academics. For example, Goldberg (2024) notes that 10% of survey respondents experienced student threats to report them.

Further, the negative impact of this hostile environment occurs even in states where specific legislation has not been passed (Goldberg, 2024). It is important to challenge not only legislation that seeks to prevent equality, diversity, and inclusion initiatives but also the attitudes and beliefs that encourage and legitimise this sentiment (Lange & Lee, 2024). Equality, diversity, and inclusion initiatives are commonly associated with "wokeness", though the latter concept is often poorly defined or misrepresented (Prasad & Śliwa, 2024). "Wokeness" is typically presented as a threat to the integrity of the higher education sector, with particular emphasis on free speech and censorship (Garry, 2023; Ketzl, 2025). Rzepka, Fazlagić, and Ahamed (2023) propose a "diagnostic tool" to assess the extent and impact of "wokeism" within universities. The tool is structured into five core areas (Management, Organizational Culture, Faculty, Curricula, and Students) and "*is intended to weed out the most characteristic manifestations of wokeisim*" (p. 498). Though the authors claim to take a neutral stance on the subject of "wokeism", it is clear that such measures could easily be weaponised against institutions.

Language and Positionality

Language is important. Language can shape the way we think about ourselves, social or cultural groups, and specific issues (Entman, 2007; Kelly, Dow, & Westerhoff, 2010). The language that is used and recommended also evolves, especially in areas associated with equality, diversity, and inclusion (Andrews, Powell, & Ayers, 2022). For example, terms such as "queer", "mad", and "crip" have been reclaimed by the communities initially attacked with those words. Whilst a full discussion of equality, diversity, and inclusion language is beyond the scope of this book, I wish to clarify my rationale for the language adopted in three core areas. I recognise, however, that as language continues to develop, accepted terminology (and my own use of language) will further change. Therefore, the language used throughout the book represents current practice and has the potential to become outdated.

Firstly, I adopt the term "equality, diversity, and inclusion" throughout this book, consistent with common practice in the United Kingdom and related legislation. There is, however, substantial variation in the field (Liu, 2024; Wolbring & Nguyen, 2023); for example, the term "diversity, equity, and inclusion" is more typically used in the United States. Further, though I have chosen to retain the use of "equality" rather than "equity", I do not propose that all people should receive the same treatment. Clearly, for example, those with caring responsibilities and underlying health conditions are in greater need of flexible working policies. Further, an identity-blind approach (i.e., treating all employees the same) communicates basic tolerance rather than valuing and appreciating a person's identity (Mor, Gündemir, & van der Toorn, 2025). Recommendations are provided in each chapter, intended both to promote a positive working environment for all employees and to address existing inequalities in order to ensure equity of opportunity. Similarly, though "diversity", "equality", and "equity" are often discussed together, it is important to recognise that a diverse organisation is not necessarily equitable, and some employees are required to work harder to achieve the same level of success (Sotto-Santiago, 2020). It is essential, therefore, that a superficial approach to equality, diversity, and inclusion is avoided (e.g., simply reporting the number of employees with a specific protected characteristic) in favour of more meaningful change (Liu, 2024).

Secondly, the language used to refer to disability varies both globally and across specific disabled communities. I typically adopt "identity-first" language (i.e., "disabled person") rather than "person-first" language (i.e., "person with disabilities"). In part, this reflects consistency with the British disability justice movement (Kelly, Dow, & Westerhoff, 2010). It also represents my lived experience as a disabled person, the importance of disability to my identity, and the desire to remove the stigma associated with disability. Indeed, policies mandating the use of person-first language in academic texts have been criticised (Peers, Spencer-Cavaliere, & Eales, 2014; Thorley, 2025). Though the term "disability" may itself be problematic (e.g., implying that a disabled person is "without ability"), I have chosen to retain the term "disabled" for consistency with the sector and widespread use of the term by disabled activists and community groups. Indeed, avoidance of the term is also problematic (Andrews et al., 2019).

Further, it is important to recognise that many people who meet the legal requirements for disability do not identify as disabled. For example, a person may not consider their condition to be a disability, or they may fear that they are not "disabled enough" to use the term (Brewer, 2025). Internalised ableism may also deter identification as disabled. In this book, when adopting the term "disability", I refer to the experiences of those who meet the (British) legal definition of "disabled" (i.e., including neurodiversity and chronic illness) regardless of whether a person chooses to identify as disabled. I recognise different language preferences and support the right of each individual to adopt the terminology they choose (e.g., chronically ill or disabled) to describe their own condition/s and circumstance. It is important that we recognise the power of language and the right of people and communities to self-identify.

Thirdly, numerous terms and acronyms have been used to discuss race and ethnicity. In the United Kingdom, the term "Black, Asian, and Minority Ethnic" (BAME) has historically been adopted in research, policy, and practice. The term is, however, outdated and problematic. For example, the term did not originate with the communities it claims to represent, and naming some ethnic groups and not others may serve to further marginalise and exclude some communities. In other regions, including the United States, terms such as "people of colour" or "Black, indigenous, and people of colour" have been adopted. Though those terms are (at present) more widely adopted, they are not without issue. For example, collective discussion fails to recognise the disparate experiences of those from different ethnic groups (Khunti et al., 2020). In this book, I predominantly use the term "racially minoritised" (unless referring to a specific group) in order to emphasise the experience of employees who are marginalised and othered in academia. I recognise that this contrasts with terminology (e.g., "global majority") that has sought to promote solidarity and emphasise that those often referred to as a minority represent a majority of the global population.

References

Abrica, E. J., & Andrew, R. O. (2024). The racial politics of Diversity, Equity, and Inclusion (DEI) work. *Journal of Diversity in Higher Education*, *18*(1), S259–S268. https://doi.org/10.1037/dhe0000566

Akala, B. M. (2021). A critical reflection on neoliberalism policies and neo-colonialism at African universities. *Journal of Decolonising Disciplines*, *3*. https://doi.org/10.35293/jdd.v3i2.3546

Andrews, E. E., Forber-Pratt, A. J., Mona, L. R., Lund, E. M., Pilarski, C. R., & Balter, R. (2019). #SaytheWord: A disability culture commentary on the erasure of "disability". *Rehabilitation Psychology*, *64*(2), 111–118. https://doi.org/10.1037/rep0000258

Andrews, E. E., Powell, R. M., & Ayers, K. (2022). The evolution of disability language: Choosing terms to describe disability. *Disability and Health Journal*, *15*(3), 101328. https://doi.org/10.1016/j.dhjo.2022.101328

Austin Henry, R., & Beserra, B. (2022). Neoliberalism and higher education in Latin America. *Latin American Perspectives*, *49*(3), 3–17. https://doi.org/10.1177/0094582X221084299

Bal, E., Grassiani, E., & Kirk, K. (2014). Neoliberal individualism in Dutch universities. *Learning and Teaching*, *7*(3), 46–72. https://doi.org/10.3167/latiss.2014.070303

Berg, L. D., Huijbens, E. H., & Larsen, H. G. (2016). Producing anxiety in the neoliberal university. *The Canadian Geographer*, *60*(2), 168–180. https://doi.org/10.1111/cag.12261

Bleijenbergh, I. L., van Engen, M. L., & Vinkenburg, C. J. (2013). Othering women: Fluid images of the ideal academic. *Equality, Diversity and Inclusion*, *32*(1), 22–35. https://doi.org/10.1108/02610151311305597

Bol, T., De Vaan, M., & Van De Rijt, A. (2018). The Matthew effect in science funding. *Proceedings of the National Academy of Sciences*, *115*(19), 4887–4890. https://doi.org/10.1073/pnas.1719557115

Bowman, N. A. (2010). College diversity experiences and cognitive development: A meta-analysis. *Review of Educational Research*, *80*(1), 4–33. https://doi.org/10.3102/0034654309352495

Bowman, N. A. (2011). Promoting participation in a diversity democracy: A meta-analysis of college diversity experiences and civic engagement. *Review of Educational Research*, *81*(1), 29–68. https://doi.org/10.3102/0034654310383047

Brewer, G. (2025). The lived experience of female academics with long-term conditions impacting on energy levels and/or cognitive function. *Disability & Society*, *40*(2), 419–444. https://doi.org/10.1080/09687599.2023.2287412

Burke, S. E., Dovidio, J. F., Perry, S. P., Burgess, D. J., Hardeman, R. R., Phelan, S. M., … & Van Ryn, M. (2017). Informal training experiences and explicit bias against African Americans among medical students. *Social Psychology Quarterly*, *80*(1), 65–84. https://doi.org/10.1007/s11606-017-4127-6

Burrows, R. (2012). Living with the h-index? Metric assemblages in the contemporary academy. *The Sociological Review*, *60*(2), 355–372. https://doi.org/10.1111/j.1467-954X.2012.02077.x

Cech, E. A. (2022). The intersectional privilege of white able-bodied heterosexual men in STEM. *Science Advances*, *8*(24), eabo1558. https://doi.org/10.1126/sciadv.abo1558

Corsino, L., & Fuller, A. T. (2021). Educating for diversity, equity, and inclusion: A review of commonly used educational approaches. *Journal of Clinical and Translational Science*, *5*(1), e169. https://doi.org/10.1017/cts.2021.834

Davies, H. C., & MacRae, S. E. (2023). An anatomy of the British war on woke. *Race & Class*, *65*(2), 3–54. https://doi.org/10.1177/03063968231164905

Dhanani, L. Y., Arena Jr, D. F., & Bogart, S. M. (2024). The unequal burden of DEI bans. *Industrial and Organizational Psychology*, *17*(4), 503–506. https://doi.org/10.1017/iop.2024.44

Entman, R. M. (2007). Framing bias: Media in the distribution of power. *Journal of Communication*, *57*(1), 163–173. https://doi.org/10.1111/j.1460-2466.2006.00336.x

Erickson, M., Hanna, P., & Walker, C. (2021). The UK higher education sector management survey: A statactivist response to managerialist governance. *Studies in Higher Education*, *46*(11), 2134–2151. https://doi.org/10.1080/03075079.2020.1712693

Garry, P. M. (2023). Threats to academic freedom in higher education. *Society*, *60*(2), 176–180. https://doi.org/10.1007/s12115-023-00821-4

Goldberg, A. E. (2024). *The impact of anti-dei legislation on LGBTQ+ faculty in higher education*. UCLA Williams Institute. Retrieved from: https://escholarship.org/content/qt81z418hx/qt81z418hx.pdf

Gurin, P., Dey, E. L., Hurtado, S., & Gurin, G. (2002). Diversity and higher education: Theory and impact on educational outcomes. *Harvard Educational Review*, *72*(3), 330–367. https://doi.org/10.17763/haer.72.3.01151786u134n051

Hardeman, R. R., Przedworski, J. M., Burke, S., Burgess, D. J., Perry, S., Phelan, S., … & van Ryn, M. (2016). Association between perceived medical school diversity climate and change in depressive symptoms among medical students: A report from the medical student CHANGE study. *Journal of the National Medical Association*, *108*(4), 225–235. https://doi.org/10.1016/j.jnma.2016.08.005

Harper, S. (2025). Leveraging research and demanding proof in response to legislative attacks on DEI in US higher education. *AERA Open*, *11*, 23328584251355514. https://doi.org/10.1177/23328584251355514

Kelly, J. F., Dow, S. J., & Westerhoff, C. (2010). Does our choice of substance-related terms influence perceptions of treatment need? An empirical investigation with two commonly used terms. *Journal of Drug Issues*, *40*(4), 805–818. https://doi.org/10.1177/002204261004000403

Ketzl, A. D. (2025). Knowledge censorship in 21st century academia: An overview with attention to the trends of wokeism and cancel culture. *Open Journal of Social Sciences*, *13*(3), 330–345. https://doi.org/10.4236/jss.2025.133023

Khunti, K., Routen, A., Pareek, M., Treweek, S., & Platt, L. (2020). The language of ethnicity. *British Medical Journal*, *371*. https://doi.org/10.1136/bmj.m4493

Lange, A. C., & Lee, J. A. (2024). Centering our humanity: Responding to anti-DEI efforts across higher education. *Journal of College Student Development*, *65*(1), 113–116. https://doi.org/10.1353/csd.2024.a919356

Liu, T. (2024). The economics of identity: How EDI initiatives treat racialized identities as currency in academic libraries. *Canadian Journal of Academic Librarianship*, *10*, 1–22. https://doi.org/10.33137/cjal-rcbu.v10.43088

McGowan, B. L., Hopson, R., Epperson, L., & Leopold, M. (2025). Navigating the backlash and reimagining diversity, equity, and inclusion in a changing sociopolitical and legal landscape. *Journal of College and Character*, *26*(1), 1–11. https://doi.org/10.1080/2194587X.2024.2441300

Merton, R. K. (1968). The Matthew effect in science: The reward and communication systems of science are considered. *Science*, *159*(3810), 56–63. https://doi.org/10.1126/science.159.3810.56

Miles, M. L., Agger, C. A., Roby, R. S., & Morton, T. R. (2022). Who's who: How "women of color" are (or are not) represented in stem education research. *Science Education*, *106*(2), 229–256. https://doi.org/10.1002/sce.21694.

Mor, K., Gündemir, S., & van der Toorn, J. (2025). "Are they just putting up with me"? How diversity approaches impact LGBTQ+ employees' sense of being tolerated at work. *British Journal of Social Psychology*, *64*(4) e70006. https://doi.org/10.1111/bjso.70006

Morgan, H. (2022). Neoliberalism's influence on American universities: How the business model harms students and society. *Policy Futures in Education*, *20*(2),149–165. https://doi.org/10.1177/14782103211006655

Peers, D., Spencer-Cavaliere, N., & Eales, L. (2014). Say what you mean: Rethinking disability language in Adapted Physical Activity Quarterly. *Adapted Physical Activity Quarterly*, *31*(3), 265–282. https://doi.org/10.1123/apaq.2013-0091

Phelan, S. M., Burke, S. E., Hardeman, R. R., White, R. O., Przedworski, J., Dovidio, J. F., ... & van Ryn, M. (2017). Medical school factors associated with changes in implicit and explicit bias against gay and lesbian people among 3492 graduating medical students. *Journal of General Internal Medicine*, *32*, 1193–1201.

Prasad, A., & M. Śliwa. (2024). Critiquing the backlash against wokeness: In defense of DEI scholarship and practice. *Academy of Management Perspectives*, *38*(2), 245–259. https://doi.org/10.5465/amp.2023.0066

Roper, B. (2018). Neoliberalism's war on New Zealand's universities. *New Zealand Sociology*, *33*(2), 9–39.

Rossiter, M. W. (1993). The Matthew Matilda effect in science. *Social Studies of Science*, *23*(2), 325–341. https://doi.org/10.1177/030631293023002004

Rzepka, A., Fazlagić, J., & Ahamed, I. (2023). Measuring woke culture in universities: A diagnostic approach. *Journal of Modern Science*, *54*(5), 488–509.

Sang, K., Powell, A., Finkel, R., & Richards, J. (2015). 'Being an academic is not a 9-5 job': Long working hours and the 'ideal worker' in UK academia. *Labour & Industry*, *25*(3), 235–249. https://doi.org/10.1080/10301763.2015.1081723

Schoorman, D. (2024). Waking up to the 'anti-woke' agenda. *Journal of Educational Administration and History*, *56*(4), 404–410. https://doi.org/10.1080/00220620.2024.2364632

Shaw, S. (2025). Reclaiming the narrative: A cartographic analysis of diversity, equity, and inclusion (DEI) and critical race theory (CRT) misinformation campaigns. *Journal of College and Character*, *26*(1), 84–95. https://doi.org/10.1080/2194587X.2024.2441296

Sotto-Santiago, S. (2020). Black and Latinx faculty perspectives on equity, diversity, and inclusion initiatives. *Journal of Best Practices in Health Professions Diversity*, *13*(1), 44–55.

Thorley, M. (2025). The importance of disability-inclusive language. *Widening Participation and Lifelong Learning*, *27*(2), 164–175. https://doi.org/10.5456/WPLL.27.2.164

Toren, N. (2009). Intersection of ethnicity, gender and class: Oriental faculty women in Israel. *Gender Issues*, *26*, 152–166. https://doi.org/10.1007/s12147-009-9073-0

Turner, C. S. V., González, J. C., & Wood, J. L. (2008). Faculty of color in academe: What 20 years of literature tells us. *Journal of Diversity in Higher Education*, *1*(3), 139–168. https://doi.org/10.1037/a0012837

Wolbring, G., & Nguyen, A. (2023). Equity/equality, diversity and inclusion, and other EDI phrases and EDI policy frameworks: A scoping review. *Trends in Higher Education*, *2*(1), 168–237. https://doi.org/10.3390/higheredu2010011

Chapter 1

Monitoring, Competition, and Workload

The higher education sector is challenging and competitive. Increased student numbers (i.e., the massification of higher education), limited funding and resources, and greater use of external measures (e.g., league tables) to rank and compare institutions (Rossi, 2010) have each contributed to a neoliberal academic culture that closely monitors staff, department, and institutional performance (Ball, 2012; Giroux, 2014, 2015). The current chapter highlights the pressures experienced by those working in the higher education sector, with particular emphasis on the measurement of performance and prominent stressors (e.g., workload and peer review).

Monitoring, Metrics, and the Pressure to Publish

For academics, there is a significant pressure to publish, and metrics such as the h-index are often used to guide the appointment and promotion of academic staff (Burrows, 2012). The research outputs expected of academic staff are, however, often perceived to be unrealistic and unfair (Kenny, 2018). Indeed, academics are expected not only to publish but to publish in the "right" (i.e., high-status) journals. The focus on a limited list of "acceptable" journals in which academics should publish has been described as a fetishism that restricts and perverts traditional scholarly practice (Hussain, 2015; Willmott, 2011).

Factors influencing the perceived quality of a journal include official rankings and a high rejection rate (Macdonald & Kam, 2007). Though particular weight is afforded to journal impact factors, these may reflect the frequent citation of a relatively small number of articles (with the remainder "free-riding"). As a consequence, journal impact factors may have little validity as a measure of the quality of individual studies published by that journal (Baum et al., 2011). There is also circularity in the assessment of journal quality. For example, high-quality journals feature articles from higher-status academics and/or institutions, and higher-status academics and/or institutions are those who publish in high-quality journals. Similarly, high-status journals typically have high rejection rates, and as the perceived quality of the journal increases,

DOI: 10.4324/9781032639321-2

more academics are encouraged to publish in the journal, further increasing the submission (and hence rejection) rates (Macdonald & Kam, 2007, 2008).

In the United Kingdom, the pressure to publish is also driven by the Research Excellence Framework (formerly the Research Assessment Exercise), which periodically rates research outputs and has both a financial and reputational impact for institutions. Academics are often instructed that only outputs classified as 3* (internationally excellent) or 4* (world leading) "count". Indeed, 1* (recognised nationally) and 2* (recognised internationally) outputs are regularly perceived to be of little consequence. Despite the significant impact of submission ratings, the research assessment process is highly pressured, with panel members tasked to read approximately 700 publications in 40 days (Macdonald & Kam, 2007). As a consequence, panel members may rely on proxy measures of research quality (e.g., the journal in which an article is published) rather than a close reading of the article itself, undermining the validity of the assessment process.

The formal assessment of research has a significant impact on both individual academics and the higher education sector more broadly. Research decisions, such as the topic to be researched and the journal in which it is published, are increasingly influenced by the research assessment process (Butler & Spoelstra, 2014). Further, research assessments that are so closely tied to prestige and financial reward increase the likelihood of disputes over article authorship and academic misconduct (e.g., data fabrication and redundant publication) (Sheikh, 2000). To some extent, academics appear to have resigned themselves to the process of assessment and evaluation. As one academic reported, "*The REF is the part that I don't like, but it's an unavoidable part of where we are now*" (Butler & Spoelstra, 2014, p. 545).

Though academics experience substantial pressure, it is important to recognise that there is a degree of prestige and flexibility associated with the academic role. Other university employees, though making a substantial contribution to the individual institution, subject discipline, and sector, are not necessarily afforded the same status. For example, research administrators report feeling invisible or being dismissed as "non-academics" who are unappreciated and only acknowledged when problems arise (Collinson, 2006; Szekeres, 2004). As summarised by one administrator, "*There are some who treat anyone who is not an academic as if you are a cleaning lady*" (Collinson, 2006, p. 278). Greater acknowledgement and reward of the contribution made by non-academic staff (e.g., administrators, technicians) is required.

Peer Review and Rejection

The importance placed on journal article publication and grant funding (especially publication in high-ranking journals and funding from favoured funding bodies) fails to recognise bias in the peer review system (Manchikanti et al., 2015; Mavrogenis, Quaile, & Scarlat, 2020; Tvina, Spellecy, & Palatnik, 2019). For example, inviting over 3,300 researchers to review a paper, Huber et al.

(2022) report that reviewers are more likely to recommend acceptance or minor revisions when a prominent Nobel laureate is listed as the author (59% recommending acceptance) compared to a relatively unknown author (fewer than 10% recommending acceptance). Indeed, both the objectiveness and the integrity of the system can be questioned. For example, editors are faster to accept the submissions of their collaborators (Liu, AlShebli, & Rahwan, 2023), and academics are commonly asked to review a manuscript that they are not competent to evaluate (Bedeian, 2003).

The quality of individual reviewer assessments and editorial decisions to accept or reject an article or funding application remains unclear. Despite this, authors may feel under pressure to make the requested revisions. In one study, over one-third of lead authors believed that the requested revisions were based on the personal preference of a reviewer or editor, almost 25% of those surveyed believed that they had made changes they felt were incorrect during the revision process, and over one-third believed that they had been treated as an inferior by an editor or referee (Bedeian, 2003). Indeed, there has been relatively little focus on the "social nature" of the peer review process and the extent to which the final article represents a compromise between the author, reviewers, and editor (Bedeian, 2004). Further, the peer review process is not consistent. Peters and Ceci (1982) resubmitted 12 (already published) manuscripts to academic journals using fictitious names and institutions. As three resubmissions were detected, nine manuscripts continued to full peer review. Of the nine resubmitted articles, eight were rejected, and 16 of the 18 reviewers recommended against publication.

Rejection (e.g., with respect to journal submissions, grant applications, or applications for promotion) forms part of academic life. It can, however, be a distressing experience that compromises academic identity and impacts engagement (Horn, 2016). For example, an academic may be reluctant to submit new grant applications if they have previously been unsuccessful. It can be especially difficult to process rejection in a sector where success (e.g., publication in a prestigious journal) is well publicised and inherently linked to academic identity. Rejection, and the emotional impact of this, is rarely acknowledged within academia (Day, 2011), perhaps because academics believe they must maintain an image of a successful scholar. Practical support (e.g., a writing mentor) and effective coping strategies (e.g., reframing the rejection) may lessen the likelihood or impact of rejection. It is, of course, also important that journal editors monitor the tone and appropriateness of peer review. Reviews that are unnecessarily hostile to a subject, finding, or methodology fail to provide the objectivity and rigour that should be central to peer review.

Competition, Comparison, and the Imposter Phenomenon

The competitive nature of academia, requiring researchers to compete for valuable resources and recognition, creates an environment in which people routinely compare themselves to others, exacerbated by formal metrics and ranking.

Feelings of inadequacy and inferiority may develop from such comparisons and from the failure and rejection which constitute routine aspects of the academic role (Woolston, 2016). In particular, the imposter phenomenon is well-documented in higher education students and staff (Parkman, 2016).

The imposter phenomenon refers to intense feelings of intellectual fraudulence, whereby success is attributed to luck or temporary effort rather than intelligence or expertise, and fear of exposure (Clance & Imes, 1978). It is also referred to as imposter syndrome, especially in the non-academic literature. Those experiencing imposter phenomenon are less likely to believe themselves "worthy" of rewards and recognition, which may impact their confidence to pursue specific roles or promotion and to apply for more competitive, prestigious grants and awards. Clance and Imes (1978) suggest that those experiencing imposter phenomenon display four types of behaviour. These include working hard to ensure others do not uncover their fraudulent status, using charm to gain the approval of others, avoiding overt displays of confidence, and concealing their true beliefs and opinions in favour of those most likely to be well received by their peers. This concealment restricts independent and original thought.

Researchers have highlighted the incidence, experience, and consequences of imposter phenomenon in academia. For example, research suggests that academics experience moderate levels of imposter phenomenon, with higher levels among non-tenured faculty (Hutchins, 2015). The phenomenon has been examined especially in relation to the STEM (i.e., Science, Technology, Engineering, and Mathematics) field (Stone-Sabali et al., 2023). It has been argued that the academic culture actively contributes to the imposter phenomenon. For example, Zorn (2005) highlights the negative impact of a lack of mentoring, scholarly isolation, valuing the product rather than the process, aggressive competitiveness, and specialist fields that do not value interdisciplinary work.

Insecurity and feelings of academic fraudulence may be further exacerbated by criticism during peer review and the broad range of activities that form part of the academic role (e.g., quality assurance, public engagement) (Abdelaal, 2020). Examining faculty experiences of the imposter phenomenon, Hutchins and Rainbolt (2017) identify a range of "imposter incidents" that led faculty to doubt themselves and question their academic identity. These included colleagues questioning their expertise, the publication and grant funding process (including submitting work for review and responding to rejection or review), comparisons with colleagues (both in terms of expertise and productivity), and objective indicators of success. As with other areas of academic culture, research on the imposter phenomenon is more likely to focus on academic staff or students than non-academic staff. It is, of course, important to recognise the incidence and importance of the imposter phenomenon in non-academic employees. For example, Clark, Vardeman, and Barba (2014) document imposter phenomenon in librarians, with 12.8% of those surveyed experiencing feelings of imposter phenomenon to a significant degree.

Though imposter phenomenon is often conceptualised as an individual issue, it is important to acknowledge the extent to which the academic environment can make people, and some groups in particular, feel that they do not belong and are "less than" their peers. As a consequence, marginalised staff such as Black academics may feel under pressure to "perform" in order to conform to expectations of academic faculty and manage audience responses (McGee & Kazembe, 2015). Edwards (2019) describes her experiences of academia as a young Black woman and explains that she overcame imposter phenomenon by reconceptualising the definition of a scholar to include underrepresented groups. Such findings highlight the importance of representation and role modelling and suggest that programmes aimed at increasing diversity within the higher education sector may have limited success if they fail to address the imposter phenomenon and associated feelings of belonging.

Fields and Cunningham-Williams (2021) interviewed Black female faculty, exploring their experiences of management of the self in response to institutional and internalised racism, with particular consideration of experiences of imposter phenomenon. Participants described a range of strategies to "prove" themselves, such as overpreparing for meetings. Though behaviour such as additional preparation for meetings may at first appear either harmless or beneficial to those experiencing imposter phenomenon, it is important to recognise both the emotional or psychological consequences of such behaviour (e.g., increased stress and anxiety), together with the amount of time spent on this type of overpreparation, time which is not available for other activities such as research. Those who are most confident in their abilities and do not feel the need to read all preparatory materials for meetings (believing that they are fully able to "wing it") are able to spend their time on the activities (such as research) that are more likely to be valued and rewarded.

Indeed, there are a range of negative consequences associated with the imposter phenomenon. These include anxiety when starting new roles and responsibilities, a reluctance to engage in long-term career planning, and discomfort serving as a role model (Brems et al., 1994; Dahlvig, 2013). For example, Wilkinson (2020) provides an autobiographical account of her experiences of imposter phenomenon as an early-career lecturer and the ways in which imposter phenomenon impacts her teaching practice, including a lack of confidence and performance anxiety. Training and mentoring may support academics and reduce feelings associated with imposter phenomenon (Hutchins, 2015; Wilkinson, 2020). Recognising the value of collaborative networks, with each person bringing their own knowledge and skills to the group, may also encourage people to value individual contribution and reduce competition. It is important that formal reward and recognition schemes do not undermine this approach, for example, by requiring researchers to evidence grant applications as a principal investigator rather than a co-investigator.

Online Abuse and Public Engagement

Targeted online abuse of academics has become more frequent (Ferber, 2018). In one large-scale study involving 2,492 university employees, 30% had experienced online harassment in the previous six months, with excessive criticism and personal attacks (including attacks on values or personal life) especially common (Celuch et al., 2022). Abuse may take many forms and involve a range of platforms. Those with experience of online harassment identify email as the most common forum for this abuse (42%), followed by Twitter (35%), and Facebook (Gosse et al., 2021). Of course, as the nature of the online environment and specific forums change (such as the move from Twitter to X), the level and nature of abuse in each online platform may also change.

Those posting academic, teaching, and political content online are most likely to experience online harassment (Eslen-Ziya, Giorgi, & Ahi, 2023). Though social media posts created by academics are most commonly (47%) identified as a trigger of online harassment, other triggers include teaching activities (30%), something created and shared on social media (30%), and something created but not shared on social media (28%) (Gosse et al., 2021). It is, therefore, important to recognise that academics are also targeted for their offline work. Staff experiencing online harassment may employ a range of coping strategies, including self-protection (e.g., use of social media security settings) (Veletsianos et al., 2018). Though adjusting social media security settings may limit exposure to abuse on social media, it does not, of course, address abuse received via email (on which the individual is dependent for work) or abuse that extends offline (e.g., voicemail messages). Ferber (2018) notes that the abuse experienced by academics includes voicemails and on-campus graffiti. Those targeted in this manner feared for their own safety and the safety of others. There was also a significant impact on the mental health of staff subjected to abuse, further exacerbated when required to read each abusive email or post. Institutions should, therefore, ensure that alternate arrangements are made to document the abuse experienced.

Factors Impacting the Likelihood of Abuse

Factors contributing to the rise in online abuse directed at academics include the higher education environment and broader sociopolitical culture. In the competitive academic environment, academics are encouraged to establish an online presence. Online activity may have a number of benefits, including increased opportunities to disseminate research, establish external networks, and learn of opportunities within the sector (Mewburn & Thomson, 2013). Online activity may also be motivated by a desire to promote public understanding of specific subjects or academic research more broadly. In some circumstances, academics may also be called upon to communicate with the general public or feel compelled to do so in order to promote public safety and wellbeing. Nölleke, Leonhardt, and Hanusch (2023) highlight the abuse targeted at medical scientists who served as media experts during the COVID-19 pandemic, with some subjects (e.g., vaccinations) especially likely to prompt abuse. This is consistent with other research suggesting that two-thirds of scientists interviewed by the media about COVID-19 were subject to online abuse, with 15% receiving death threats and 22% receiving threats of physical or sexual violence (Nogrady, 2021).

Indeed, the type of work conducted by academics (e.g., climate change, racism) may make them especially vulnerable to online attention and abuse (Ferber, 2018). Barlow and Awan (2016) provide auto-ethnographic accounts of their experiences of online abuse and hate. Targeted because of their own identities and work on oppressed groups, they received comments such as "*No-one cares. You just need a good raping to shut you up*" (p. 5) and "*You need to be sorted out with a knife*" (p. 6). They report being overwhelmed by the volume of abuse, on one occasion receiving over 100 tweets in one hour, the majority of which were abusive. Similarly, Colley and Moore (2022) document the abuse targeted at the authors following the delivery of an in-person workshop focused on the 4chan online community and the association with the Alt-Right. Institutional support is clearly required for those working in such areas.

In recent years, online abuse has been emboldened by an increasingly polarised, fragmented, and extremist political climate in which prejudice is openly accepted and endorsed by a substantial proportion of the general population. Further, in the current "post-truth" political climate, trust in traditional experts such as academics has declined, also contributing to the online abuse directed at academic researchers (Galpin & Vernon, 2024). Ferber (2018) provides a chilling account of the hostile environment experienced by many academics, including the range of websites (e.g., Professor Watchlist) to identify academics who "advance leftist propaganda" and books with titles such as "The Professors: The 101 Most Dangerous Academics in America" (Horowitz, 2006) and "Brainwashed: How Universities Indoctrinate America's Youth" (Shapiro, 2004).

Consequences of Abuse and Support

This type of targeted abuse can have a significant personal and professional impact. In one online survey, the most common personal consequences of online abuse included feelings of anxiety and distress (69%), irritability (47%), difficulty concentrating (46%), and feeling depressed (44%) (Gosse et al., 2021). Professional consequences of online abuse include a loss of confidence in academic work (56%), a loss of productivity (51%), a reluctance to go to the university (44%), a desire to leave their role (35%), and reputational damage (34%) (Gosse et al., 2021). Further, of those experiencing online harassment, 32% of academics consider limiting their contribution to online discussions, and 20% consider changing the focus of their work. (Eslen-Ziya, Giorgi, & Ahi, 2023). There are, therefore, important consequences of abuse for specific subject areas and public understanding of those subjects.

Despite the prevalence and impact of online abuse, universities may be ill-equipped to respond to this issue or more likely to focus on online abuse from a public relations perspective (Ferber, 2018). Faculty appear to be aware of the lack of institutional support available. For example, Hodson et al. (2024) report that those experiencing online abuse are reluctant to report harassment to their employer, believing that there is little that the institution can or will do to address the issue. They also find that academics are concerned that they will be perceived as a problem or liability by the institution and do not wish to make themselves vulnerable (Hodson et al., 2024). It is important that the higher education sector protects staff who conduct public engagement work as part of their academic role and recognises the disproportionate impact of such abuse on some faculty. Indeed, women are both more likely to experience online abuse (see Subject in Focus 2 section) and to report that reaching out to their department was not at all helpful (23.4% vs 6.5%) (Houlden et al., 2022).

Workload

The academic role incorporates a wide and expanding range of roles and responsibilities (e.g., curriculum design, acquisition of funding, public engagement), with each activity requiring subject-specific knowledge and expertise. Indeed, academics have highlighted the (increased) time focused on administration and compliance and the time spent on tasks that are not directly related to core teaching or research (Paewai, Meyer, & Houston, 2007). Smaller departments may be especially vulnerable if, for example, all staff are expected to take on multiple roles with few opportunities to specialise in particular areas of teaching or research. As a consequence, high workloads and long working hours are commonplace. For example, in one diary study, Beckers et al. (2008) reported that approximately 90% of academics work overtime.

Whilst most studies focus on perceptions of academic workload, Forgasz and Leder (2006) used an experience sampling method to prompt academics to record their current activities. Approximately 65% of work-related activities took place during office hours (Monday-Friday, 9–5), and 35% of these activities occurred outside office hours, with an estimated 55 hours worked in the week. Many departmental or university meetings were held outside standard office hours. There may also be a gender difference in the type of overtime completed. Men are more likely to spend time at off-campus lectures, conferences, or professional society events and engage in research or committee work, and women are more likely to be with students, advising them on their work or preparing and evaluating their work (Forgasz & Leder, 2006).

Long working hours have become normalised, with overtime and evening and weekend work perceived by academics as unavoidable (Bos et al., 2013). Further, the nature of the academic role means that when annual or sick leave is taken, work is rarely redistributed. As a consequence, workload often accumulates, and academics either work whilst on leave or have an increased workload on return. As one academic states,

> you stay at home or you might call in sick because you know you're not working. However, that work didn't get done. So you're lying there anxious thinking 'I'm going to have to do this work at another time. No-one else is going to do it for me'.
>
> (Remnant et al., 2023, p. 13)

Workload is central to the job stress experienced by academics (Adriaenssens, De Prins, & Vloeberghs, 2006). Excessive academic workloads can also impact collegiality, morale, and academic integrity (Jensen & Morgan, 2009). As stated by one academic, "*I love my job but fear that it may kill me*" (Kenny & Fluck, 2014, p. 590). The lack of time for reflection and discussion with colleagues can also reduce opportunities for formal and informal mentorship of less experienced staff (Bos et al., 2013). As a consequence, academics may work in relative isolation, reducing opportunities to learn from and collaborate with other staff (Bos et al., 2013).

Workload Models

Many institutions adopt a workload model to quantify the time spent on various roles and responsibilities (e.g., module coordination, supervision, marking). Broadly, there are three forms of workload model based on either contact hours, actual hours, or a points system (Vardi, 2009). It is argued that such workload models identify the amount of time each employee should spend on specific aspects of their role and promote a fair allocation of roles and responsibilities across the department and institution. Indeed, identifying staff who are under- or overloaded with work is an important aspect of workload models (Vardi, 2009). Involving staff in the design and implementation of the workload model may help to establish credibility and fairness (Kenny & Fluck, 2014).

It is, of course, important to ensure that workload models are fair, transparent, and account for all aspects of the academic role. In one study, only 50% of academics questioned reported that workload models were published and freely available, whilst only 40% and 20%, respectively, believed that the model was easy to understand and applied transparently (Kenny & Fluck, 2014). Perhaps most importantly, only 14% of academics felt that the model was based on realistic estimates of the time required to complete academic duties (Kenny & Fluck, 2014).

The extent to which workload models accurately represent the work conducted by academics is questionable. For example, when academics secure competitive funding, universities may not release them from other duties in order to conduct the research, compromising their ability to deliver agreed project outputs (Kenny & Fluck, 2014). Further, academics may adopt a range of external roles in order to enhance their skills, drive change, or demonstrate the impact of their work. Though these roles may be personally and professionally rewarding, external roles may not be compensated for within workload models, contributing to excessive workloads. Further, this practice encourages an environment where only those who are relatively privileged and able to invest the time in these roles (e.g., without caring responsibilities) are able to demonstrate external engagement and progress in their careers.

The failure to recognise some activities in formal workload models and the need for academics to demonstrate a range of responsibilities and experience in order to gain a permanent position or promotion can leave some academics especially vulnerable to exploitation. As explained by one academic,

> I feel unsupported and exploited; paid to teach only, but in the knowledge that I will probably do research in my own time. As an ECR [early career researcher] it is expected that I will make myself competitive so do research for free to get publications up.
>
> (Kenny & Fluck, 2014, p. 596)

It is, therefore, essential that workload models are realistic and allow time for all expected academic activities. Workload models should also consider factors such as the distribution of allocated work, with models often documenting workloads across the academic year but failing to consider "pinch points" where workloads become unmanageable.

Recommendations

Institutions should,

- Avoid the use of arbitrary metrics and recognise the value of work published in varied formats and for a range of audience types. For example, a journal targeted at practitioners may have a lower impact factor but be more likely to influence practice and result in meaningful change.
- Recognise bias in the peer review process and the impact of this on individual researchers, subject disciplines, and institutions. Ensure that important research areas of a lower status (and those who conduct them) are supported.
- Provide support and mentoring focused on developing confidence and addressing feelings of inferiority and intellectual fraudulence. Such support should include guidance for coping with rejection, setbacks, and negative feedback.

- Ensure diverse role models and representation. Provide varied examples of thriving in the higher education sector and promote a culture in which rejection and setbacks can be openly discussed.
- Acknowledge the potential for online abuse to occur and the disproportionate impact of this on marginalised staff. Ensure that staff are not compelled to publicise their work in open forums and provide support where they choose to do so. Social media accounts and emails associated with projects or groups (rather than individual staff) should be available where preferred. Institutions should publicise the support available to all staff.
- Workloads should be equitable and realistic. Allowing staff to anonymously view the workloads of other staff can promote transparency and allow identification of inequalities. When staff are unwell or absent for other reasons (e.g., bereavement), work should be reallocated. Workloads should be adjusted where external funding has been obtained, and external activities should be included in workload models.

In addition,

- Journal publishers have a responsibility to ensure that the peer review process is fair and constructive. Regular audits should be conducted to address this. Reviewers should be fairly compensated for their time, ensuring that all researchers are able to contribute to the process. Where reviewers request citation of specific work, they should clearly state if they have a connection to the work recommended.

Subject in Focus 1: Predatory Journals

Though not without issue, the traditional peer review and publication model is intended to maintain the scientific rigour and quality of research that is shared with the broader scientific community and general public. Increasingly, the financial cost of this publication has been borne by the author or their institution rather than the consumer (i.e., the open access model), placing another pressure on academic researchers. Capitalising on this trend and the pressure to publish within academia, the presence and reach of predatory journals offering rapid 'review' and publication for a fee have risen (Perlin et al., 2018; Shen & Björk, 2015).

Central to the success of predatory journals, the review and editorial process is often minimal, failing to recognise serious issues with the quality of the research submitted (Bohannon, 2013). Such journals are also often characterised by aggressive marketing (especially with unsolicited emails) and false information (e.g., the editorial board, inclusion in databases) (Beall, 2016; Grudniewicz et al., 2019). Features such as emails and homepages that include spelling and grammatical errors and direct submission via email rather than an online submission system are more common in predatory journals, though these features are not always present. It can, therefore, be difficult to distinguish between predatory and legitimate journals, especially for inexperienced researchers (Demir, 2018), though authors at all levels may inadvertently fall victim to predatory journals (Cobey, 2017). Indeed, confusion is exacerbated by the tendency for predatory journals to adopt titles similar to those of legitimate publications.

Motivation and Consequences

Increasingly, research has been conducted to examine motivations for publication in predatory journals and the factors encouraging this practice (see Mertkan, Onurkan Aliusta, & Suphi, 2021 for a review). Competition within the institution, the pressure to publish, fear of job loss, and desire for promotion may each encourage publication in these journals (Demir, 2018; Kurt, 2018). Specific academic practices such as requiring PhD candidates to publish their work to be eligible for the doctoral degree and financial incentives to publish may also encourage publication in predatory journals (Demir, 2018; Pyne, 2017). Those publishing in predatory journals are disproportionately likely to be based in developing countries (Demir, 2018; Xia et al., 2015), highlighting the inequalities of this practice. These authors have reported feeling that traditional (typically Western based) journals may be bias against them, contributing to a preference for predatory journals, often based in developing countries (Kurt, 2018).

Predatory journals can have a negative impact on our knowledge and understanding and undermine confidence in the research literature and open access publications in particular (Ferris & Winker, 2017). For example, research published in predatory journals that has not undergone rigorous review is cited by authors publishing in legitimate journals (Akça & Akbulut, 2021; Manca et al., 2017). As a consequence, this work enters the scientific and public domain without rigorous review. Though researchers may themselves actively avoid publication in predatory journals, it may not be feasible for authors, editors, or reviews to check whether research cited by other academics is published in predatory journals (Roberts, 2016).

Subject in Focus 2: Women and Online Abuse

Women, and other minoritized groups, are more likely to be targeted for online abuse. For example, female hosted YouTube science channels are more likely to receive hostile feedback, comments on presenter appearance, and sexist or sexual comments (Amarasekara & Grant, 2019). Similarly, in a survey of female science popularisers, McDonald, Barriault, and Merritt (2020) report that all respondents had personally experienced or witnessed at least one gender harassing behaviour and 47% of those questioned had experienced or witnessed at least one of the behaviours often or very often. Most women (78%) surveyed believed that gender harassment had impacted on their behaviour (e.g., avoiding controversial subjects or wearing more conservative clothing). As a consequence, there has been a call for further research examining the online harassment experienced by female academics (Kavanagh & Brown, 2020).

The disproportionate abuse directed at some groups (e.g., women) serves to silence those who are already marginalised and underrepresented. In general populations, women may be cautious expressing their opinions online as women are more likely than men to be the subject of comments based on group characteristics such as gender or sexuality (Nadim & Fladmoe, 2021). Women are less likely to feature as experts within the media, reflecting both media bias in selection and women's reluctance to be perceived as self-promoting (Howell & Singer, 2017), and abuse further impacts on their presence. Despite abuse from members of the public following media appearances, female academics often remain committed to public engagement reporting a sense of responsibility to both science communication and the representation of female experts (Samer, Lacombe, & Calmy, 2021). It is essential that measures are in place to both reduce the abuse experienced and support women where this occurs.

References

Abdelaal, G. (2020). Coping with imposter syndrome in academia and research. *The Biochemist*, *42*(3), 62–64. https://doi.org/10.1042/BIO20200033

Adriaenssens, L., De Prins, P., & Vloeberghs, D. (2006). Work experience, work stress and HRM at the university. *Management Revue*, *17*(3), 344–363.

Akça, S., & Akbulut, M. (2021). Are predatory journals contaminating science? An analysis on the Cabells' Predatory Report. *The Journal of Academic Librarianship*, *47*(4), 102366. https://doi.org/10.1016/j.acalib.2021.102366

Amarasekara, I., & Grant, W. J. (2019). Exploring the YouTube science communication gender gap: A sentiment analysis. *Public Understanding of Science*, *28*(1), 68–84. https://doi.org/10.1177/0963662518786654

Ball, S. J. (2012). Performativity, commodification and commitment: An I-Spy guide to the neoliberal University. *British Journal of Educational Studies*, *60*(1), 17–28. https://doi.org/10.1080/00071005.2011.650940

Barlow, C., & Awan, I. (2016). "You need to be sorted out with a knife": The attempted online silencing of women and people of Muslim faith within academia. *Social Media+ Society*, *2*(4), 2056305116678896. https://doi.org/10.1177/2056305116678896

Baum, J. A. C. (2011). Free-riding on power laws: Questioning the validity of the impact factor as a measure of research quality in organization studies. *Organization*, *18*(4), 449–466. https://doi.org/10.1177/1350508411403531

Beall, J. (2016). Essential information about predatory publishers and journals. *International Higher Education*, *86*, 2–3. https://doi.org/10.6017/ihe.2016.86.9358

Beckers, D. G., van Hooff, M. L. M., van der Linden, D., Kompier, M. A. J., Taris, T. W., & Geurts, S. A. E. (2008). A diary study to open up the black box of overtime work among university faculty members. *Scandinavian Journal of Work, Environment & Health*, *34*(3), 213–223.

Bedeian, A. G. (2003). The manuscript review process: The proper roles of authors, referees, and editors. *Journal of Management Inquiry*, *12*(4), 331–338. https://doi.org/10.1177/1056492603258974

Bedeian, A. G. (2004). Peer review and the social construction of knowledge in the management discipline. *Academy of Management Learning & Education*, *3*(2), 198–216. https://doi.org/10.5465/amle.2004.13500489

Bohannon, J. (2013). Who's afraid of peer review? *Science*, *342*(6154), 60–65. http://doi.org/10.1126/science.342.6154.60

Bos, J. T., Donders, N. C., van der Velden, K., & van der Gulden, J. W. (2013). Perceptions of mental workload in Dutch university employees of different ages: A focus group study. *BMC Research Notes*, *6*, 102. https://doi.org/10.1186/1756-0500-6-102

Brems, C., Baldwin, M. R., Davis, L., & Namyniuk, L. (1994). The imposter syndrome as related to teaching evaluations and advising relationships of university faculty members. *The Journal of Higher Education*, *65*(2), 183–193. https://doi.org/10.1080/00221546.1994.11778489

Burrows, R. (2012). Living with the h-Index? Metric assemblages in the contemporary academy. *The Sociological Review*, *60*(2), 355–372. https://doi.org/10.1111/j.1467-954X.2012.02077.x

Butler, N., & Spoelstra. S. (2014). The regime of excellence and the erosion of ethos in critical management studies. *British Journal of Management*, *25*(3), 538–550. https://doi.org/10.1111/1467-8551.12053

Celuch, M., Savela, N., Oksa, R., Latikka, R., & Oksanen, A. (2022). Individual factors predicting reactions to online harassment among Finnish professionals. *Computers in Human Behavior*, *127*, 107022. https://doi.org/10.1016/j.chb.2021.107022

Clance, P. R., & Imes, S. A. (1978). The imposter phenomenon in high achieving women: Dynamics and therapeutic intervention. *Psychotherapy: Theory, Research & Practice*, *15*(3), 241–247. https://doi.org/10.1037/h0086006

Clark, M., Vardeman, K., & Barba, S. (2014). Perceived inadequacy: A study of the imposter phenomenon among college and research librarians. *College & Research Libraries*. *75*(3), 255–271. https://doi.org/10.5860/crl12-423

Cobey, K. (2017). Illegitimate journals scam even senior scientists. *Nature*, *549*, 7. https://doi.org/10.1038/549007a

Colley, T., & Moore, M. (2022). The challenges of studying 4chan and the Alt-right: 'Come on in the water's fine'. *New Media & Society*, *24*(1), 5–30. https://doi.org/10.1177/1461444820948803

Collinson, J. A. (2006). Just 'non-academics'? Research administrators and contested occupational identity. *Work, Employment and Society*, *20*(2), 267–288. https://doi.org/10.1177/0950017006064114

Dahlvig, J. E. (2013). A narrative study of women leading within the Council for Christian Colleges & Universities. *Christian Higher Education*, *12*(1–2), 93–109. https://doi.org/10.1080/15363759.2013.739435

Day, N. E. (2011). The silent majority: Manuscript rejection and its impact on scholars. *Academy of Management Learning & Education*, *10*(4), 704–718. https://doi.org/10.5465/amle.2010.0027

Demir, S. B. (2018). Predatory journals: Who publishes in them and why? *Journal of Informetrics*, *12*(4), 1296–1311. https://doi.org/10.1016/j.joi.2018.10.008

Edwards, C. W. (2019). Overcoming imposter syndrome and stereotype threat: Reconceptualizing the definition of a scholar. *Taboo: The Journal of Culture and Education*, *18*(1), 3. https://doi.org/10.31390/taboo.18.1.03

Eslen-Ziya, H., Giorgi, A., & Ahi, C. J. (2023). Digital vulnerabilities and online harassment of academics, consequences, and coping strategies: An exploratory analysis. *Feminist Media Studies*, *24*(6), 1422–1427. https://doi.org/10.1080/14680777.2023.2281268

Ferber, A. L. (2018). "Are you willing to die for this work?" Public targeted online harassment in higher education: SWS presidential address. *Gender & Society*, *32*(3), 301–320. https://doi.org/10.1177/0891243218766831

Ferris, L. E., & Winker, M. A. (2017). Ethical issues in publishing in predatory journals. *Biochemia Medica*, *27*(2), 279–284. https://doi.org/10.11613/BM.2017.030

Fields, L. N., & Cunningham-Williams, R. M. (2021). Experiences with imposter syndrome and authenticity at research-intensive schools of social work: A case study on Black female faculty. *Advances in Social Work*, *21*(2/3), 354–373. https://doi.org/10.18060/24124

Forgasz, H. J., & Leder, G. C. (2006). Academic life: Monitoring work patterns and daily activities. *The Australian Educational Researcher*, *33*(1), 1–22. https://doi.org/10.1007/BF03246278

Galpin, C., & Vernon, P. (2024). Post-truth politics as discursive violence: Online abuse, the public sphere and the figure of 'the expert'. *The British Journal of Politics and International Relations*, *26*(2), 423–443. https://doi.org/10.1177/13691481231202641

Giroux, H. A. (2014). *Neoliberalism's war on Higher Education*. Haymarket Books.

Giroux, H. A. (2015). *Education and the crisis of public values: Challenging the assault on teachers, students, and public education* (2nd ed.). Peter Lang.

Gosse, C., Veletsianos, G., Hodson, J., Houlden, S., Dousay, T. A., Lowenthal, P. R. (2021). The hidden costs of connectivity: Nature and effects of scholars' online harassment. *Learning, Media and Technology*, *46*(3), 264–280. https://doi.org/10.1080/17439884.2021.1878218

Grudniewicz, A., Moher, D., Cobey, K. D., Bryson, G. L., Cukier, S., Allen, K., … & Lalu, M. M. (2019). Predatory journals: No definition, no defence. *Nature*, *576*(7786), 210–212. https://doi.org/10.1038/d41586-019-03759-y

Hodson, J., O'Meara, V., Owen, J., Veletsianos, G., & Morales, E. (2024). Why don't faculty members report incidents of online abuse and what can be done about it? *Computers in Human Behavior Reports*, *15*, 100469. https://doi.org/10.1016/j.chbr.2024.100469

Horn, S. A. (2016). The social and psychological costs of peer review: Stress and coping with manuscript rejection. *Journal of Management Inquiry*, *25*(1), 11–26. https://doi.org/10.1177/1056492615586597

Horowitz, D. (2006). *The professors: The 101 most dangerous academics in America*. Regnery Publishing.

Houlden, S., Hodson, J., Veletsianos, G., Gosse, C., Lowenthal, P., Dousay, T., & Hall, N. C. (2022). Support for scholars coping with online harassment: An ecological framework. *Feminist Media Studies*, *22*(5), 1120–1138. https://doi.org/10.1080/14680777.2021.1883086

Howell, L., & Singer, J. B. (2017). Pushy or a princess? Women experts and British broadcast news. *Journalism Practice*, *11*(9), 1062–1078. https://doi.org/10.1080/17512786.2016.1232173

Huber, J., Inoua, S., Kerschbamer, R., König-Kersting, C., Palan, S., & Smith, V. L. (2022). Nobel and novice: Author prominence affects peer review. *Proceedings of the National Academy of Sciences*, *119*(41), e2205779119. https://doi.org/10.1073/pnas.2205779119

Hussain, S. (2015). Journal list fetishism and the 'sign of 4' in the ABS guide: A question of trust? *Organization*, *22*(1), 119–138. https://doi.org/10.1177/1350508413506763

Hutchins, H. M. (2015). Outing the imposter: A study exploring imposter phenomenon among higher education faculty. *New Horizons in Adult Education and Human Resource Development*, *27*(2), 3–12. https://doi.org/10.1002/nha3.20098

Hutchins, H. M., & Rainbolt, H. (2017). What triggers imposter phenomenon among academic faculty? A critical incident study exploring antecedents, coping, and development opportunities. *Human Resource Development International*, *20*(3), 194–214. https://doi.org/10.1080/13678868.2016.1248205

Jensen, A. L., & Morgan, K. (2009). The vanishing idea of a scholarly life: Workload calculations and the loss of academic integrity in Western Sydney. *Australian Universities Review*, *51*(2), 62–69.

Kavanagh, E., & Brown, L. (2020) Towards a research agenda for examining online gender-based violence against women academics. *Journal of Further and Higher Education*, *44*(10), 1379–1387. https://doi.org/10.1080/0309877X.2019.1688267

Kenny, J. (2018). Re-empowering academics in a corporate culture: An exploration of workload and performativity in a university. *Higher Education*, *75*, 365–380. https://doi.org/10.1007/s10734-017-0143-z

Kenny, J. D. J., & Fluck, A. E. (2014). The effectiveness of academic workload models in an institution: A staff perspective. *Journal of Higher Education Policy and Management*, *36*(6), 585–602. https://doi.org/10.1080/1360080X.2014.957889

Kurt, S. (2018). Why do authors publish in predatory journals? *Learned Publishing*, *31*(2), 141–147. https://doi.org/10.1002/leap.1150

Liu, F., AlShebli, B., & Rahwan, T. (2023). Editors handle their collaborators' submissions despite explicit policies. Preprint. https://doi.org/10.48550/arXiv.2307.00794

Macdonald, S., & Kam, J. (2007). Ring a ring o'roses: Quality journals and gamesmanship in management studies. *Journal of Management Studies*, *44*(4), 640–655. https://doi.org/10.1111/j.1467-6486.2007.00704.x

Macdonald, S., & Kam, J. (2008). Quality journals and gamesmanship in Management Studies. *Management Research News*, *31*(8), 595–606. https://doi.org/10.1108/01409170810892154

Manca, A., Martinez, G., Cugusi, L., Dragone, D., Dvir, Z., & Deriu, F. (2017). The surge of predatory open-access in neurosciences and neurology. *Neuroscience*, *353*, 166–173. https://doi.org/10.1016/j.neuroscience.2017.04.014

Manchikanti, L., Kaye, A. D., Boswell, M., & Hirsch, J. A. (2015). Medical journal peer review: Process and bias. *Pain Physician*, *18*(1), E1–E14.

Mavrogenis, A. F., Quaile, A., & Scarlat, M. M. (2020). The good, the bad, and the rude peer-review. *International Orthopaedics*, *44*, 413–415. https://doi.org/10.1007/s00264-020-04504-1

McDonald, L., Barriault, C., & Merritt, T. (2020). Effects of gender harassment on science popularization behaviors. *Public Understanding of Science*, *29*(7), 718–728. https://doi.org/10.1177/0963662520946667

McGee, E. O., & Kazembe, L. (2015). Entertainers or education researchers? The challenges associated with presenting while Black. *Race Ethnicity and Education*, *19*(1), 96–120. https://doi.org/10.1080/13613324.2015.1069263

Mertkan, S., Onurkan Aliusta, G., & Suphi, N. (2021). Profile of authors publishing in 'predatory' journals and causal factors behind their decision: A systematic review. *Research Evaluation*, *30*(4), 470–483. https://doi.org/10.1093/reseval/rvab032

Mewburn, I., & Thomson, P. (2013). Why do academics blog? An analysis of audiences, purposes and challenges. *Studies in Higher Education*, *38*(8), 1105–1119. https://doi.org/10.1080/03075079.2013.835624

Nadim, M., & Fladmoe, A. (2021). Silencing women? Gender and online harassment. *Social Science Computer Review*, *39*(2), 245–258. https://doi.org/10.1177/0894439319865518

Nogrady, B. (2021). "I hope you die": How the COVID pandemic unleashed attacks on scientists. *Nature*, *598*(7880), 250–253. https://doi.org/10.1038/d41586-021-02741-x

Nölleke, D., Leonhardt, B. M., & Hanusch, F. (2023). "The chilling effect": Medical scientists' responses to audience feedback on their media appearances during the COVID-19 pandemic. *Public Understanding of Science*, *32*(5), 09636625221146749. https://doi.org/10.1177/09636625221146749

Paewai, S. R., Meyer, L. H., & Houston, D. (2007). Problem solving academic workloads management: A university response. *Higher Education Quarterly*, *61*(3), 375–390. https://doi.org/10.1111/j.1468-2273.2007.00360.x

Parkman, A. (2016). The imposter phenomenon in Higher Education: Incidence and impact. *Journal of Higher Education Theory and Practice*, *16*(1), 51–60.

Perlin, M. S., Imasato, T., & Borenstein, D. (2018). Is predatory publishing a real threat? Evidence from a large database study. *Scientometrics*, *116*, 255–273. https://doi.org/10.1007/s11192-018-2750-6

Peters, D. P., & Ceci, S. J. (1982). Peer-review practices of psychological journals: The fate of published articles, submitted again. *Behavioral and Brain Sciences*, *5*(2), 187–255. https://doi.org/10.1017/S0140525X00011213

Pyne, D. (2017). The rewards of predatory publications at a small business school. *Journal of Scholarly Publishing*, *48*(3), 137–160. http://doi.org/10.3138/jsp.48.3.137

Remnant, J., Sang, K., Myhill, K., Calvard, T., Chowdhry, S., & Richards, J. (2023). Working it out: Will the improved management of leaky bodies in the workplace create a dialogue between medical sociology and disability studies? *Sociology of Health & Illness*, *45*(6), 1276–1299. https://doi.org/10.1111/1467-9566.13519

Roberts, J. (2016). Predatory journals: Illegitimate publishing and its threat to all readers and authors. *The Journal of Sexual Medicine*, *13*(12), 1830–1833. https://doi.org/10.1016/j.jsxm.2016.10.008

Rossi, F. (2010). Massification, competition and organizational diversity in higher education: Evidence from Italy. *Studies in Higher Education*, *35*(3), 277–300. https://doi.org/10.1080/03075070903050539

Samer, C., Lacombe, K., & Calmy, A. (2021). Cyber harassment of female scientists will not be the new norm. *The Lancet Infectious Diseases*, *21*(4), 457–458. https://doi.org/10.1016/S1473-3099(20)30944-0

Shapiro, B. (2004). *Brainwashed: How universities indoctrinate America's youth*. Thomas Nelson.

Sheikh, A. (2000). Publication ethics and the research assessment exercise: Reflections on the troubled question of authorship. *Journal of Medical Ethics*, *26*(6), 422–426. https://doi.org/10.1136/jme.26.6.422

Shen, C., & Björk, B. C. (2015). 'Predatory' open access: A longitudinal study of article volumes and market characteristics. *BMC Medicine*, *13*, 230. http://doi.org/10.1186/s12916-015-0469-2

Stone-Sabali, S., Bernard, D. L., Mills, K. J., & Osborn, P. R. (2023). Mapping the evolution of the impostor phenomenon research: A bibliometric analysis. *Current Psychology*, *42*, 32097–32109. https://doi.org/10.1007/s12144-022-04201-9

Szekeres, J. (2004). The invisible workers. *Journal of Higher Education Policy and Management*, *26*(1), 7–22. https://doi.org/10.1080/1360080042000182500

Tvina, A., Spellecy, R., & Palatnik, A. (2019). Bias in the peer review process: Can we do better? *Obstetrics & Gynecology*, *133*(6), 1081–1083. https://doi.org/10.1097/AOG.0000000000003260

Vardi, I. (2009). The impacts of different types of workload allocation models on academic satisfaction and working life. *Higher Education*, *57*, 499–508. https://doi.org/10.1007/s10734-008-9159-8

Veletsianos, G., Houlden, S., Hodson, J., & Gosse, C. (2018). Women scholars' experiences with online harassment and abuse: Self-protection, resistance, acceptance, and self-blame. *New Media & Society*, *20*(12), 4689–4708. https://doi.org/10.1177/1461444818781324

Wilkinson, C. (2020) Imposter syndrome and the accidental academic: An autoethnographic account. *International Journal for Academic Development*, *25*(4), 363–374. https://doi.org/10.1080/1360144X.2020.1762087

Willmott, H. (2011). Journal list fetishism and the perversion of scholarship: Reactivity and the ABS list. *Organization*, *18*(4), 429–442. https://doi.org/10.1177/1350508411403532

Woolston, C. (2016). Faking it. *Nature*, *529*, 555–557. https://doi.org/10.1038/nj7587-555a.

Xia, J., Harmon, J. L., Connolly, K. G., Donnelly, R. M., Anderson, M. R., & Howard, H. A. (2015). Who publishes in "predatory" journals? *Journal of the Association for Information Science and Technology*, *66*(7), 1406–1417. https://doi.org/10.1002/asi.23265

Zorn, D. (2005). Academic culture feeds the imposter phenomenon. *Academic Leader*, *21*(8).

Chapter 2

Health, Wellbeing, and Burnout

Historically, academia has been perceived as a "low-stress profession". There has, however, been a significant change in the higher education sector, and high levels of stress, distress, and burnout now exist. Indeed, important indicators of staff satisfaction (e.g., intentions of leaving the sector) appear to have become more rather than less concerning over time (Kinman, Jones, & Kinman, 2006). Workload also remains a persistent issue. In one national survey, 62% of those employed in the higher education sector reported regularly working over 40 hours per week, 22% reported working at least 50 hours per week, and 52% of respondents experienced unrealistic time pressures often or always (Wray & Kinman, 2021). Chapter 2 provides an overview of the occupational stress that exists across the higher education sector and the impact of this on employees. There is a particular emphasis on employee mental health and burnout.

Stress, Health, and Wellbeing

Academia constitutes a challenging and competitive environment increasingly characterised by performance management and close monitoring of staff. In part, this environment reflects broader financial pressures and increased assessment of the student experience and student outcomes. Research indicates that increased competition and the expectations placed on staff have contributed to elevated stress levels (Priyadarshini, Ponnam, & Banerjee, 2015). The "student-as-consumer" model of education has also negatively impacted staff wellbeing (O'Brien & Guiney, 2018). As a consequence, higher education staff report higher levels of stress compared to normative data (Tytherleigh et al., 2005).

Gillespie et al. (2001) explore experiences of occupational stress in university employees, identifying five sources of stress. These were (1) inadequate funding and resources (e.g., inadequate teaching spaces and IT support), (2) excessive workload (e.g., increased numbers of students and administrative responsibilities), (3) poor management (e.g., frequent organisational change and a lack of consultation), (4) job insecurity (e.g., threat of redundancy and

DOI: 10.4324/9781032639321-3

precarious contracts), and (5) inadequate recognition and reward (e.g., few opportunities for promotion and low recognition of teaching excellence compared to research). Overall, the increased stress reported by academics reflects both increased demands (e.g., administrative burdens) and fewer resources or support (e.g., role clarity).

It is important to recognise that research in this area often focuses on higher education in North America and Western Europe. There is, of course, likely to be substantial variation in the academic experience, influenced, for example, by regional levels of job security and the extent to which teaching and research performance are assessed. In countries such as the United States that operate a tenure-track system, a lack of tenure may be especially stressful, with non-tenured academics aware that their ongoing appointment is contingent on research funding, student recruitment, or individual performance. Adopting a longitudinal design, Reevy and Deason (2014) explore the experiences of non-tenured faculty, with those employees identifying workplace stressors directly related to the non-tenured nature of their role. Stressors included a lack of support (e.g., physical space to work), not being able to contribute to departmental activities (e.g., governance), a lack of recognition, and a lack of benefits (e.g., healthcare).

The development and communication of stress-based interventions is, therefore, important. Pignata et al. (2016) report that awareness of stress interventions predicted job satisfaction, affective organisational commitment, and trust in senior management in non-academic university employees. In academic employees, awareness of stress-based interventions predicted job satisfaction and organisational trust only. Further, those who had worked for the institution for an intermediate period were most aware of stress-related interventions and most positive about the institution.

Given the stressors associated with the academic environment, it is perhaps not surprising that those employed in higher education report relatively poor health and wellbeing. For example, Catano et al. (2010) surveyed academic staff from 56 universities in Canada, with 13% and 22% of respondents reporting high psychological distress and elevated physical health symptoms, respectively. In a national study of over 2,000 higher education staff (85.9% academic staff, 14.1% academic-related staff), Wray and Kinman (2021) report that those employed in the higher education sector report lower than average wellbeing for all Health and Safety Executive (HSE) work hazard categories.

Workplace stress, especially in relation to workload, facilities, and student management, also impacts the wellbeing and performance of professional services staff, for example, in relation to poor concentration, forgetfulness, and anxiety (Uzoechina & Onuselogu, 2009). Relatively few studies have, however, focused on the wellbeing of university administrators compared to students or academics (Górak-Sosnowska, & Piwowar-Sulej, 2023). Though Winefield et al. (2003) report poorer wellbeing in academic than non-academic staff, Ablanedo-Rosas et al. (2011) report similar levels of stress experienced by academic and non-academic university staff. Additional research addressing the causes, experience, and consequences of poor health and wellbeing in non-academic higher education employees is, therefore, required.

The consequences of stress and ill health extend beyond the individual, with research highlighting the relationships between workplace stress, ill health and job performance (e.g., Gillespie et al., 2001). For example, if staff wellbeing is compromised, this has a direct impact on interactions with students and the ability to provide academic and pastoral support (Brewster et al., 2022), though across the sector there is relatively little acknowledgement of the impact of staff wellbeing on the student experience.

Coping

Both organisational stressors and the strategies employed to cope with those stressors impact employee wellbeing. For example, academics with higher levels of self-efficacy and optimism report lower levels of stress and higher levels of life satisfaction (Darabi, Macaskill, & Reidy, 2017). Relatively few studies have, however, examined the coping strategies used within the higher education sector (Urbina-Garcia, 2020), and additional research is required. Research suggests that communication with loved ones and exercise are the adaptive strategies most commonly used by university employees, and alcohol consumption and increased consumption of food are the most frequently employed maladaptive strategies (Holton, Barry, & Chaney, 2016). Findings suggest appropriate areas for potential intervention and staff support (see Health and Wellbeing Interventions and Support section).

Coping strategies may also influence behaviour within the workplace. In a survey of academic and administrative staff employed at one university, Melin, Astvik, and Bernhard-Oettel (2014) identified three patterns of coping styles: Compensatory, restrictive, and self-supporting. Those in the first group, *compensatory*, were most likely to work through lunch breaks, evenings, and vacations and tended to deprioritise specific meetings and tasks. Those adopting a *restrictive* coping pattern were more likely to prioritise tasks (sometimes asking for support from supervisors to do so), set limits, seek assistance from colleagues, and object to taking on tasks and responsibilities when workload was already excessive. Employees in the final, *self-supporting* group tended not to take on work that they did not have time for. Perhaps unsurprisingly, each group differed in the average number of hours worked. Those adopting a compensatory approach worked the most hours each week (49.3), followed by those with restrictive (43.2) and self-supporting (38.9) styles.

Mental Health

There is particular concern relating to the mental health of higher education employees, and researchers have consistently documented significant anxiety and depression among university employees (e.g., Manaf et al., 2021; Meeks, Peak, & Dreihaus, 2023). Though such research has often focused on academic mental health, reporting that academics are more likely to experience psychological distress than other professions (Kinman, Jones, & Kinman, 2006), mental health is also of concern for administrators (Borges et al., 2023). A range of stressors, such as job insecurity and overwork, may negatively impact mental health in the higher education sector (Johnson & Lester, 2022; Nicholls et al., 2022). In addition to these general work-related stressors, university staff often provide support to others for psychological distress. In one study, Margrove et al. (2014) report that over 60% of university staff had provided support for students in distress, and over 40% of university staff had provided this support to their colleagues. The routine provision of such support may be difficult and further exacerbate mental health issues.

Despite the prevalence of mental distress in the higher education sector, there is a lack of open discourse on the subject (Nicholls et al., 2022). There has, however, been an increased willingness to share personal experiences of mental ill health in academia. For example, higher education employees have published personal accounts detailing their experiences of mental ill health (Butler, 2022; England, 2016; Fox & Gasper, 2020). High-profile cases of suicide have also drawn attention to the academic work environment and mental distress (Parr, 2014). Smith and Ulus (2020) explore the blogs and news articles written by academics that discuss mental health or distress. These describe the extent to which emotional distress occurs, the role of stigma and social inequality, and the pressure to hide these. For example, the author comments, "*I have chosen not to disclose the diagnosis and for many years I have hidden the symptoms. They are masked, veiled, denied by me – because being depressed is incompatible with the identity of an academic*" (p. 849) and

> I smiled, I chatted. I conveyed (I hoped authority). And then I would close my office door, curl up in the corner, and cry silently, only to get up again and present a competent self. Day after day this would happen.
>
> (p. 849)

Burnout

"Burnout" describes a state of physical, emotional, and mental exhaustion which develops in response to chronic job-related stressors. Research indicates high levels of burnout in academia, and in one study, 81% of academic Chairs experienced moderate levels of burnout (Johns & Ossoff, 2005). Action is therefore required, both to address the causes of academic burnout and to support those experiencing or at risk of burnout. According to MacDougall (2000), there are four stages of the burnout process. These are (1) emotional warning signs (e.g., vague anxiety, fatigue), (2) mild physical and emotional symptoms (e.g., sleep disturbance, social withdrawal), (3) entrenched symptoms (e.g., excessive irritability, emotional outbursts), and (4) debilitating emotional and physical symptoms (e.g., severe depression, inability to function). Interventions could, therefore, be implemented at each stage of the burnout process.

There are three well-established components of burnout: (1) Emotional exhaustion, (2) cynicism or depersonalisation, and (3) lack of accomplishment or ineffectiveness (Maslach, Schaufeli, & Leiter, 2001). Emotional exhaustion refers to the feeling of fatigue as emotional energy becomes depleted. Depersonalisation is experienced when the person becomes indifferent to or cynical towards work and the people (e.g., students) they support. As people no longer feel that they are making a meaningful contribution, a lack of personal accomplishment and self-efficacy is experienced. Levels of emotional exhaustion are especially high in the higher education sector. In one national survey, Wray and Kinman (2021) report that 65.3% of those employed in higher education feel emotionally drained from work at least once per week, with 25.6% and 28.6% reporting feeling emotionally drained a few times each week and every day, respectively. Burnout appears to be a developmental process, though the causal relationships between each component of burnout have been debated (Taris et al., 2005).

As discussed in Chapter 1, the higher education sector is challenging, and numerous aspects of the academic or academic-related (e.g., professional services) role may contribute to burnout. Perhaps unsurprisingly, high workloads and role conflict consistently predict academic burnout (Sabagh et al., 2018). In addition, the number of students taught, time spent assessing students, and student evaluation also predict burnout (Lackritz, 2004; Watts & Robertson, 2011). For those in advanced positions (e.g., Chairs), factors such as departmental budget deficits, loss of faculty, and time spent on administrative duties contribute to burnout (Johns & Ossoff, 2005). Additional recognition is required for the burnout that may result from specific responsibilities and the increased likelihood of burnout experienced by some people. For example, those at greater personal risk of discrimination and engaging in activism may be more likely to experience burnout, though there is little recognition of this issue in research, practice, and policy (Wolbring & Lillywhite, 2023).

It is important to note that though research (as illustrated by this book) typically focuses on the negative aspects of higher education, some aspects of the academic role can be personally meaningful and rewarding. Research indicates that academics who spend a relatively low proportion of their time on the most personally meaningful activities are at greater risk of burnout (Shanafelt et al., 2009). As a consequence, allowing academics to specialise and shape their role may promote health and wellbeing. It is, of course, important to ensure that if providing specific routes through higher education (e.g., distinct teaching and scholarship and teaching and research contracts), equal opportunities for promotion and reward are available.

Research indicates that specific academic groups, such as younger academics and those with less experience or of a lower academic rank, are at greater risk of burnout (Sabagh, Hall, & Saroyan, 2018). There has, however, been relatively little recognition of the incidence of burnout in administrators working in the higher education sector. Burnout is often associated with employees in public-facing or caring roles, suggesting that professional services staff in direct contact with students may be at elevated risk of burnout. Initial research has identified significant levels of burnout in research administrators (Tabakakis et al., 2020). Factors such as emotional job demands, role ambiguity, and management ineffectiveness may contribute to burnout in university administrators (Lei, Alam, & Hassan, 2023; Noor, Aslam, & Md Isa, 2024), and more recognition of this issue is required.

Burnout has significant consequences for both the individual employee (e.g., mental and physical ill health) and the institution (e.g., low productivity). For example, research consistently demonstrates that burnout is associated with low levels of organisational commitment, lowered personal identification with the academic role, and higher intentions to leave the organisation and/or sector (Sabagh, Hall, & Saroyan, 2018). Despite this, burnout has been conceptualised as a common academic experience that is simply not discussed (Jaremka et al., 2020).

Burnout in Health-Related Disciplines

In some disciplines, academics may combine their faculty (teaching and/or research) role with clinical practice. These faculty are, therefore, exposed to both the pressures of academia and the challenges of a practitioner role. For example, staff may be expected to engage in professional development relating to programme design, maintain clinical skills, and conduct subject-specific research. Perhaps unsurprisingly, such staff are at elevated risk of burnout. There has been particular examination of burnout in relation to such academic disciplines as nursing (Boamah et al., 2023; Hosseini et al., 2022), medicine (Kavanagh & Spiro, 2018; Summers et al., 2019), and pharmacy (Darbishire, Isaacs, & Miller, 2020; El-Ibiary, Yam, & Lee, 2017).

In addition to more generalised workplace pressures such as workload, the consequences of a mistake are far greater for those in clinical fields (e.g., harm to patients, accusations of professional misconduct). Clinical academics must both maintain their own professional standards and ensure the competency and ethical practice of their students; this may represent a significant emotional burden. Greater support is required for clinical academics and recognition of these issues. These issues may, of course, also impact recruitment and retention in the wider discipline. For example, in one study of early career (i.e., four or fewer years of teaching experience) nursing faculty, the emotional exhaustion and depersonalisation aspects of burnout predicted intentions to leave nursing academia (Aquino et al., 2018).

Risk Factors and Vulnerability

A range of environmental, social, and individual factors may exacerbate or lessen the impact of work-related stressors and job strain on academic wellbeing (Achour, Mohd Nor, & MohdYusoff, 2016). Marginalised groups may be especially vulnerable to workplace stress and ill health, both as students and as academic or non-academic staff. For example, marginalisation and discrimination negatively impact health and wellbeing, which may be further compounded by a lack of culturally appropriate services (Stoll et al., 2022). Utilising the narratives of academic and professional services staff, Arday (2022) explores the specific issues experienced by Black and minority ethnic communities. As stated by one person, "*The isolation… I experience as a Black person in the Academy is debilitating, you end up residing in this prism which becomes a downward spiral. Consequently, the violence of these racialised cultures affects your mental wellbeing*". (p. 91).

Specific networks for minoritised staff could lessen the impact of isolation within academia. Ensuring that mental health services understand the importance of cultural context and experiences of discrimination is important and should inform service provision. Further, interventions and services are required that specifically address racial, ethnic, and cultural discrimination. Similarly, social class (referring to overall social status and including social and cultural capital) can impact experiences of higher education in a range of ways, including financial freedom to pursue opportunities such as conference attendance. Indeed, poor wellbeing is more than twice as likely amongst university staff from lower-class backgrounds, and status, inclusion and autonomy appear to mediate the relationship between social class and wellbeing (Dougall, Weick, & Vasiljevic, 2021). Social class also impacts the extent to which those from lower social classes and socioeconomic backgrounds experience isolation and exclusion or acceptance and respect (Binns, 2019), and greater recognition of this issue is required.

COVID-19

The COVID-19 pandemic presented additional challenges to academics and professional services staff already experiencing high workloads and substantial work-related stress (Wray & Kinman, 2022). For example, universities were required to change programme delivery in response to national lockdowns, requiring a shift to online learning and assessment using unfamiliar software. This took place whilst academics and professional service staff sought to support students in distress, often struggling to cope with isolation, anxiety, and increased financial pressures. The occupational stress experienced by academics during the pandemic negatively impacted emotional wellbeing and mental health (Shen & Slater, 2021). For some disciplines (e.g., nursing, medicine), staff and students also placed themselves at direct risk of infection by working on the "front-line" of the pandemic.

In one longitudinal study (collecting data twice in 2020 and once in 2021), Wood et al. (2022) explored the health and wellbeing of academics and professional services staff employed by British universities during the pandemic. Uncertainty (focused on the job and employer support) predicted poorer wellbeing, including increased levels of anxiety and depression. This uncertainty may include both short- and long-term aspects of employment. For example, short-term uncertainty regarding programme delivery and long-term uncertainty relating to job security in the context of reduced university funding. Similarly, Charoensukmongkol and Phungsoonthorn (2021) also report that uncertainty contributed to the emotional exhaustion reported by university employees.

The pandemic was, of course, especially difficult for some faculty and professional services staff. A substantial number of higher education employees had caring responsibilities during the pandemic (Dinu et al., 2021), and parents were required to balance their university role with childcare and homeschooling. Those with pre-existing health conditions or a compromised immune system often experienced disruption to treatment and/or were required to isolate for longer periods of time. During the COVID-19 pandemic, female university staff, those with comorbid conditions, and administrative staff were more likely to experience psychological distress (Van Niekerk & van Gent, 2021). Similarly, though the blurred boundaries between work and home weakened existing social hierarchies, it was problematic for those from lower socioeconomic backgrounds. For example, whilst some people had access to a private office space with a comfortable office chair and necessary computer equipment, others were working at a kitchen table with little privacy or personal space. As a consequence, the quality of the home office space and equipment available had an important impact on staff experiences of home working (Dinu et al., 2021).

Health and Wellbeing Interventions and Support

Recognising the incidence of stress and ill health in the higher education sector, institutions have increasingly developed health- and wellbeing-related interventions. Such interventions can include specific events (e.g., a "wellbeing week") intended to draw attention to a health issue, focus attention on available services, or prompt behavioural change. In one review of health interventions targeted at university staff, Plotnikoff et al. (2015) report that interventions focusing on weight loss, physical activity, or nutrition are most common. It is important to note, however, that interventions focused on employee wellbeing remain less prevalent than interventions intended to improve productivity or student satisfaction (Ohadomere & Ogamba, 2021).

Interventions introduced and evaluated include apps (e.g., Lahtinen et al., 2023) and exercise (e.g., Hartfiel et al., 2011). For example, it has been suggested that one 60-minute yoga class per week for six weeks can improve the mood and wellbeing of university employees (Hartfiel et al., 2011). Similarly, Lemola et al. (2021) introduced a "rewards for activity" app specifically targeted at university employees with low to moderate physical activity levels. Self-reported steps were converted to a virtual currency that could be used in university outlets or within the app. During the three-month trial, there was an increase in self-reported physical activity, sleep quality, life satisfaction, and positive affect. The positive impact of the intervention was not, however, observed at a 12-month follow-up. A range of individual, occupational, and environmental factors may also influence awareness of and responses to workplace interventions (Pignata et al., 2016).

Of course, whilst such interventions may be popular with institutions, they often focus on individual responses to stress and personal resilience, implying that experiencing stress or ill health is a personal "failure" to cope and failing to recognise or address the structural and systemic issues which impact on employee wellbeing (Brewster et al., 2022). For example, a time management course does not actually reduce the duties and responsibilities required by an excessive workload. Perhaps reflecting this issue, the least helpful sources of support identified by those employed in higher education include health promotion (39%), telephone or online support for wellbeing (36%), goal-setting and coping skills (36%), guidance on wellbeing and self-care (35%), culturally appropriate counselling (35%), time management and personal organisation training (31%), guidance on work-life balance (31%), individual-focused stress-management training (e.g., mindfulness) (30%), support and guidance for personal difficulties (e.g., finance) (23%), and group counselling (15%) (Wray & Kinman, 2021).

Further, though universities often have support available to staff, employees may be reluctant to access it. In one national survey, 71% of respondents agreed or strongly agreed that seeking support for their wellbeing would harm their career (Wray & Kinman, 2021). In part, this may reflect the inconsistency between institutional guidance and workplace culture. As summarised by Evans et al. (2024), "*The academic job market is brutal and highly competitive; it is naive to believe a CV with sparse publications but a solid commitment to ethics and well-being will fare better than one with more conventional achievements*". (p. 13). Wray and Kinman (2021) also note that the vast majority of staff questioned (92%) report that they are able to discuss work-related stress with co-workers, suggesting important avenues for intervention and support. The most beneficial sources of support identified were feeling appreciated and respected (92%), the ability to work from home (86%), opportunities for informal chats with colleagues (86%), encouragement to take time off when unwell (83%), timetabling that ensures adequate breaks between teaching (81%), and managers who are aware of the pressures of the job (81%).

Recommendations

Institutions should,

- Acknowledge the extent to which stress impacts employees and the role of institutional issues such as workload and communication. Staff training often focuses on "staff awareness" of occupational health without accepting institutional responsibility for significant occupational stressors. Stress-reduction interventions should be introduced and publicised.

- Ensure that staff are not penalised for issues that are beyond their control. For example, high importance is placed on markers of student satisfaction such as the National Student Survey. Though some aspects of the student experience can be improved by individual staff and departments (e.g., how intellectually stimulating a course is), other areas (e.g., timetabling of teaching sessions) are more likely to be under central university control. Institutions must take responsibility for initiatives that have negatively impacted student satisfaction.
- Implement measures to address staff workload. Where workload increases for a fixed period (e.g., increased marking due to a large student intake), the additional resources required (e.g., additional staff) should be provided without delay. Initiatives to reduce bureaucracy are welcomed. However, it is important to introduce these in consultation and collaboration with staff. Measures intended to reduce bureaucracy can often inadvertently increase workloads. For example, changes to programme assessment intended to reduce marking can increase the workload of staff involved in the quality assurance process, and this should be compensated for.
- Provide clear opportunities for the promotion of academic and non-academic staff. This should include clear promotion criteria and mentorship. Non-academic staff are often provided with less support than their academic colleagues, and this inequity must be addressed. Other forms of reward and recognition are also encouraged (e.g., staff awards) for academic and non-academic staff to ensure that staff contributions feel valued.
- Prioritise staff mental health. For example, trained mental health advocates should be present in all departments who are able to provide initial support and guidance. Counselling should be available to staff (including those on fixed-term contracts), and staff should be able to self-refer (i.e., without informing Human Resources or a line manager). It is especially important that staff who provide front-line support for students (and their mental health) are informed of and able to access this support.
- Support staff to recognise the early signs of burnout. It is essential that early support and intervention be available. The additional stress associated with clinical roles should also be recognised. Support should include a review of workload, roles, and responsibilities. For example, staff should be able to continue with rewarding and meaningful activities whilst being provided with relief for stressful or burdensome areas of the role.
- Provide additional support for marginalised staff (e.g., staff networks) and recognise the impact of additional stressors such as racism on campus or national discussions that negatively represent marginalised groups such as immigrants or members of the LGBTQIA community.

Subject in Focus 1: Work-Life Balance and Work-Life Conflict

There is a well-established literature examining "work-life balance" in the higher education sector (Fauzi et al., 2024). For example, in one study involving 1,474 academic and 1,953 non-academic staff employed across nine universities in the United Kingdom, Fontinha, Easton, and Van Laar (2019) identified a negative relationship between work-life balance and additional hours worked. Work-life balance policies are, therefore, commonplace in academia. It is important to note that whilst such policies are often in place, the impact of work-life policies may be limited by a culture that rewards commitment to the academic role and excessive working hours. Indeed, engagement with work-life policies may have a negative impact on academic identity and perceived character (Cannizzo, Mauri, & Osbaldiston, 2019). Further, though institutional policies (such as those providing opportunities for flexible working) may provide some support for higher education staff, they also extend the reach of the institution beyond the workplace and can further blur the boundaries between employment and personal life (Saltmarsh & Randell-Moon, 2015).

When work-related pressures are not compatible with the pressures of personal life, conflict occurs. This may take the form of work-life conflict, with work interfering with personal life, or life-work conflict where the personal life impacts on work. These two forms of conflict should be conceptualised as related but distinct (Mesmer-Magnus & Viswesvaran, 2005). Work-life conflict may be especially common among academics (who often have high workloads and long working hours). For example, in a national survey conducted by Wray and Kinman (2021), 36% of those surveyed report that they always or almost always neglect their personal needs due to work demands and 28% reported missing important personal activities due to work almost or almost always.

Work-life conflict has a range of negative consequences for the individual academic (e.g., life dissatisfaction, conflict with loved ones, and stress) and institution (e.g., low productivity, dissatisfaction with work, and intentions to leave the institution or sector). Indeed, work-life conflict (but not life-work conflict) negatively impacts on job satisfaction (Dorenkamp & Ruhle, 2019). Such issues do not, of course, impact all higher education employees equally. For example, reflecting greater caregiving and academic housekeeping responsibilities etc, female academics typically report a poorer work-life balance and greater work-life conflict than their male colleagues (Fauzi et al., 2024; Rosa, 2022). Similarly, those on precarious contracts who are regularly expected to move institutions and geographical area may find it particularly difficult to create a stable home life (e.g., be unable to secure a mortgage or require children to change their school). It is, therefore, important to recognise and address this inequality.

Subject in Focus 2: Healthy Universities

Greater recognition of the health and wellbeing issues experienced by higher education staff has resulted in additional guidance for institutions targeted at this area. In 1998, the World Health Organisation published 'Health Promoting Universities: Concept, Experience and Framework for Action' (Tsouros et al., 1998). The document outlines the principles that underpin healthy universities, includes a series of detailed case studies, and provides a framework to support the strategic development of health-promoting higher education projects.

Similarly, the UK Healthy Universities Network provides a toolkit for higher education institutions planning to adopt a healthy university approach including a self-review tool, guidance packages, and case studies (see https://healthyuniversities.ac.uk/ for more information). Despite this, there has arguably been less interest in the concept or implementation of "healthy universities" compared to similar initiatives in other sectors such as "healthy schools" (Dooris & Doherty, 2010). In part, this may reflect a lack of high-level international leadership and support compared to other initiatives as well as the complex organisational structures and diverse goals associated with higher education (Newton, Dooris, & Wills, 2016).

Work in this area has continued, however, and in 2020 Universities UK published the Mentally Healthy Universities Framework (de Pury & Dicks, 2020) encouraging institutions to make the mental health and wellbeing of staff and students a strategic priority. A self-assessment tool is also available. There is, therefore, substantial guidance for institutions wishing to support the health and wellbeing of its staff and students.

References

Ablanedo-Rosas, J. H., Blevins, R. C., Gao, H., Teng, W. Y., & White, J. (2011). The impact of occupational stress on academic and administrative staff, and on students: An empirical case analysis. *Journal of Higher Education Policy and Management*, *33*(5), 553–564. https://doi.org/10.1080/1360080X.2011.605255

Achour, M., Mohd Nor, M. R., & MohdYusoff, M. Y. Z. (2016). Islamic personal religiosity as a moderator of job strain and employee's well-being: The case of Malaysian academic and administrative staff. *Journal of Religion and Health*, *55*, 1300–1311. https://doi.org/10.1007/s10943-015-0050-5

Aquino, E., Lee, Y. M., Spawn, N., & Bishop-Royse, J. (2018). The impact of burnout on doctorate nursing faculty's intent to leave their academic position: A descriptive survey research design. *Nurse Education Today*, *69*, 35–40. https://doi.org/10.1016/j.nedt.2018.06.027

Arday, J. (2022). No one can see me cry: Understanding mental health issues for Black and minority ethnic staff in higher education. *Higher Education*, *83*(1), 79–102. https://doi.org/10.1007/s10734-020-00636-w

Binns, C. (2019). *Experiences of academics from a working-class heritage: Ghosts of childhood habitus.* Cambridge Scholars Publishing.

Boamah, S. A., Kalu, M., Stennett, R., Belita, E., & Travers, J. (2023). Pressures in the ivory tower: An empirical study of burnout scores among nursing faculty. *International Journal of Environmental Research and Public Health, 20*(5), 4398. https://doi.org/10.3390/ijerph20054398

Borges, L. d. O., Motta, G. M. V., Garcia-Primo, G. M., Barros, S. C., & Heleno, C. T. (2023). Working conditions and mental health in a Brazilian university. *International Journal of Environmental Research and Public Health, 20*(2), 1536. https://doi.org/10.3390/ijerph20021536

Brewster, L., Jones, E., Priestley, M., Wilbraham, S. J., Spanner, L., & Hughes, G. (2022). 'Look after the staff and they would look after the students' cultures of wellbeing and mental health in the university setting. *Journal of Further and Higher Education, 46*(4), 548–560. https://doi.org/10.1080/0309877X.2021.1986473

Butler, R. M. (2022). Serious mental illness in healthcare and academia: A lived experience. *Journal of Psychiatric and Mental Health Nursing, 29*(5), 624–629. https://doi.org/10.1111/jpm.12862

Cannizzo, F., Mauri, C., & Osbaldiston, N. (2019). Moral barriers between work/life balance policy and practice in academia. *Journal of Cultural Economy, 12*(4), 251–264. https://doi.org/10.1080/17530350.2019.1605400

Catano, V., Francis, L., Haines, T., Kirpalani, H., Shannon, H., Stringer, B., & Lozanzki, L. (2010). Occupational stress in Canadian universities: A national survey. *International Journal of Stress Management, 17*(3), 232–258. https://doi.org/10.1037/a0018582

Charoensukmongkol, P., & Phungsoonthorn, T. (2021). The effectiveness of supervisor support in lessening perceived uncertainties and emotional exhaustion of university employees during the COVID-19 crisis: The constraining role of organizational intransigence. *The Journal of General Psychology, 148*(4), 431–450. https://doi.org/10.1080/00221309.2020.1795613

Darabi, M., Macaskill, A., & Reidy, L. (2017). Stress among UK academics: Identifying who copes best. *Journal of Further and Higher Education, 41*(3), 393–412. https://doi.org/10.1080/0309877X.2015.1117598

Darbishire, P., Isaacs, A. N., & Miller, M. L. (2020). Faculty burnout in pharmacy education. *American Journal of Pharmaceutical Education, 84*(7), 7925. https://doi.org/10.5688/ajpe7925

de Pury, J., & Dicks, A. (2020). *Stepchange: Mentally healthy universities.* Universities UK. Retrieved from: https://www.universitiesuk.ac.uk/sites/default/files/field/downloads/2021-07/uuk-stepchange-mhu.pdf

Dinu, L. M., Dommett, E. J., Baykoca, A., Mehta, K. J., Everett, S., Foster, J. L., & Byrom, N. C. (2021). A case study investigating mental wellbeing of university academics during the COVID-19 pandemic. *Education Sciences, 11*(11), 702. https://doi.org/10.3390/educsci11110702

Dooris, M., & Doherty, S. (2010). Healthy universities-time for action: A qualitative research study exploring the potential for a national programme. *Health Promotion International, 25*(1), 94–106. https://doi.org/10.1093/heapro/daq015

Dorenkamp, I., & Ruhle, S. (2019). Work-life conflict, professional commitment, and job satisfaction among academics. *The Journal of Higher Education, 90*(1), 56–84. https://doi.org/10.1080/00221546.2018.1484644

Dougall, I., Weick, M., & Vasiljevic, M. (2021). Social class and wellbeing among staff and students in higher education settings: Mapping the problem and exploring underlying mechanisms. *Journal of Applied Social Psychology, 51*(10), 965–986. https://doi.org/10.1111/jasp.12814

El-Ibiary, S. Y., Yam, L., & Lee, K. C. (2017). Assessment of burnout and associated risk factors among pharmacy practice faculty in the United States. *American Journal of Pharmaceutical Education, 81*(4), 75. https://doi.org/10.5688/ajpe81475

England, M. R. (2016). Being open in academia: A personal narrative of mental illness and disclosure. *Canadian Geographies, 60*(2), 226–231. https://doi.org/10.1111/cag.12270

Evans, B., Allam, A., Bê, A., Hale, C., Rose, M., & Ruddock, A. (2024). Being left behind beyond recovery: 'Crip time' and chronic illness in neoliberal academia. *Social & Cultural Geography*, In Press. https://doi.org/10.1080/14649365.2024.2410262

Fauzi, M. A., Rahamaddulla, S. R., Lee, C. K., Ali, Z., & Alias, U. N. (2024). Work pressure in higher education: A state-of-the-art bibliometric analysis on academic work-life balance. *International Journal of Workplace Health Management, 17*(2), 175–195. https://doi.org/10.1108/IJWHM-01-2023-0002

Fontinha, R., Easton, S., & Van Laar, D. (2019). Overtime and quality of working life in academics and nonacademics: The role of perceived work-life balance. *International Journal of Stress Management, 26*(2), 173–183. https://doi.org/10.1037/str0000067

Fox, J., & Gasper, R. (2020). The choice to disclose (or not) mental health ill health in UK Higher Education Institutions: A duoethnography by two female academics. *Journal of Organizational Ethnography, 9*(3), 295–309. https://doi.org/10.1108/JOE-11-2019-0040

Gillespie, N. A., Walsh, M., Winefield, A. H., Dua, J., & Stough, C. (2001). Occupational stress in universities: Staff perceptions of the causes, consequences and moderators of stress. *Work & Stress, 15*(1), 53–72. https://doi.org/10.1080/02678370117944

Górak-Sosnowska, K., & Piwowar-Sulej, K. (2023). The well-being of female administrative staff in managerial positions in Polish Higher Education Institutions. *Central European Management Journal, 31*(2), 207–221. https://doi.org/10.1108/CEMJ-12-2021-0151

Hartfiel, N., Havenhand, J., Khalsa, S. B., Clarke, G., & Krayer, A. (2011). The effectiveness of yoga for the improvement of well-being and resilience to stress in the workplace. *Scandinavian Journal of Work, Environment & Health*, 37(1), 70–76.

Holton, M. K., Barry, A. E., & Chaney, J. D. (2016). Employee stress management: An examination of adaptive and maladaptive coping strategies on employee health. *Work, 53*(2), 299–305. https://doi.org/10.3233/WOR-152145

Hosseini, M., Soltanian, M., Torabizadeh, C., & Shirazi, Z. H. (2022). Prevalence of burnout and related factors in nursing faculty members: A systematic review. *Journal of Educational Evaluation for Health Professions, 19*. https://doi.org/10.3352/jeehp.2022.19.16

Jaremka, L. M., Ackerman, J. M., Gawronski, B., Rule, N. O., Sweeny, K., Tropp, L. R., … & Vick, S. B. (2020). Common academic experiences no one talks about: Repeated rejection, impostor syndrome, and burnout. *Perspectives on Psychological Science, 15*(3), 519–543. https://doi.org/10.1177/1745691619898848

Johns, M. M., & Ossoff, R. H. (2005). Burnout in academic chairs of otolaryngology: Head and neck surgery. *The Laryngoscope, 115*(11), 2056–2061. https://doi.org/10.1097/01.MLG.0000181492.36179.8B

Johnson, A. P., & Lester, R. J. (2022). Mental health in academia: Hacks for cultivating and sustaining wellbeing. *American Journal of Human Biology, 34*(S1), e23664. https://doi.org/10.1002/ajhb.23664

Kavanagh, K. R., & Spiro, J. (2018). Faculty wellness: Educator burnout among otolaryngology graduate medical educators. *Otolaryngology: Head and Neck Surgery, 158*(6), 991–994. https://doi.org/10.1177/0194599818770647

Kinman, G., Jones, F., & Kinman, R. (2006). The well-being of the UK Academy, 1998–2004. *Quality in Higher Education*, *12*(1), 15–27. https://doi.org/10.1080/13538320600685081

Lackritz, J. R. (2004). Exploring burnout among university faculty: Incidence, performance, and demographic issues. *Teaching and Teacher Education*, *20*(7), 713–729. https://doi.org/10.1016/j.tate.2004.07.002

Lahtinen, O., Aaltonen, J., Kaakinen, J., Franklin, L., & Hyönä, J. (2023). The effects of app-based mindfulness practice on the well-being of university students and staff. *Current Psychology*, *42*(6), 4412–4421. https://doi.org/10.1007/s12144-021-01762-z

Lei, M., Alam, G. M., & Hassan, A. (2023). Job burnout amongst university administrative staff members in China: A perspective on sustainable development goals (SDGs). *Sustainability*, *15*(11), 8873. https://doi.org/10.3390/su15118873

Lemola, S., Gkiouleka, A., Read, B., Realo, A., Walasek, L., Tang, N. K. Y., & Elliott, M. T. (2021). Can a 'rewards-for-exercise app' increase physical activity, subjective well-being and sleep quality? An open-label single-arm trial among university staff with low to moderate physical activity levels. *BMC Public Health*, *21*(1), 782. https://doi.org/10.1186/s12889-021-10794-w

MacDougall, M. (2000). Meltdown: Avoiding executive burnout. *Executive Excellence*, *17*(1), 14–14.

Manaf, M. R. A., Shaharuddin, M. A. A., Nawi, A. M., Tauhid, N. M., Othman, H., Rahman, M. R. A., … & Ganasegeran, K. (2021). Perceived symptoms of depression, anxiety and stress amongst staff in a Malaysian public university: A workers survey. *International Journal of Environmental Research and Public Health*, *18*(22), 11874. https://doi.org/10.3390/ijerph182211874

Margrove, K. L., Gustowska, M., & Grove, L. S. (2014). Provision of support for psychological distress by university staff, and receptiveness to mental health training. *Journal of Further and Higher Education*, *38*(1), 90–106. https://doi.org/10.1080/0309877X.2012.699518

Maslach, C., Schaufeli, W. B., & Leiter, M. P. (2001). Job burnout. *Annual Review of Psychology*, *52*, 397–422.

Meeks, K., Peak, A. S., & Dreihaus, A. (2023). Depression, anxiety, and stress among students, faculty, and staff. *Journal of American College Health*, *71*(2), 348–354. https://doi.org/10.1080/07448481.2021.1891913

Melin, M., Astvik, W., & Bernhard-Oettel, C. (2014). New work demands in higher education. A study of the relationship between excessive workload, coping strategies and subsequent health among academic staff. *Quality in Higher Education*, *20*(3), 290–308. https://doi.org/10.1080/13538322.2014.979547

Mesmer-Magnus, J. R., & Viswesvaran, C. (2005). Convergence between measures of work-to-family and family-to-work conflict: A meta-analytic examination. *Journal of Vocational Behavior*, *67*(2), 215–232. https://doi.org/10.1016/j.jvb.2004.05.004

Newton, J., Dooris, M., & Wills, J. (2016). Healthy universities: An example of a whole-system health-promoting setting. *Global Health Promotion*, *23*(1), 57–65. https://doi.org/10.1177/1757975915601037

Nicholls, H., Nicholls, M., Tekin, S., Lamb, D., & Billings, J. (2022). The impact of working in academia on researchers' mental health and well-being: A systematic review and qualitative meta-synthesis. *PLoS ONE*, *17*(5), e0268890. https://doi.org/10.1371/journal.pone.0268890

Noor, S., Aslam, A., & Md Isa, F. (2024). Causes of occupational stress and burnout amongst administrative staff in public universities: Case of Pakistan. *Journal of Applied Research in Higher Education*, In press. https://doi.org/10.1108/JARHE-03-2024-0120

O'Brien, T., & Guiney, D. (2018). *Staff wellbeing in Higher Education: A research study for education support partnership*. Education Support Partnership. Retrieved from: https://www.voced.edu.au/content/ngv%3A83125

Ohadomere, O., & Ogamba, I. K. (2021). Management-led interventions for workplace stress and mental health of academic staff in higher education: A systematic review. *The Journal of Mental Health Training, Education and Practice*, *16*(1), 67–82. https://doi.org/10.1108/JMHTEP-07-2020-0048

Parr, C. (2014). *Imperial College professor Stefan Grimm 'was given grant income target'*. Times Higher Education. Retrieved from: https://www.timeshighereducation.com/news/imperial-college-professor-stefan-grimm-was-given-grant-income-target /2017369.article

Pignata, S., Winefield, A. H., Provis, C., & Boyd, C. M. (2016). Awareness of stress-reduction interventions on work attitudes: The impact of tenure and staff group in Australian universities. *Frontiers in Psychology*, *7*, 1225. https://doi.org/10.3389/fpsyg.2016.01225

Plotnikoff, R., Collins, C. E., Williams, R., Germov, J., & Callister, R. (2015). Effectiveness of interventions targeting health behaviors in university and college staff: A systematic review. *American Journal of Health Promotion*, *29*(5), e169–e187. https://doi.org/10.4278/ajhp.130619-LIT-313

Priyadarshini, C., Ponnam, A., & Banerjee, P. (2015). Role stress and coping among business school professors: A phenomenological study. *Qualitative Report*, *20*(12), 2050–2066.

Reevy, G. M., & Deason, G. (2014). Predictors of depression, stress, and anxiety among non-tenure track faculty. *Frontiers in Psychology*, *5*, 701. https://doi.org/10.3389/fpsyg.2014.00701

Rosa, R. (2022). The trouble with 'work–life balance' in neoliberal academia: A systematic and critical review. *Journal of Gender Studies*, *31*(1), 55–73. https://doi.org/10.1080/09589236.2021.1933926

Sabagh, Z., Hall, N. C., & Saroyan, A. (2018). Antecedents, correlates and consequences of faculty burnout. *Educational Research*, *60*(2), 131–156. https://doi.org/10.1080/00131881.2018.1461573

Saltmarsh, S., & Randell-Moon, H. (2015). Managing the risky humanity of academic workers: Risk and reciprocity in university work-life balance policies. *Policy Futures in Education*, *13*(5), 662–682. https://doi.org/10.1177/1478210315579552

Shanafelt, T. D., West, C. P., Sloan, J. A., Novotny, P. J., Poland, G. A., Menaker, R., ... & Dyrbye, L. N. (2009). Career fit and burnout among academic faculty. *Archives of Internal Medicine*, *169*(10), 990–995.

Shen, P., & Slater, P. (2021). The effect of occupational stress and coping strategies on mental health and emotional well-being among university academic staff during the COVID-19 outbreak. *International Education Studies*, *14*(3), 82–95. https://doi.org/10.5539/ies.v14n3p82

Smith, C., & Ulus, E. (2020). Who cares for academics? We need to talk about emotional well-being including what we avoid and intellectualise through macro-discourses. *Organization*, *27*(6), 840–857. https://doi.org/10.1177/1350508419867201

Stoll, N., Yalipende, Y., Byrom, N. C., Hatch, S. L., & Lempp, H. (2022). Mental health and mental well-being of Black students at UK universities: A review and thematic synthesis. *BMJ Open*, *12*(2), e050720. https://doi.org/10.1136/bmjopen-2021-050720

Summers, S. M., Nagy, C. J., April, M. D., Kuiper, B. W., Rodriguez, R. G., & Jones, W. S. (2019). The prevalence of faculty physician burnout in military graduate medical education training programs: A cross-sectional study of academic physicians in the United States Department of Defense. *Military Medicine*, *184*(9-10), e522–e530. https://doi.org/10.1093/milmed/usz055

Tabakakis, K., Sloane, K., Besch, J., & To, Q. G. (2020). Burnout and its correlates in research administrators. *Research Management Review*, *24*(1), 1.

Taris, T. W., Le Blanc, P. M., Schaufeli, W. B., & Schreurs, P. J. (2005). Are there causal relationships between the dimensions of the Maslach Burnout Inventory? A review and two longitudinal tests. *Work & Stress*, *19*(3), 238–255. https://doi.org/10.1080/02678370500270453

Tsouros, A. D., Dowding, G., Thompson, J., & Dooris, M. (1998). *Health promoting universities: Concept, experience and framework for action. Target 14.* World Health Organization. Regional Office for Europe. Retrieved from: https://iris.who.int/bitstream/handle/10665/108095/9789289012850-eng.pdf?sequence=1&isAllowed=y

Tytherleigh, M. Y., Webb, C., Cooper, C. L., & Ricketts, C. (2005). Occupational stress in UK higher education institutions: A comparative study of all staff categories. *Higher Education Research & Development*, *24*(1), 41–61. https://doi.org/10.1080/0729436052000318569

Urbina-Garcia, A. (2020). What do we know about university academics' mental health: A systematic literature review. *Stress & Health*, *36*(5), 563–585. https://doi.org/10.1002/smi.2956

Uzoechina, G., & Onuselogu, A. (2009). Stressors and their influence on job performance of career administrative staff in university reform implementation in Anambra state. *African Research Review*, *3*(4), 338–350. https://doi.org/10.4314/afrrev.v3i4.47569

Van Niekerk, R. L., & van Gent, M. M. (2021). Mental health and well-being of university staff during the coronavirus disease 2019 levels 4 and 5 lockdown in an Eastern Cape university, South Africa. *South African Journal of Psychiatry*, *27*, 1589. https://doi.org/10.4102/sajpsychiatry.v27i0.1589

Watts, J., & Robertson, N. (2011). Burnout in university teaching staff: A systematic literature review. *Educational Research*, *53*(1), 33–50. https://doi.org/10.1080/00131881.2011.552235

Winefield, A. H., Gillespie, N., Stough, C., Dua, J., Hapuarachchi, J., & Boyd, C. (2003). Occupational stress in Australian university staff: Results from a national survey. *International Journal of Stress Management*, *10*(1), 51–63. https://doi.org/10.1037/1072-5245.10.1.51

Wolbring, G., & Lillywhite, A. (2023). Burnout through the lenses of Equity/Equality, Diversity and Inclusion and disabled people: A scoping review. *Societies*, *13*(5), 131. https://doi.org/10.3390/soc13050131

Wood, S., Michaelides, G., Daniels, K., & Niven, K. (2022). Uncertainty and well-being amongst homeworkers in the COVID-19 pandemic: A longitudinal study of university staff. *International Journal of Environmental Research and Public Health*, *19*(16), 10435. https://doi.org/10.3390/ijerph191610435

Wray, S., & Kinman, G. (2021). *Supporting staff wellbeing in higher education.* Project Report. Education Support, London. Retrieved from: https://eprints.bbk.ac.uk/id/eprint/47038/1/FINALES%20Supporting%20Staff%20Wellbeing%20in%20HE%20Report.pdf

Wray, S., & Kinman, G. (2022). The challenges of COVID-19 for the well-being of academic staff. *Occupational Medicine*, *72*(1), 2–3. https://doi.org/10.1093/occmed/kqab007

Chapter 3

Precarious Contracts, Doctoral Students, and Postdoctoral Researchers

Those employed on precarious (i.e., casual or fixed-term) contracts represent a significant and increasing proportion of the academic workforce (e.g., Brown, Goodman, & Yasukawa, 2008; Dobbie & Robinson, 2008). Factors contributing to the increase in casualised staff include the reduced funding available to universities and the significant increase in student numbers, often referred to as the massification of higher education. Despite the prevalence of these contracts, research, practice, and policy have paid relatively little attention to those on casual contracts, in comparison to their permanent colleagues. The current chapter considers the experiences of precariously employed academics, addressing both the use of casual teaching-focused contracts and the use of research-orientated fixed-term postdoctoral positions.

Precarious Teaching Positions

The use of precarious (e.g., casual, fixed-term, or zero-hour) contracts to support teaching and learning is commonplace, and a range of non-traditional (i.e., full-time permanent) contract types may exist. These include hourly payment to teach specific sessions, payment to teach a particular module or course over a semester, and fixed-term contracts involving part-time or full-time work for a limited period. The use of each contract type and the terminology used to describe these positions may vary by country and institution type. For example, academics employed on casual contracts may be referred to as "sessional staff" or "adjunct faculty" in Australia and North America, respectively.

It is often argued that casualised, fixed-term, and zero-hour teaching contracts provide academics with a degree of flexibility, for example, allowing employees to tailor the amount of teaching they complete to other personal or professional demands. The notion that casual contracts provide flexibility is rejected by many precariously employed academics; however, employees are typically unable to negotiate the hours worked or their salary. When asked to identify their preferred contract type, less than one-third of casual academic staff select casual contracts, with over half preferring full-time or part-time

DOI: 10.4324/9781032639321-4

permanent contracts (Junor, 2004), suggesting that the widespread use of non-permanent contracts is not driven by employee demand.

Casually employed academics experience a number of challenges related to their precarious position (Brown, Goodman, & Yasukawa, 2008). In particular, though highly skilled and experienced, staff employed on casual contracts are often paid less than their permanent colleagues and may be perceived as the "cheaper alternative" to those appointed to permanent positions. In addition to lower pay and a lack of financial security, those on casual contracts may not have access to important benefits (e.g., paid sickness leave). Further, academics employed on casual contracts are often recruited for a relatively narrow range of academic activities (e.g., marking and teaching of first-year undergraduate students), limiting autonomy, personal development, and opportunities for progression and promotion.

Limited opportunities for career progression are further exacerbated by practice beyond individual institutions. In particular, it has been argued that funding structures in the United Kingdom systematically exclude long-term casualised staff (Menard & Wånggren, 2025). It is perhaps not surprising then that casually employed academics identify a number of stressors related to their precarious position. When Reevy and Deason (2014) asked employees to report the most stressful aspects of their job, 31% highlighted the contingency/precariousness of their status. Other stressors arguably related to their contract type include a lack of support, including the physical space available (30%); pay inequity or low pay (27%); not being permitted to engage in departmental governance (19%); invisibility/a lack of recognition (16%); and a lack of benefits such as health or retirement benefits (11%).

As a consequence, it has been argued that a "class divide" has developed between casual and permanent academics. For example, Kimber (2003) refers to the tenured core and tenuous periphery to highlight the two-tier system that exists within higher education. Highlighting the nature and extent of this class divide, only 38% of casual staff report being included in meetings and decision-making processes (Ryan et al., 2013). Such exclusion both restricts the knowledge and expertise available to management and has a significant impact on the casually employed staff. For example, those employed on casual contracts may become isolated from colleagues on more secure contracts, limiting opportunities for research and collaboration.

Financial Insecurity

Despite the increased numbers of students enrolling in higher education programmes, austerity and competition across the sector have had a negative impact on the funds available to higher education institutions. In part, the increased use of precarious contracts is a response to this broader financial situation, with fixed-term positions used to meet teaching and learning demands without a long-term commitment to increased staffing budgets. For those employed on casual contracts, typically dependent on institutional or departmental budgets and student enrolment numbers, this position is fundamentally precarious.

Financial insecurity is central to the experience of academics employed on casual or fixed-term contracts. Insecurity is exacerbated further by the nature of recruitment to such contracts. For example, student numbers may not be confirmed until the start of the semester, resulting in last-minute demand and requests for teaching. This approach makes it difficult for those employed on precarious contracts to plan their time and may be especially challenging for those with caring responsibilities. There is, of course, no guarantee of future employment and associated income for those employed on casual contracts, and there may be extended periods (e.g., over the summer vacation) with no academic income available. Reflecting the "last-minute" nature of many casual contracts, recruitment to those positions is often informal (Crimmins, 2017). As a consequence, people may be dependent on their networks for employment, and there is potential for significant bias, favouritism, and discrimination in the recruitment and selection process.

It is perhaps of no surprise then that 57% of academics employed on casual contracts regard employment and financial insecurity as significant issues, and of those, 81% disclose moderate to severe levels of financial worry (Junor, 2004). This is echoed by research with sessional staff in Australia who identify a range of concerns as moderately to very important, including discontinuity of employment (84%), insufficient notice of teaching allocation (81%), impact of income uncertainty on financial planning (80%), risks in refusing unreasonable demands (72%), and impact of hours on family life (64%) (Ryan et al., 2013). As illustrated in Table 3.1 (data from Junor, 2004), the impact of issues related to precarious contracts is similar for academic and non-academic staff.

Table 3.1 The Impact of Insecure Contacts as Reported by Academic and Non-Academic Staff

Issue	*Staff Type*	*Very Minor (%)*	*Minor (%)*	*Moderate (%)*	*Major (%)*
Discontinuity	Academic	7	22	34	38
	Non-academic	6	19	36	39
Income insecurity and difficulty with financial planning	Academic	5	14	31	50
	Non-academic	6	15	29	51
Limited notice of appointment	Academic	5	21	36	38
	Non-academic	9	18	28	34

The Work Environment

Those employed on casual or precarious contracts may feel pressured to accept all teaching opportunities, anxious that student numbers may not justify their position in future semesters. Their workload, as a consequence, may be excessive. In some circumstances, tutors may be employed on a separate contract for each module they support, and these may extend across different institutions or campuses (Crimmins, 2017). There may, therefore, be little oversight of their overall workload. Further, academics are often expected to undertake work that exceeds their allocated roles and responsibilities. For example, a lecturer may adopt leadership roles commensurate with senior lecturer status in order to apply for promotion to senior lectureship. Academics may also take on additional work because they feel pressured to do so and/or fear that their reputation will suffer if they do not. Those on precarious contracts are especially susceptible to this type of pressure, aware that they are dependent on favourable references and fearful that rejecting an offer of employment may make them appear less reliable or committed than those who accept.

Further, there may be some uncertainty regarding the boundaries of casual contracts, such as the extent to which academics are expected to engage with student queries outside the teaching session (Brown, Goodman, & Yasukawa, 2008). Staff on precarious or part-time contracts may have less time available to prepare for their teaching or to interact with students than their permanent full-time colleagues (Umbach, 2007), though metrics such as student evaluations do not take this into account. As a consequence, those on casual contracts often undertake tasks without payment. In one survey of Australian casual academics, Ryan et al. (2013) report that whilst 91% of casual staff are paid for marking, only 50% receive payment for preparation for teaching. Further, a relatively small number were paid for student consultation (33%) and responding to emails (16%). Even if staff are not explicitly instructed to complete unpaid work, failure to do so (e.g., not responding to student requests for additional feedback on their grade) may negatively impact student evaluations of that employee and the likelihood that they will be rehired in the future.

Resources and Professional Development

A relatively small proportion of casually employed academics are provided with useful performance feedback (32%), opportunities for training and development (23%), and are advised on their career options (15%) (Ryan et al., 2013). Indeed, the careers support provided varies considerably, with over 25% of sessional academics surveyed in one study reporting receiving no support from their institution (Heffernan, 2018). It is perhaps unsurprising then that casual staff report low satisfaction with the training and development opportunities available to them (Ryan & Bhattacharyya, 2012). The support provided to casual academic staff impacts their overall job and career satisfaction (May, Strachan, & Peetz, 2013) and has broader potential consequences for the higher education workforce. For example, if casual employees are not supported and become less satisfied with higher education, fewer highly skilled academics are available to fill vacant roles. It is also important to recognise that there is significant variation in access to basic physical resources such as a desk or computer. For example, May, Strachan, and Peetz (2013) report that 57% of casual academic staff have access to a suitable space to meet with students, with some gender disparity (women 55%, men 60%).

Of course, a broad range of casual contract types exists, and the circumstances of those employed on a casual basis may also vary. For example, Junor (2004) distinguishes Academic Apprentices (enrolled on a full-time or part-time postgraduate programme in addition to their casual contract and intending on a traditional academic career following graduation), Qualified Academic Jobseekers (holding a higher degree and preferring permanent full-time or part-time academic work), and Outside Industry Experts (e.g., employed full-time in a non-education industry). Each group may have different motivations for casual work, long-term plans, and access to resources. In particular, academic staff employed on casual contracts who are studying full-time typically have financial support for research (women 66%, men 73%), though access to support for research is significantly lower for those studying on a part-time basis (women 32%, men 32%) or not studying (women 16%, men 13%) (May, Strachan, & Peetz, 2013). Findings suggest that the financial support received for research is largely a consequence of their student status rather than academic role, and research, practice, and policy should acknowledge the variation in casually employed staff experience.

Doctoral Students

It may be especially difficult for doctoral students who are both employed on a casual contract and enrolled in a postgraduate programme to navigate the competing pressures on their time. For example, they are required to spend time on their doctoral research (and may have a limited period of time in which to complete this or access to funds for a limited period), but feel unable to turn down requests to engage in teaching or marking made by their Head of Department (and prospective employer). Such role conflict can cause considerable distress and may be especially difficult for those with other demands on their time, such as doctoral students with caring responsibilities or energy-limiting conditions.

Of course, even doctoral students who are not also employed on a casual teaching or research contract experience a degree of precarity. Supervisors have considerable power in their relationship with doctoral students. In addition to control over valuable resources such as lab equipment, bursaries for conference attendance, and mentorship, supervisors can limit access to collaborative opportunities such as co-authorship of journal publications and grant funding. Students may experience a range of supervisory issues, including incompetent, inadequate, or exploitative supervision (Goodyear, Crego, & Johnston, 1992). Supervisory bullying also occurs, involving unrealistic work demands, criticism, inappropriate attention, and abuse of power (Morris, 2011).

Interviewing PhD students about their PhD programme and experiences of supervision, Löfström and Pyhältö (2014) identify over 100 ethical issues associated with the individual supervisory relationship or broader academic community. These included exploitation (e.g., high workloads unrelated to the PhD research), abuse (e.g., public criticism and humiliation), and misappropriation (e.g., supervisors presenting the student's ideas as their own). Doctoral students may be especially reluctant to challenge inappropriate behaviour, conscious that they are dependent on their supervisor for a supportive reference and access to academic networks. As described by one doctoral student, "*They are really tricky, these hierarchies here, and when you are a beginner, you are always the one without power*" (Löfström & Pyhältö, 2014, p. 204).

Attrition and Outcomes

Doctoral programmes have relatively high levels of student attrition, and Nettles and Millet (2006) report doctorate attrition rates ranging from 40 to 70%. Gardner (2008) explores the extent to which "fitting the mold" impacts the attrition of doctoral students from underrepresented groups. Five categories of doctoral students who reported not "fitting the mold" were identified, including women, students of colour, students with children, part-time students, and older students, describing the way in which they felt "different" from their peers. For example, women referred to the "old boys club", male-dominated discipline, and widespread sexist attitudes. In addition to the consequences of attrition for the specific subject discipline and broader research environment, there is a substantial cost to the individual doctoral student. For example, students who do not complete their doctorate may experience a sense of loss, guilt, and failure. The support available to doctoral students (both from the supervisor and at a broader departmental level) is essential and can reduce intentions to leave academia (Hunter & Devine, 2016).

Relatively few doctoral students become full-time academics or professors. Further, though the number of academic positions is unlikely to increase to a significant degree, the number of doctoral graduates continues to rise. Despite this, doctoral programmes often fail to prepare people for a non-academic career or acknowledge the number of graduates who opt for a non-academic career (Harris, 2012). In part, this may reflect the perception that doctorates are training for academic careers only and that those who do not enter academia are "wasting their talent". The focus on academic career pathways may also reflect doctoral students' initial perceptions of an academic career, sometimes later described as naïve or idealistic (Guerin, 2020).

Sauermann and Roach (2012) explore the career preferences of PhD students in the life sciences, physics, and chemistry. They report that, despite the fact that academic advisors strongly encourage an academic career, the attractiveness of an academic career to students decreases over the course of the PhD programme. The decision to leave the academic career pathway may, of course, reflect both a process of being "pushed out" of academia (e.g., inability to secure an academic position) as well as being "pulled out" by more attractive opportunities (Guerin, 2020). Doctoral students should, therefore, be encouraged to view their doctoral programme as preparation for a range of careers, including non-academic careers.

Postdoctoral Researchers

The term "postdoc" is used to refer to postdoctoral fellows or scholars who enter a fixed-term period of supervised/mentored research following successful completion of their doctoral studies. Postdoc positions are research-intensive, with the postdoc researcher typically focused on activities such as journal publication, grant writing, and supervision of less-experienced researchers. Though postdoc positions may provide valuable training, mentorship, and opportunities (e.g., opportunities to establish an academic profile, develop project management skills, and network with potential collaborators or employers), the system has been criticised as exploitative. In particular, postdocs receive a relatively low wage (for their experience and qualifications) and are often expected to work excessive hours.

Academics may complete a series of postdoc contracts, with an implicit expectation that they obtain experience in a range of research departments prior to securing a more permanent faculty position and demonstrating an ability to publish impactful research articles and secure research funding. As a consequence, postdocs can spend a substantial amount of their time searching for appropriate positions and preparing applications and, as many positions require relocation, also making the necessary personal arrangements.

Of course, the expectation that academics must gain postdoc experience in a range of departments or countries is especially problematic for some academics, including those with caregiving responsibilities or without the financial resources to support relocation. For disabled postdocs, relocation may require finding accessible housing and medical care and requesting accommodations in the new institution, which may take considerable time to implement. For gay, lesbian, and transgender postdocs, relocation may be restricted by laws pertaining to sexual orientation and gender identity and societal acceptance or discrimination in the new area. Clearly, it may be difficult to obtain reliable information relating to an institution's willingness to implement accommodations for disabled postdocs or acceptance for gay, lesbian, and transgender postdocs, increasing the stress and anxiety associated with this type of relocation.

It is also important to recognise that though moving institutions can provide access to a broader network of potential collaborators, moving institutions may also negatively impact the research activity (e.g., publication) of non-tenured researchers (Bäker, 2015). This may reflect a number of factors, including distance from existing collaborators and the time taken to establish access to equipment. Indeed, the research agenda of a postdoc position is likely to focus on the specific interests of the principal investigator rather than the postdoc themselves, and frequent relocation may create distance between the postdoc and their original specialism. It is also difficult for postdocs to assess the quality of the experience available prior to appointment, with significant variation in the support available to postdocs, such as support for conference attendance and mentorship (Baader et al., 2017). Postdocs make a substantial contribution to academic research and are responsible for a relatively large proportion of research and innovation; it is important that research practice and policy reflect this with greater consideration of the postdoc experience.

Postdoctoral Outcomes

Postdoctoral positions have historically been regarded as a temporary stage of academic employment, prior to appointment to a permanent position. Indeed, Andalib, Ghaffarzadegan and Larson (2018) describe postdocs as "*a labour force in waiting*" (p. 675) who either leave the postdoc "queue" when they secure a tenure-track academic position or when they decide to pursue an alternate career. Academics are, however, spending greater periods of time on postdoc contracts due to the difficulty securing a faculty role (Puljak & Sharif, 2009), with salaries that do not reflect the increased cost of living. This trend impacts financial security and the ability of researchers to purchase a property or establish a family and may lead accomplished researchers to pursue a non-academic career.

Using data from the US Survey of Doctorate Recipients, Andalib, Ghaffarzadegan and Larson (2018) report that the mean time spent in the "postdoc queue" is 2.9 years (though there is substantial variation across academic disciplines), with only approximately 17% of postdocs securing the desired tenure-track position. In another study exploring the postdoc experience at Dutch universities, 85% of postdocs reported wanting to remain in academia, though fewer than 3% were offered a tenure-track position (van der Weijden et al., 2016). Despite this, only 34.6% of postdocs reported receiving career guidance from a mentor, and just 21.3% reported receiving career guidance from the institution (Puljak & Sharif, 2009). Uncertain prospects and work stress may also lead postdocs to leave academia, with job strain and job satisfaction especially important (Dorenkamp & Weiß, 2018). Despite this, relatively few postdocs prepare for a non-academic career (van der Weijden et al., 2016).

Gendered Postdoctoral Inequality

The postdoc experience is inherently gendered, and women report a range of negative postdoc experiences. For example, being seen as less "academic" than male colleagues, being less likely to be offered opportunities such as high-profile projects and networking with male colleagues being misinterpreted as romantic interest (Ysseldyk et al., 2019). The scale of this issue is perhaps illustrated by the fact that women frequently perceive such treatment as a part of the academic role and environment that they must "get used to" (Ysseldyk et al., 2019). Further, research indicates that male postdocs receive higher salaries than female postdocs, even when controlling for institution type, years since graduation, age and other relevant factors (McConnell et al., 2018).

Family commitments and maternity leave are especially prominent issues for female postdocs, and women with children are especially underrepresented in postdoctoral positions (Martinez et al., 2007). Women reported not being able to take up academic opportunities because of family commitments, postponing having children, or being penalised (explicitly or through "lagging behind") for taking maternity leave. As explained by one woman,

> You sort of reach the postdoc stage where you're supposed to launch academically at the same time that you have to decide whether or not to have kids. And most women have put it off because they've been studying so long.
>
> (Ysseldyk et al., 2019, p. 7)

Such issues are exacerbated by the fact that male postdocs are more likely to report having a spouse who does not work outside the home (male 36% vs. female 8%) and are more likely to report that a partner or relative provides childcare during the day (male 42.5% vs. female 15.5%) or after school (male 71.5% vs. female 25%) (Martinez et al., 2007).

As summarised by one female postdoc

> Well I'd often talked with colleagues, male and female, and what we've always ended up with at some point is that what you actually need, in order to pull off an academic career fairly safely, what you'd ACTUALLY need, is a wife.
>
> (Baader et al., 2017, p. 290)

As a consequence, it has been argued that fellowships targeted at postdoc mothers should be available to allow postdoc mothers to maintain their academic work during a challenging period (Keller & Garry, 2016).

Recommendations

Institutions should,

- Minimise the use of fixed-term contracts. Provide those on fixed-term contracts with the same career development and progression support available to permanent staff. For example, appraisal and support to gain teaching qualifications and accreditation. Enabling precariously employed staff to feed into policy and practice (e.g., attendance at staff meetings) is also of direct benefit to the department and institution.
- Where precarious contracts exist, recognise the expertise of precariously employed staff. Ensure all staff are paid commensurate with their skills and experience, have access to relevant benefits (e.g., sickness pay), and are provided the resources (e.g., printing, office space) to perform their role. Induction and training completed for the role should be paid.
- Recognise the stress associated with precarious contracts and financial insecurity in particular. Clearly communicate the schedule for determining the availability and advertising of precarious contracts and the future likelihood of such positions.
- Clearly define contract boundaries and the work that staff on precarious contracts are and are not expected to complete. For example, staff employed to mark assessments should not be expected to provide students with further verbal feedback unless they are also paid to do so. Module coordinators should ensure that students understand tutor roles (e.g., who they should contact for support and guidance) to avoid precariously employed staff being placed in a difficult position or being perceived as unhelpful.
- Evaluate precarious staff experiences. Evaluations should consider the importance of contract type (e.g., if staff are enrolled as students when employed on precarious contracts).
- Provide doctoral students with advice and guidance relating to both academic and non-academic career pathways.
- Appreciate that for many people, it is not feasible to undertake a series of postdoctoral contracts or work in a variety of institutions before applying for a permanent position. Recognise the advantages associated with moving directly to a permanent position rather than postdoctoral contracts (e.g., pursuing their original research interests) and provide the training and support (e.g., research grant guidance) that may have otherwise been obtained during a postdoctoral position.
- Implement additional measures to ensure the safety and wellbeing of those in precarious contracts. For example, allocation to an alternative lab group when bullying has taken place. Ensure all safeguarding measures and institutional processes are clearly communicated to all staff, including those on precarious contracts.

Subject in Focus 1: Doctoral Student Mental Health

In one large European study Levecque et al. (2017) assessed the mental health of over 3,500 PhD students. Of those surveyed, 51% experienced at least two symptoms (indicative of psychological distress) and 32% reported at least four symptoms (at risk of having or developing a common psychiatric disorder). Further, the likelihood of experiencing at least two or at least four symptoms was 34% and 27% higher in women than in men. Both the immediate environment and broader academic culture may increase the likelihood of mental distress and mental ill health (Casey et al., 2023). As mental health impacts engagement with the programme, risk of interruption of studies, number of publications produced, and research self-efficacy (Berry, Niven, & Hazell, 2023; González-Betancor, & Dorta-González, 2020; Zhang et al., 2022), the wellbeing of doctoral students may have long-term career and employability consequences.

Despite the prevalence of mental health issues such as anxiety and depression in doctoral student samples, relatively few specialised interventions have been introduced or evaluated (Mackie & Bates, 2019). Many doctoral students do not engage with the mental health support services provided by their institution (Waight & Giordano, 2018), instead favouring external online resources. Of course, where institutions provide mental health support, this may be primarily targeted at undergraduate students, with little consideration for the specific doctoral context (e.g., relative ambiguity re the expectations of doctoral research). Doctoral students who engage in undergraduate teaching may be particularly reluctant to use services that are also accessed by their students.

Our knowledge of this subject may have been hindered by the tendency to consider the mental health of "graduate students" (e.g., Andrade, Ribeiro, & Máté, 2023; Grady et al., 2014) without distinguishing between different student groups. For example, Masters students on a one year taught programme, PhD students on a three or four year research programme, and Professional Doctorate students whose programmes may combine taught, research, and practice elements may each have different stressors associated with their programme.

In recent years, there has been greater recognition of doctoral student mental health. In 2018, a Vitae report, funded by the Higher Education Funding Council for England (now Research England) highlighted the prevalence of mental distress and mental ill health in postgraduate research students, and issues associated with mental health support (Metcalfe, Wilson, & Levecque, 2018). The particular vulnerability of international, part-time and disabled students was noted together with recommendations for future action. A subsequent catalyst funding call from Research England and the Office for Students supported 17 projects focused on doctoral student mental health and wellbeing, including training, peer networks, and mentoring programmes (Metcalfe et al., 2020).

Subject in Focus 2: Doctoral Student Experiences of Bullying and Harassment

Research indicates that doctoral students are more likely to experience bullying and harassment than other academic groups. Bullying and harassment may have a range of negative consequences, both for the individual and broader higher education sector. For example, graduate students experiencing bullying report lower levels of student interest and greater intentions to leave their studies (Martin, Goodboy, & Johnson, 2015). Investigating the workplace bullying experienced by graduate students, Yamada, Cappadocia, and Pepler (2014) identify three forms of bullying behaviour, (1) work-management (e.g., setting impossible deadlines, undue pressure to produce work), (2) threatening-dismissive (e.g., verbal or non-verbal threats, persistent attempts to belittle and undermine work), and (3) passive-aggressive interpersonal (e.g., making inappropriate jokes, persistent attempts to humiliate in front of colleagues or other faculty). As shown in Table 3.2, experience of each bullying type varied by supervisor status (data from Yamada, Cappadocia, and Pepler, 2014).

In order to address the bullying experienced by those in precarious academic positions (including doctoral students) it is important to consider the types of bullying specific to the academic context. In one study, Moss and Mahmoudi (2021) examine academic bullying in a sample comprised largely of graduate students (21.6%) and postdocs (22.8%) using both a single item measure of bullying and items specific to academia. Using the single item measure, targets and witnesses indicate that graduate students are especially vulnerable to academic bullying. Using the scale specific to academic science, the most frequent forms of bullying were 'encouraged others to mistreat me' (53.1%), 'cancelled or threatened to cancel my current appointment/position' (52.1%), and 'gave me a bad/unfair recommendation' (48.0%). Other behaviour specific to academia such as 'took away my funding or threatened to take

Table 3.2 Mean Bullying Score by Bullying Type and Supervisor Status

Bullying Type	*Supervisor Status*	*Mean Score*
Work-management	Assistant Professor	.35
	Associate Professor	.47
	Full Professor	.28
Threatening-dismissive	Assistant Professor	.25
	Associate Professor	.33
	Full Professor	.20
Passive-aggressive interpersonal	Assistant Professor	.15
	Associate Professor	.26
	Full Professor	.10

away my finding' (43.1%) and 'violated authorship contribution guidelines (if existed)' (41.0%) were also prevalent.

A number of strategies have been proposed to address specific issues such as publication authorship including scoring systems and identifying individual author roles and contributions (Oberlander & Spencer, 2006). It may, however, be more difficult to address the underlying issues of power imbalance and exploitation in the competitive individualistic academic environment. Wang (2024) highlights the incidence of racialized academic bullying targeted at international doctoral students, with ethnic stereotypes of Asian students as hardworking and compliant forming a part of the exploitative treatment. As recalled by one student "*They said Chinese students here worked like cows. And they are more willing to hire those who are from China.*" (Wang, 2024, p. 688). These students were especially vulnerable to bullying that capitalized on their international status, for example some supervisors threatened to cancel the student's visa, demonstrating that these students require additional support and protection.

References

Andalib, M. A., Ghaffarzadegan, N., & Larson, R. C. (2018). The Post-doc queue: A labour force in waiting. *Systems Research and Behavioral Science*, *35*(6), 675–686. https://doi.org/10.1002/sres.2510

Andrade, D., Ribeiro, I. J. S., & Máté, O. (2023). Academic burnout among master and doctoral students during the COVID-19 pandemic. *Scientific Reports*, *13*, 4745. https://doi.org/10.1038/s41598-023-31852-w

Baader, M. S., Böhringer, D., Korff, S., & Roman, N. (2017). Equal opportunities in the postdoctoral phase in Germany? *European Educational Research Journal*, *16*(2–3), 277–297. https://doi.org/10.1177/1474904117694624

Bäker, A. (2015). Non-tenured post-doctoral researchers' job mobility and research output: An analysis of the role of research discipline, department size, and co-authors. *Research Policy*, *44*(3), 634–650. https://doi.org/10.1016/j.respol.2014.12.012

Berry, C., Niven, J. E., & Hazell, C. M. (2023). Predictors of UK postgraduate researcher attendance behaviours and mental health-related attrition intention. *Current Psychology*, *42*, 30521–30534. https://doi.org/10.1007/s12144-022-04055-1

Brown, T., Goodman, J., & Yasukawa, K. (2008). Casualisation of academic work: Industrial justice and quality education. *Dialogue*, *27*(1), 17–29.

Casey, C., Taylor, J., Knight, F., & Trenoweth, S. (2023). Understanding the mental health of doctoral students. *Encyclopedia*, *3*(4), 1523–1536. https://doi.org/10.3390/encyclopedia3040109

Crimmins, G. (2017). Feedback from the coal-face: How the lived experience of women casual academics can inform human resources and academic development policy and practice. *International Journal for Academic Development*, *22*(1), 7–18, https://doi.org/10.1080/1360144X.2016.1261353

Dobbie, D. & Robinson, I. (2008). Reorganizing higher education in the United States and Canada. *Labor Studies Journal*, *33*(2), 117–140. https://doi.org/10.1177/0160449X07301241

Dorenkamp, I., Weiß, E. E. (2018). What makes them leave? A path model of postdocs' intentions to leave academia. *Higher Education*, *75*, 747–767. https://doi.org/10.1007/s10734-017-0164-7

Gardner, S. K. (2008). Fitting the mold of graduate school: A qualitative study of socialization in doctoral education. *Innovative Higher Education*, *33*, 125–138. https://doi.org/10.1007/s10755-008-9068-x

González-Betancor, S. M., & Dorta-González, P. (2020). Risk of interruption of doctoral studies and mental health in PhD students. *Mathematics*, *8*(10), 1695. https://doi.org/10.3390/math8101695

Goodyear, R. K., Crego, C. A., & Johnston, M. W. (1992). Ethical issues in the supervision of student research: A study of critical incidents. *Professional Psychology: Research and Practice*, *23*(3), 203–210. https://doi.org/10.1037/0735-7028.23.3.203

Grady, R. K., La Touche, R., Oslawski-Lopez, J., Powers, A., & Simacek, K. (2014). Betwixt and between: The social position and stress experiences of graduate students. *Teaching Sociology*, *42*(1), 5–16. https://doi.org/10.1177/0092055X13502182

Guerin, C. (2020). Stories of moving on HASS PhD graduates' motivations and career trajectories inside and beyond academia. *Arts and Humanities in Higher Education*, *19*(3), 304–324. https://doi.org/10.1177/1474022219834448

Harris, M. (2012). The academic pyramid. *Physics World*, *25*(10), 54–57. https://doi.org/10.1088/2058-7058/25/10/40

Heffernan, T. A. (2018) Approaches to career development and support for sessional academics in higher education. *International Journal for Academic Development*, *23*(4), 312–323. https://doi.org/10.1080/1360144X.2018.1510406

Hunter, K. H., & Devine, K. (2016). Doctoral students' emotional exhaustion and intentions to leave academia. *International Journal of Doctoral Studies*, *11*, 35–61.

Junor, A. (2004). Casual university work: Choice, risk, inequity and the case for regulation. *The Economic and Labour Relations Review*, *14*(2), 276–304. https://doi.org/10.1177/103530460401400208

Keller, U., & Garry, A. (2016). Retaining Postdoc mothers in an academic career. *Optics & Photonics News*, 19–21.

Kimber, M. (2003). The tenured "core" and the tenuous "periphery": The casualisation of academic work in Australian Universities. *Journal of Higher Education Policy and Management*, *25*(1), 41–50. https://doi.org/10.1080/13600800305738

Levecque, K., Anseel, F., De Beuckelaer, A., Van der Heyden, J., & Gisle, L. (2017). Work organization and mental health problems in PhD students. *Research Policy*, *46*(4), 868–879. https://doi.org/10.1016/j.respol.2017.02.008

Löfström, E., & Pyhältö, K. (2014). Ethical issues in doctoral supervision: The perspectives of PhD students in the natural and behavioral sciences. *Ethics & Behavior*, *24*(3), 195–214. https://doi.org/10.1080/10508422.2013.830574

Mackie, S. A., & Bates, G. W. (2019). Contribution of the doctoral education environment to PhD candidates' mental health problems: A scoping review. *Higher Education Research & Development*, *38*(3), 565–578. https://doi.org/10.1080/07294360.2018.1556620

Martin, M. M., Goodboy, A. K., & Johnson, Z. D. (2015). When professors bully graduate students: Effects on student interest, instructional dissent, and intentions to leave graduate education. *Communication Education*, *64*(4), 438–454. https://doi.org/10.1080/03634523.2015.1041995

Martinez, E. D., Botos, J., Dohoney, K. M., Geiman, T. M., Kolla, S. S., Olivera, A., Qiu, Y., Rayasam, G. V., Stavreva, D. A., & Cohen-Fix, O. (2007). Falling off the academic bandwagon: Women are more likely to quit at the postdoc to principal investigator transition. *EMBO Reports*, *8*, 977–981. https://doi.org/10.1038/sj.embor.7401110

May, R., Strachan, G., & Peetz, D. (2013). Workforce development and renewal in Australian universities and the management of casual academic staff. *Journal of University Teaching & Learning Practice*, *10*(3), 1–26. https://doi.org/10.53761/1.10.3.3

McConnell, S. C., Westerman, E. L., Pierre, J. F., Heckler, E. J., & Schwartz, N. B. (2018). United States National Postdoc Survey results and the interaction of gender, career choice and mentor impact. *eLife*, *7*, e40189. https://doi.org/10.7554/eLife.40189

Menard, C., & Wånggren, L. (2025). *Recognising long-term casualised academics in the funding landscape: Evidence-based report on exclusionary and discriminatory funding criteria.* Retrieved from: https://edicaucus.ac.uk/wp-content/uploads/2025/08/Long-term-casualised-academics-report-for-funders.pdf

Metcalfe, J., Day, E., de Pury, J., & Dicks, A. (2020). *Catalyst fund. Supporting mental health and wellbeing for postgraduate research students. Programme evaluation.* Vitae and Universities UK. Retrieved from: https://www.ukri.org/wp-content/uploads/2021/12/RE-141221-CatalystFundProgrammeEvaluation.pdf

Metcalfe, J., Wilson, S., & Levecque, K. (2018). *Exploring wellbeing and mental health and associated support services for postgraduate researchers.* Vitae. Retrieved from: https://www.ukri.org/wp-content/uploads/2018/05/RE_141221-MentalHealthReportFinal.pdf

Morris, S. E. (2011). Doctoral students' experiences of supervisory bullying. *Pertanika Journal of Social Sciences and Humanities*, *19*(2), 547–555.

Moss, S. E., & Mahmoudi, M. (2021). STEM the bullying: An empirical investigation of abusive supervision in academic science. *EClinicalMedicine*, *40*, 101121. https://doi.org/10.1016/j.eclinm.2021.101121

Nettles, M. T., & Millet, C. M. (2006). *Three magic letters, getting the Ph.D.* John Hopkins University Press.

Oberlander, S. E., & Spencer, R. J. (2006). Graduate students and the culture of authorship. *Ethics & Behavior*, *16*(3), 217–232. https://doi.org/10.1207/s15327019eb1603_3

Puljak, L., & Sharif, W. D. (2009). Postdocs' perceptions of work environment and career prospects at a US academic institution. *Research Evaluation*, *18*(5), 411–415. https://doi.org/10.3152/095820209X483064

Reevy, G. M., & Deason, G. (2014). Predictors of depression, stress, and anxiety among non-tenure track faculty. *Frontiers in Psychology*, *5*, 701. https://doi.org/10.3389/fpsyg.2014.00701

Ryan, S., & Bhattacharyya, A. (2012). Barriers to professional development among contingent academic employees: An Australian case study. *International Journal of Learning*, *18*(4), 247–262.

Ryan, S., Burgess, J., Connell, J., & Groen, E. (2013). Casual academic staff in an Australian university: Marginalised and excluded. *Tertiary Education and Management*, *19*(2), 161–175. http://dx.doi.org/10.1080/13583883.2013.783617

Sauermann, H., & Roach, M. (2012). Science PhD career preferences: Levels, changes, and advisor encouragement. *PLoS ONE* *7*(5), e36307. https://doi.org/10.1371/journal.pone.0036307

Umbach, P. D. (2007). How effective are they? Exploring the impact of contingent faculty on undergraduate education. *The Review of Higher Education*, *30*(2), 91–123. https://doi.org/10.1353/rhe.2006.0080

van der Weijden, I., Teelken, C., de Boer, M., & Drost, M. (2016). Career satisfaction of postdoctoral researchers in relation to their expectations for the future. *Higher Education*, *72*, 25–40. https://doi.org/10.1007/s10734-015-9936-0

Waight, E., & Giordano, A. (2018). Doctoral students' access to non-academic support for mental health. *Journal of Higher Education Policy and Management*, *40*(4), 390–412. https://doi.org/10.1080/1360080X.2018.1478613

Wang, P. (2024). Academic bullying as a racialized phenomenon in STEM Higher Education: Centering the experiences of Asian international doctoral students. *Journal of International Students*, *14*(4), 679–701.

Yamada, S., Cappadocia, M. C., & Pepler, D. (2014). Workplace bullying in Canadian graduate psychology programs: Student perspectives of student-supervisor relationships. *Training and Education in Professional Psychology*, *8*(1), 58–67. https://doi.org/10.1037/tep0000015

Ysseldyk, R., Greenaway, K. H., Hassinger, E., Zutrauen, S., Lintz, J., Bhatia, M. P., Frye, M., Starkenburg, E., & Tai, V. (2019). A leak in the academic pipeline: Identity and health among Postdoctoral women. *Frontiers in Psychology*, *10*, 1297. https://doi.org/10.3389/fpsyg.2019.01297

Zhang, F., Litson, K., & Feldon, D. F. (2022). Social predictors of doctoral student mental health and well-being. *PLoS ONE* *17*(9), e0274273. https://doi.org/10.1371/journal.pone.0274273

Chapter 4

Disability, Chronic Illness, and Neurodivergence

In higher education, research, practice, and policy are more likely to focus on disabled students than disabled staff (Friedensen et al., 2021; Saltes, 2020). Further, disabled students are better supported by universities than disabled staff (Emira et al., 2018; Remnant et al., 2024). Where research addressing the disabled staff experience has been conducted, the hostile environment experienced by disabled staff is clear. For example, Shigaki et al. (2012) report that 26% of university staff experienced job discrimination and 20% experienced harassment because of their disability. This hostility has both a physical and psychological impact on disabled people (Lindsay & Fuentes, 2022) in a sector where the workplace environment and associated stress already negatively impact employee wellbeing (Nicholls et al., 2022; Urbina-Garcia, 2020). Ill treatment is also evident through other measures. For example, in a large-scale study of doctoral recipients (N = 1,148,817), Castro et al. (2024) highlight the salary disparities experienced by disabled people. Disabled academics working in Science, Technology, Engineering, and Mathematics (STEM) earned $14,360 less than their non-disabled colleagues. The current chapter outlines the environment and barriers to inclusion experienced by disabled staff, including particular issues associated with disclosure and obtaining workplace accommodations.

The Physical, Social, and Cultural Academic Environment

Disability is less prevalent in the higher education sector than in the general population (Brewer et al., 2025). It is, of course, important to recognise that data are likely to underestimate the presence of disabled staff. Those who meet formal criteria (e.g., the Equality Act, 2010 definition of "disabled") may not wish to disclose a disability. This may reflect the stigma associated with disability and fear of discrimination, the belief that their condition is not a disability, or that they are not "disabled enough" to "count" as disabled (Brewer, 2025). Though the number of disabled people working in higher education remains uncertain, it is clear that disabled academics are either less present in the sector

DOI: 10.4324/9781032639321-5

than in the general population or unwilling to disclose their disabled status, indicating an environment that is hostile to people with disabilities.

Academic workplaces are often inaccessible. In part, this may reflect the fundamental assumption that those working in the higher education sector are not disabled, with disabled academics characterised as unexpected workers (Stone, Crooks, & Owen, 2013) and misfits (Waterfield, Beagan, & Weinberg, 2018). For example, a lecture theatre may be classified as "accessible" for wheelchair users if it is appropriate for disabled students, failing to consider whether the lectern is accessible for academic wheelchair users (Inckle, 2018). As a consequence, disabled staff often spend additional time physically checking the teaching rooms they are allocated in advance to avoid later disruption and embarrassment. Indeed, inaccessible spaces have a significant impact on employee performance and productivity; for example, open-plan offices may be problematic for those with concentration or hearing difficulties (Van Laer, Jammaers, & Hoeven, 2022). Inaccessible work environments can also force disabled people to become dependent on their non-disabled colleagues (Van Laer, Jammaers, & Hoeven, 2022). Such dependence may further impair productivity, undermine confidence, and lead non-disabled employees to view their disabled colleagues as less competent or capable.

The neoliberal environment (see introduction and Chapter 1) is especially problematic. Drawing on the experiences of disabled academics, university stakeholders (e.g., human resources professionals, trade union representatives, and line managers), and policy documents, Remnant et al. (2024) investigate the consequences of the neoliberal environment for disabled academics. The authors demonstrate that disabled academics are required to navigate hostile policies and procedures. For example, workplace policies pertaining to disability typically focus on staff presence, performance, and legal obligations, minimising flexibility and characterising disabled staff as unproductive and less capable of meeting performance standards (Remnant et al., 2024). In one recent survey, 32% of respondents (employed in higher education in academic or non-academic roles) felt that the way disability is viewed by others had negatively impacted their career progression, and 44% of respondents had thought about leaving their institution because of a lack of disability inclusion (Evans & Brewer, 2025).

Assumptions that disabled employees will be less productive are consistent with broader stereotypes of disability. For example, disabled people are often perceived as less competent or capable than their non-disabled peers. In academia, there is an assumption that some tasks are too demanding for disabled scholars (Swenor, 2019), and when issues arise, disabled employees are more likely to have their competence questioned than be offered support (Best, 2025). As a consequence, disabled academics are often eager to prove themselves, demonstrate motivation and commitment to their role, and reassure senior staff that disability will not impede their productivity (Jammaers, Zanoni, & Hardonk, 2016; Waterfield, Beagan, & Weinberg, 2018). Indeed, ableism (i.e., the negative attitudes and behaviour targeted at disabled people because they do not display the "ideal" state of non-disabled) is well documented in academia (e.g., Brown & Leigh, 2020, 2021; Dolmage, 2017). Clearly, change is required at a cultural and sector level, with issues extending beyond individual departments or institutions.

Many disabled people also possess other marginalised identities, though relatively little attention has been paid to the specific experiences of disabled women, disabled racialised minorities, etc. (Vernon, 1999). Though the present chapter focuses on disability, it is important to recognise the importance of intersectionality. For example, Shaw, Chan, and McMahon (2012) explore formal allegations of disability harassment, with particular attention to the ethnicity, gender, and age of those experiencing harassment. There was significant variation in the experience of disability-orientated harassment; for example, women were more likely to report disability harassment than men. Though data covered a range of industries (e.g., retail, manufacturing), the identification of specific characteristic groups that place individuals at greater or lower risk of disability harassment may highlight those who are most likely to be marginalised and subjected to hostile treatment in academia.

Relatively few studies address the experiences of non-academic disabled university employees. In one exception, Mousa (2022) highlights the issues experienced by disabled non-academic employees in public universities. Barriers to inclusion were evident at a range of levels, including a lack of understanding of the needs of disabled employees and poor infrastructure (at the macro level), a lack of representation at senior levels and disproportionate access to university resources (at the meso level), and a lack of confidence in applying for promotion and barriers to networking (at the micro level). Clearly, a range of structural and systemic issues exists that requires consideration and intervention. In part, the current hostile environment that exists for disabled staff reflects the relative importance afforded to disability, chronic ill health, and neurodivergence. Though a substantial proportion of the general population is disabled, equality, diversity, and inclusion practice and policy are arguably less focused on disability than other protected characteristics (Wolbring & Lillywhite, 2021). It is essential, therefore, that disability is afforded the same attention and status as other protected characteristics.

Further, compared to other protected characteristics, disability is most likely to be discussed and defined in negative terms. In particular, a "deficit model" is typically adopted whereby specific conditions and disability more broadly are described in relation to difficulty and limitation. For example, neurodivergence may be explained with reference to "difficulties with social communication" rather than "strengths of creative thinking". Though it is important to recognise the barriers experienced by people with disabilities (in order to address these), it is also important to recognise the strengths associated with disability. The Affirmation Model provides a non-tragic perspective, incorporating a positive disabled identity (Swain & French, 2000). Institutions are encouraged to promote disability pride, which research indicates has a protective effect against stigma (Bogart, Lund, & Rottenstein, 2018; Qin et al., 2025).

Academic Conferences and Networking

As outlined above, the working environment is problematic for disabled employees. Workspaces may also impede social inclusion, negatively impacting opportunities for professional networking and social support (Van Laer, Jammaers, & Hoeven, 2022). Networking is an essential part of academia, providing opportunities to collaborate, disseminate research, and build the reputation often required for promotion. For example, in one survey of 109 academics, Heffernan (2021) reports that 42 obtained publication opportunities from their networks, 38 acknowledged career advancements, and 13 achieved direct employment. Conferences represent one of the most important opportunities for networking in higher education. These are, however, often problematic for disabled academics (Brewer, 2025).

For example, academic conferences frequently require long-distance travel, and for many delegates, public transport is inaccessible, requiring additional planning, travelling time, and financial resources. Conference venues are typically noisy, and social activities or meetings may be scheduled for "free" time. These environments are especially difficult for attendees sensitive to noise, subject to fatigue, or likely to be overwhelmed. Such issues even occur at equality, diversity, and inclusion-focused conferences (Callus, 2017), where delegates may expect greater accessibility and support. There are a number of reports highlighting the issues experienced by disabled conference delegates, such as the additional expense often incurred, and important recommendations to address these barriers to inclusion (e.g., Brown, Thompson, & Leigh, 2018; De Picker, 2020; McClurg, 2024).

Though conference delegates may be provided with an opportunity to secure accommodations (e.g., through contacting conference organisers prior to the event), this approach requires disclosure of the disability and specific needs. Attendees may be unwilling to disclose such personal information, especially to those most closely connected to their specific research field. For example, conference organisers may be most likely to review their research publications, grant proposals, or job applications. Further, requests for accommodations provide no guarantee that support will be provided, and organisers may indicate their irritation and annoyance with disabled attendees (Hodge, 2014). It is, therefore, important to build accessibility into conference organisation rather than depend on individual disclosure and accommodation. Accessibility should not be restricted to the conference venue, with consideration for calls for abstracts and overnight accommodation also required. An inclusive approach may also benefit non-disabled delegates. For example, a hybrid approach allowing both online and in-person attendance may be of value to those with caring responsibilities or without access to the funds for travel and hotel accommodation.

Recruitment and Progression

Particular issues have been identified with regard to the recruitment and progression of disabled staff. Compared to other sectors, recruitment to academic posts involves a lengthy application and intensive interview process. Combining interviews with disabled academics and staff involved in recruitment with an analysis of job advertisements, Wilde and Fish (2025) conclude that staff involved in academic recruitment are aware of the barriers that exist for disabled applicants. Further, the commitment to equality, diversity, and inclusion that often features in recruitment advertising may be viewed as performative rather than as evidence of tangible support for marginalised applicants (Wilde & Fish, 2025).

There are particular barriers associated with recruitment or promotion to leadership and senior positions (Best, 2025; Brewster et al., 2017; Clifford, 2015). Barriers include disabled staff concerns that the long working hours associated with leadership positions exclude their participation and inaccessible development opportunities (Emira et al., 2018). For example, whilst leadership programmes are often advertised specifically for those with other protected characteristics (e.g., women and racially minoritised staff), similar initiatives targeted at disabled staff are rarely provided. Further, management may not trust disabled people to be appointed to leadership positions, perceiving them as less competent or reliable than their non-disabled peers. Indeed, disabled people commonly experience paternalistic forms of ableism, including infantilisation and pity (Nario-Redmond, Kemerling, & Silverman, 2019).

As a consequence, disabled staff may feel compelled to work harder than their peers to offset performance concerns and ensure that they are recognised for their accomplishments (Best, 2025). Reflecting such barriers to progression, disabled academics are especially underrepresented at senior levels and in secure (i.e., tenured) roles (Castro et al., 2024). The relative absence of disabled staff in leadership and management positions is especially concerning, as disabled staff in such positions may feel more comfortable disclosing such information. Of course, for disabled staff who have secured leadership positions, important institutional and personal barriers remain (Emira et al., 2018). It is, therefore, essential that disabled staff are meaningfully involved in all areas of practice and policy decision-making (Sarju, 2021).

Workload and Personal Impact

The term "crip time" is commonly used to describe the additional time required of disabled people in ableist environments and cultures. Workload models often fail to recognise the additional time required to process information, move across campus, etc., let alone the additional time required to attend medical appointments or extended periods of recovery after illness. Such issues are especially problematic in the higher education sector, where disabled staff are often required to undertake additional work not recognised in formal workloads, for example, requesting and making arrangements for workplace accommodations (Inckle, 2018; Merchant et al., 2020). A desire to support students, and especially marginalised students, further increases disabled academic workloads. As stated by one academic, "*I used to have queues of students... mostly other people's students*". (Wilde & Fish, 2025, p. 11).

For academics with energy-limiting conditions, time can be especially problematic in the productivity-focused neoliberal environment (Brewer, 2025; Evans et al. 2024). For example, academics may require regular rest, using evenings and weekends for rest and recovery. Evans et al. (2024) highlight the experience of exhaustion in academia and the feeling of being "left behind". For example, "*My experience of trying to keep up with reading for research and teaching, meet marking deadlines, respond to reports or policies for admin roles, is therefore one of constantly being left behind*". (p. 9). In particular, the authors discuss the potential to be left behind through a lack of accommodations, the normalisation of hyper-productivity, energy expenditure that may result in relapse, and a lack of career development.

There are a number of personal reflections highlighting the challenges experienced by disabled academics (e.g., England, 2016), though relatively few by non-academic staff (e.g., Pionke, 2019) employed in higher education. Individual and collective autoethnographic accounts highlight the personal impact of disability, chronic illness, and neurodivergence (e.g., Bertilsdotter Rosqvist et al., 2023; Merchant et al., 2020; Wilkinson & Wilkinson, 2023). For example, autoethnographies can convey the personal and professional cost of inequality and promote the empathy and understanding of disability required for active allyship. Such accounts require significant emotion work, however, and can leave those already marginalised in academia more vulnerable to stigma and discrimination. It is particularly important that where disabled people are asked to provide personal insight into disability, these contributions lead to meaningful change and are not used as "inspiration porn" for the entertainment of others (Haller & Preston, 2016).

Non-Visible Conditions and Disclosure

Non-visible disabilities are conditions that are not immediately observable, with many chronic illnesses, learning disabilities, and mental health conditions being non-visible. There are important differences in the lived experiences of disabled people with visible and non-visible conditions (e.g., Nario-Redmond, Kemerling, & Silverman, 2019). In particular, those with non-visible conditions can typically decide whether to share information about their disability or not. Indeed, disabled staff are often cautious when choosing to share information about their disability, both formally (e.g., to human resources) and informally (e.g., to colleagues). As a consequence, non-disabled staff may not understand the extent to which a disabled colleague is affected by their condition and the importance of accommodations. There may, of course, be significant variation in willingness to disclose, reflecting factors such as the type of disability and perceived job security (Von Schrader, Malzer, & Bruyère, 2014). For example, there may be particular concerns relating to the disclosure of stigmatised and poorly understood conditions.

Disabled employees are often marginalised and othered (Merchant et al., 2020), and for many staff, "passing" as non-disabled in order to avoid stigma and discrimination may be preferable to the disclosure required to access workplace accommodations (Best, 2025). Such concerns are not unfounded, and staff report being provided with fewer opportunities after disclosing their disabled status (Brewster et al., 2017). Reluctance to disclose highlights the importance of creating an accessible workplace environment that supports colleagues who have not shared their personal access needs. For example, ensuring that documents are available a few days prior to a meeting provides all staff with time to process relevant information without needing to disclose dyslexia, etc. It is important to recognise, however, that the fear of being "outed" as disabled can impede access to both social support and workplace accommodations (Clifford et al., 2015), and institutions must provide a supportive workplace environment in which disclosure is not detrimental.

Accommodations and Adjustments

In the United Kingdom and elsewhere, employers are legally required to provide "reasonable accommodations" to support disabled staff. Whilst it is important to provide employees with appropriate support, there are issues with the current framing of workplace accommodations and the processes through which employees request these. For example, the term "accommodations" suggests tolerance of disability (and connected stereotypes of disability as a burden to others) rather than valuing disability or simply providing the support that employees require. Further, disability is framed as an individual responsibility, with disabled academics typically required to navigate complex university systems to access workplace accommodations with little institutional support or guidance (Waterfield, Beagan, & Weinberg, 2018).

Indeed, in higher education, the services available to support disabled staff are less developed than the infrastructure in place to support disabled students (Pionke, 2019; Saltes, 2022). The process of obtaining workplace accommodations can be lengthy and bureaucratic, with employees repeatedly asking for workplace accommodations and spending months or years waiting for accommodations to be provided (Best, 2025). This is, of course, especially challenging for those on fixed-term precarious contracts who may be without support for the entirety of their position. Further, employees are often required to provide medical evidence of their condition, creating a barrier for those without a formal diagnosis (Remnant et al., 2024). It should be possible for staff to discuss their disability and access requirements without a formal diagnosis, especially as the diagnostic process can be lengthy, expensive, and distressing.

Of course, even where a diagnosis is available, management may not fully understand the impact of such conditions, and some disabilities are especially stigmatised.

Support for disabled staff, including implementation of workplace accommodations, is often dependent on line manager approval (Brewer, 2025), even if recommended by occupational health professionals working at the university.

It is not surprising, therefore, that the process of obtaining workplace accommodations can have a detrimental impact on those working in higher education, especially when it requires implicit or explicit questioning of the employee's health status and justifying their need for support. For example, research indicates that requests for workplace accommodations can be emotionally exhausting, with disabled staff concerned that they can be perceived as needy, undeserving, or asking too much (Waterfield, Beagan, & Weinberg, 2018). Further, where institutions do agree to provide workplace accommodations, disabled employees often spend a substantial proportion of their time managing these accommodations (Inckle, 2018; Merchant et al., 2020). For example, employees may be required to arrange their own interpreters or research the most appropriate assistive devices, requiring significant administrative time not commonly accounted for in workload models.

Further issues are created by the widespread misunderstanding that exists in relation to the purpose and role of workplace accommodations. Though accommodations are intended to address inequity (e.g., the additional time taken for a task), they are often perceived to be an unfair advantage. This may reflect the broader societal dialogue that surrounds disability, with media frequently discussing disability in relation to benefit fraud, adopting terms such as "scrounger" to demonise and marginalise disabled people (Briant, Watson, & Philo, 2013). Misconceptions of workplace accommodations may be especially problematic in sectors such as higher education. For example, it is often assumed that accommodations are not required if a person excels in their role, and people who excel when receiving accommodations are perceived to be unfairly advantaged or less respectable (Egan & Giuliano, 2009; Paetzold et al., 2008).

The Hierarchy of Disability

Policy and practice often discuss disability in general terms, providing a focus for activism and support. There are, of course, a range of disability types, and the Equality Act (2010) guidance makes specific reference to sensory impairments, impairments with fluctuating or recurring effects, progressive conditions, autoimmune conditions, organ-specific conditions, developmental conditions, learning disabilities, mental health conditions, mental illnesses, and conditions produced by injury to the body. It is, therefore, important to acknowledge that disability can be visible or non-visible, present from birth or acquired later in life, permanent, temporary (though long-term), or fluctuating, and impact physical and/or mental health. Such variation is likely to impact employee experiences of academia. Experiences vary according to condition type or symptom profile (e.g., Brewer, 2022, 2025; Smith & Andrews, 2015). Indeed, even those with the same condition are likely to report different experiences based on the presence or severity of each symptom, their roles and responsibilities, and their working environment. Policy and practice addressing the experiences of disabled employees working in the higher education sector should, therefore, recognise and accommodate this variation.

Further, attitudes and behaviour towards people with disabilities can vary depending on the nature of the condition (Wang et al., 2019). For example, in a vignette study involving over 2,000 participants, Timmons, McGinnity, and Carroll (2024) demonstrate that ableism is more commonly directed towards some conditions than others. Similarly, Nario-Redmond, Kemerling, and Silverman (2019) report that infantilisation, unwanted help, and invasions of privacy are more commonly directed at people with visible disabilities, whilst accusations of fraud and invalidation are more commonly targeted at people with non-visible conditions.

Indeed, research indicates a "hierarchy" of disability, with some conditions deemed to be more socially acceptable and deserving of support than others (Thomas, 2000). For example, some conditions are assumed to be a consequence of risky behaviour (such as smoking or alcohol consumption) and are less deserving of support. Other conditions are poorly defined, difficult to diagnose, and perceived to be less legitimate. This hierarchy appears to impact the attitudes and behaviour of both disabled and non-disabled people (e.g., Deal, 2006) and may have a range of consequences. For example, employees may be unwilling to disclose or discuss conditions deemed to be less deserving of support and may be more subject to stigma and discrimination from others when they do.

Recommendations

Institutions should,

- Ensure that the same support available to disabled students is available to staff. For example, increased numbers of disability support officers to assist disabled staff with workplace accommodations and accessibility reports for all teaching and research spaces that consider the staff (as well as student) experience.
- Recognise that many staff who meet the legal definition of disability do not identify as such. Ensure that documentation (e.g., equality, diversity, and inclusion background questions) reflects this and does not simply ask staff if they are or are not disabled.
- Apply the same attention to the lived experience of disability that is applied to other protected characteristics. For example, workplace surveys are more likely to address racist bullying and harassment than ableism. When analysing such data, it is important to consider the experiences of

staff with different condition types (e.g., sensory impairment, mental health conditions) or combinations of disabilities.

- Guide staff through the disclosure and workplace accommodation process. Include example accommodations for those unfamiliar with the support available (e.g., software), but recognise the importance of individual circumstances. Support needs will vary according to specific symptom profiles, the roles and responsibilities held, and the presence of comorbid conditions. Compensate staff for the additional time taken to complete duties in formal workload models (e.g., time required for training on assistive devices).
- Establish an inclusive and accessible environment that reduces the need for individual accommodations. Make the importance and value of workplace accommodations clear to all staff; this should extend beyond simple legislative requirements and include the retention and wellbeing of disabled staff. Move beyond a traditional deficit model of disability to recognise the strengths associated with disability and raise awareness of particular issues (e.g., fluctuating conditions).
- Recognise the barriers that exist for disabled staff beyond the individual institution (e.g., conference attendance) and the existence of infantilising stereotypes that disadvantage disabled staff. Provide additional resources and professional development opportunities to address barriers to inclusion. All financial resources (including funding for workplace accommodations) should be provided centrally, reducing the impact (and potential for bias) at the departmental level.
- Establish a disabled staff network that provides staff members with both practical and social support and provides a forum for shared advocacy. Ensure that such networks are consulted on all proposed changes to practice and policy (e.g., travel policy). Engage disabled staff in the planning of new spaces to enhance accessibility.

Subject in Focus 1: Research Funding

For research focused academics, the successful acquisition of external funding is essential (see Chapter 1). External funding makes an important economic contribution to the institution and can provide the necessary 'buy out' of time from other duties. Further, research funding is associated with a greater number of research outputs such as journal articles (Rosenbloom et al., 2015; Song, Sun, & Zhang, 2025) and funded articles are more likely to be cited than non-funded articles (Dorta-González & Dorta-González, 2023). Despite the importance of research funding for academic progression there have been relatively few analyses of the disproportionate funding awarded to disabled researchers, especially when compared to similar analyses of funding application and award by applicant gender and ethnicity.

In one study, Swenor, Munoz, and Meeks (2020) examine National Institute of Health (NIH) research grant applicants and successful awardees from 2008 to 2018, demonstrating that disabled academics are less likely to receive funding for their work than their non-disabled peers. Further, the funding landscape is becoming more, not less, challenging for disabled scholars, with 1.9% and 1.2% of principal investigators awarded a grant reporting a disability in 2008 and 2018 respectively (Swenor, Munoz, & Meeks, 2020). The lower likelihood of successful grant funding experienced by disabled academics may reflect a range of issues including inaccessible application processes, funding applications made less competitive by the need to cost for workplace accommodations, and disability bias within the peer review system (Iezzoni, 2018).

It is important to recognise that though the analysis of research funding awarded to disabled academics covers a broad range of disciplines and research subjects, some of this work may include equality, diversity, and inclusion research. Academics who are both experts by qualification (e.g., a PhD) and experts by experience (i.e., lived experience of a condition) have a unique insight into subjects such as access to healthcare. This is especially valuable where despite increased awareness of public and patient engagement, relatively little funded disability research is conducted in partnership with disabled people (Smith-Merry et al., 2024) and disabled people have expressed a desire for a partnership approach to research (Kitchin, 2000). Such insights should, therefore, make the work of disabled academics more rather than less attractive to research funders.

Subject in Focus 2: Laboratory Access

Laboratories can be particularly inaccessible, sending a clear message that disabled people are unexpected and unwelcome in these environments. For example, laboratory access may be denied on the premise of "health and safety" suggesting that disabled employees are a liability to themselves or others. Clearly, inaccessible laboratories hinder performance. Disabled researchers who are not permitted to conduct their own laboratory work may be dependent on collaboration with other researchers (who may demand first or prominent authorship of subsequent publications) or be forced to cost for the recruitment, training, and support of non-disabled research assistants. There may also be a significant personal cost associated with such workspaces reflecting the repeated need for disabled employees to formally disclose their condition, request appropriate accommodations, and self-advocate. Alternatively, disabled researchers may only be granted access to the laboratory when others are present, both limiting opportunities for data collection and undermining their position in the research group.

In recent years, there has been greater focus on the accessibility of laboratory spaces. As with other disability focused research, practice, and policy, work addressing the inaccessibility of laboratories have typically focused on the student rather than employee experience (e.g., Jeannis et al., 2020) again suggesting that disabled researchers do not exist or do not belong in those spaces. In one important exception, Egambaram et al. (2022) propose a number of recommendations to improve disabled access to chemistry laboratories. Physical adjustments include reducing excessive noise to prevent sensory overload and ensuring access routes are wide enough for those using mobility aids. The cultural changes to enhance inclusion such as normalising discussion of individual access needs are also identified.

References

Bertilsdotter Rosqvist, H., Hultman, L., Österborg Wiklund, S., Nygren, A., Storm, P., & Sandberg, G. (2023). ADHD in higher education and academia. *Canadian Journal on Disability Studies*, *12*(3), 1–26. https://doi.org/10.15353/cjds.v12i3.1032

Best, M. (2025). How inclusive is higher education for female disabled staff? Stigmas & stoppers. *Disability & Society*. https://doi.org/10.1080/09687599.2025.2509533

Bogart, K. R., Lund, E. M., & Rottenstein, A. (2018). Disability pride protects self-esteem through the rejection-identification model. *Rehabilitation Psychology*, *63*(1), 155–159.

Brewer, G. (2022). *Disability in higher education: Investigating identity, stigma and disclosure amongst academics*. McGraw-Hill Education.

Brewer, G. (2025). The lived experience of female academics with long-term conditions Impacting on energy levels and/or cognitive function. *Disability & Society*, *40*(2), 419–444. https://doi.org/10.1080/09687599.2023.2287412

Brewer, G., Dimitriadi, Y., Doddato, F., Haroon, H., Jolly, J., Leigh, J., Mahaut-Smith, M., Remnant, J., & Sarju, J. (2025). *Towards a fully inclusive environment for disabled people in STEMM: A NADSN White paper*. NADSN STEMM Action Group. Retrieved from: https://www.nadsn-uk.org/wp-content/uploads/2025/04/NADSN_STEMM_White_Paper_090425-v0.3.pdf

Brewster, S., Duncan, N., Emira, M., & Clifford, A. (2017). Personal sacrifice and corporate cultures: Career progression for disabled staff in higher education. *Disability & Society*, *32*(7), 1027–1042. https://doi.org/10.1080/09687599.2017.1331837.

Briant, E., Watson, N., & Philo, G. (2013). Reporting disability in the age of austerity: The changing face of media representation of disability and disabled people in the United Kingdom and the creation of new 'folk devils'. *Disability & Society*, *28*(6), 874–889. https://doi.org/10.1080/09687599.2013.813837

Brown, N. (2021). *Lived experiences of Ableism in academia*. Policy Press.

Brown, N., & Leigh, J. (2020). *Ableism in academia: Theorising experiences of disabilities and chronic illnesses in higher education*. UCL Press.

Brown, N., Thompson, P., & Leigh, J. S. (2018). Making academia more accessible. *Journal of Perspectives in Applied Academic Practice*, *6*(2). https://doi.org/10.14297/jpaap.v6i2.348

Callus, A. M. (2017). Making disability conferences more actively inclusive. *Disability & Society*, *32*(10), 1661–1665. https://doi.org/10.1080/09687599.2017.1356059

Castro, F., Stuart, E., Deal, J., Varadaraj, V., & Swenor, B. K. (2024). STEM doctorate recipients with disabilities experienced early in life earn lower salaries and are underrepresented among higher academic positions. *Nature Human Behaviour*, *8*(1), 72–81. https://doi.org/10.1038/s41562-023-01745-z

Clifford, A., Brewster, S., Duncan, N., Williams-Findlay, B., Emira, M., & Taysum, A. (2015). *Understanding leadership from a disability perspective*. Leadership Foundation for Higher Education. Retrieved from: https://wlv.openrepository.com/items/243f3c47-5f39-4b39-ae94-1018c9b2e187

De Picker, M. (2020). Rethinking inclusion and disability activism at academic conferences: Strategies proposed by a PhD student with a physical disability. *Disability & Society*, *35*(1), 163–167. https://doi.org/10.1080/09687599.2019.1619234

Deal, M. (2006). Attitudes of disabled people toward other disabled people and impairment groups. Unpublished doctoral thesis, City University, London. Retrieved from: https://openaccess.city.ac.uk/17416/

Dolmage, J. T. (2017). *Academic ableism: Disability and higher education*. University of Michigan Press.

Dorta-González, P., & Dorta-González, M. I. (2023). Citation differences across research funding and access modalities. *The Journal of Academic Librarianship*, *49*(4), 102734. https://doi.org/10.1016/j.acalib.2023.102734

Egambaram, O., Hilton, K., Leigh, J., Richardson, R., Sarju, J., Slater, A., & Turner, B. (2022). The future of laboratory chemistry learning and teaching must be accessible. *Journal of Chemical Education*, *99*(12), 3814–3821. https://doi.org/10.1021/acs.jchemed.2c00328

Egan, P. M., & Giuliano, T. A. (2009). Unaccommodating attitudes: perceptions of students as a function of academic accommodation use and test performance. *North American Journal of Psychology*, *11*(3), 487–500.

Emira, M., Brewster, S., Duncan, N., & Clifford, A. (2018). What disability? I am a leader! Understanding leadership in HE from a disability perspective. *Educational Management Administration & Leadership*, *46*(3), 457–473. https://doi.org/10.1177/1741143216662923

England, M. R. (2016). Being open in academia: A personal narrative of mental illness and disclosure. *The Canadian Geographer*, *60*(2), 226–231. https://doi.org/10.1111/cag.12270

Equality Act (2010). Retrieved from: https://www.legislation.gov.uk/ukpga/2010/15/contents

Evans, B., Allam, A., Bê, A., Hale, C., Rose, M., & Ruddock, A. (2024). Being left behind beyond recovery: 'Crip time' and chronic illness in neoliberal academia. *Social & Cultural Geography*, 1–21. https://doi.org/10.1080/14649365.2024.2410262

Evans. C., & Brewer, G. (2025). *Report by researching disability inclusion: Research strategy team for realising inclusion for disabled employees in higher education*. RIDE Higher: A NADSN initiative.

Friedensen, R. E., Horii, C. V., Kimball, E., Lisi, B., Miller, R. A., Siddiqui, S., ... & Woodman, A. (2021). A systematic review of research on faculty with disabilities. 1–25. *Journal of the Professoriate*, *12*(2).

Haller, B., & Preston, J. (2016). Confirming normalcy: 'Inspiration porn' and the construction of the disabled subject? In K. Ellis and M. Kent (Eds.), *Disability and social media* (pp. 63–78). Routledge.

Heffernan, T. (2021). Academic networks and career trajectory: 'There's no career in academia without networks'. *Higher Education Research & Development*, *40*(5), 981–994. https://doi.org/10.1080/07294360.2020.1799948

Hodge, N. (2014). Unruly bodies at conference. *Disability & Society*, *29*(4), 655–658. https://doi.org/10.1080/09687599.2014.894749

Iezzoni, L. I. (2018). Explicit disability bias in peer review. *Medical Care*, *56*(4), 277–278. https://doi.org/10.1097/MLR.0000000000000889

Inckle, K. (2018). Unreasonable adjustments: The additional unpaid labour of academics with disabilities. *Disability & Society*, *33*(8), 1372–1376. https://doi.org/10.1080/09687599.2018.1480263

Jammaers, E., Zanoni, P., & Hardonk, S. (2016). Constructing positive identities in ableist workplaces: Disabled employees' discursive practices engaging with the discourse of lower productivity. *Human Relations*, *69*(6), 1365–1386. https://doi.org/10.1177/0018726715612901

Jeannis, H., Goldberg, M., Seelman, K., Schmeler, M., & Cooper, R. A. (2020). Barriers and facilitators to students with physical disabilities' participation in academic laboratory spaces. *Disability and Rehabilitation: Assistive Technology*, *15*(2), 225–237. https://doi.org/10.1080/17483107.2018.1559889

Kitchin, R. (2000). The researched opinions on research: Disabled people and disability research. *Disability & Society*, *15*(1), 25–47. https://doi.org/10.1080/09687590025757

Lindsay, S., & Fuentes, K. (2022). It is time to address ableism in academia: A systematic review of the experiences and impact of ableism among faculty and staff. *Disabilities*, *2*(2), 178–203. https://doi.org/10.3390/disabilities2020014

McClurg, U. L. (2024). A short guide to addressing accessibility at scientific conferences. *Journal of Cell Science*, *137*(10). https://doi.org/10.1242/jcs.261858

Merchant, W., Read, S., D'Evelyn, S., Miles, C., & Williams, V. (2020). The insider view: Tackling disabling practices in higher education institutions. *Higher Education*, *80*, 273–287. https://doi.org/10.1007/s10734-019-00479-0

Mousa, M. (2022). Disability of non-academic employees in public universities: An exploration of daily work experiences. *International Journal of Educational Management*, *36*(6), 877–891. https://doi.org/10.1108/IJEM-07-2021-0287

Nario-Redmond, M. R., Kemerling, A. A., & Silverman, A. (2019). Hostile, benevolent, and ambivalent ableism: Contemporary manifestations. *Journal of Social Issues*, *75*(3), 726–756. https://doi.org/10.1111/josi.12337

Nicholls, H., Nicholls, M., Tekin, S., Lamb, D., & Billings, J (2022). The impact of working in academia on researchers' mental health and well being: A systematic review and qualitative meta synthesis. *PLoS ONE*, *17*(5), e0268890. https://doi.org/10.1371/journal.pone.0268890

Paetzold, R. L., García, M. F., Colella, A., Ren, L. R., del Triana, M. C., & Ziebro, M. (2008). Perceptions of people with disabilities: When is accommodation fair? *Basic and Applied Social Psychology*, *30*(1), 27–35. https://doi.org/10.1080/01973530701665280

Pionke, J. J. (2019). The impact of disbelief: On being a library employee with a disability. *Library Trends*, *67*(3), 423–435. https://doi.org/10.1353/lib.2019.0004

Qin, S., Isadore, K., Chun, J., Chen, R. Z., & Mears, M. (2025). Belonging and pride in people with disabilities: An approach to counteract stigma. *Stigma and Health*. https://doi.org/10.1037/sah0000619

Remnant, J., Sang, K., Calvard, T., Richards, J., & Babajide, O. (2024). Exclusionary logics: Constructing disability and disadvantaging disabled academics in the neoliberal university. *Sociology*, *58*(1), 23–44. https://doi.org/10.1177/00380385231162570

Rosenbloom, J. L., Ginther, D. K., Juhl, T., & Heppert, J. A. (2015). The effects of research & development funding on scientific productivity: Academic chemistry, 1990–2009. *PLoS ONE*, *10*(9), e0138176. https://doi.org/10.1371/journal.pone.0138176

Saltes, N. (2020). Disability barriers in academia: An analysis of disability accommodation policies for faculty at Canadian universities. *Canadian Journal of Disability Studies*, *9*(1), 53–90. https://doi.org/10.15353/cjds.v9i1.596

Saltes, N. (2022). 'It's all about student accessibility. No one ever talks about teacher accessibility': Examining ableist expectations in academia. *International Journal of Inclusive Education*, *26*(7), 674–700. https://doi.org/10.1080/13603116.2020.1712483

Sarju, J. P. (2021). Nothing about us without us: Towards genuine inclusion of disabled scientists and science students post pandemic. *Chemistry*, *27*(41), 10489–10494. https://doi.org/10.1002/chem.202100268.

Shaw, L. R., Chan, F., & McMahon, B. T. (2012). Intersectionality and disability harassment: The interactive effects of disability, race, age, and gender. *Rehabilitation Counseling Bulletin*, *55*(2), 82–91. https://doi.org/10.1177/0034355211431167

Shigaki, C. L., Anderson, K. M., Howald, C. L., Henson, L., & Gregg, B. E. (2012). Disability on campus: A perspective from faculty and staff. *Work*, *42*(4), 559–571. https://doi.org/10.3233/WOR-2012-1409

Smith, D. H., & Andrews, J. F. (2015). Deaf and hard of hearing faculty in higher education: Enhancing access, equity, policy, and practice. *Disability & Society*, *30*(10), 1521–1536. https://doi.org/10.1080/09687599.2015.1113160

Smith-Merry, J., Darcy, S., Dew, A., Hemsley, B., Imms, C., O'Donovan, M. A., … & Ellem, K. (2024). Who funds published disability research in Australia? *Journal of Disability Policy Studies*, 36(1), 52–63. https://doi.org/10.1177/10442073241228840

Song, Y., Sun, W., & Zhang, Y. (2025). The impact of research funding on academic outputs: Evidence from the personnel data in China. *Economic and Political Studies.13(3)*. 326–346. https://doi.org/10.1080/20954816.2024.2439619

Stone, S. D., Crooks, V. A., & Owen, M. (2013). Going through the back door: Chronically ill academics' experiences as 'unexpected workers'. *Social Theory and Health*, *11*(2), 151–174. https://doi.org/10.1057/sth.2013.1

Swain, J., & French, S. (2000). Towards an affirmation model of disability. *Disability & Society*, *15*(4), 569–582. https://doi.org/10.1080/09687590050058189

Swenor, B. (2019). Losing vision and gaining perspective. *JAMA*, *321*(5), 455–456. https://doi.org/10.1001/jama.2019.0076

Thomas, A. (2000). Stability of Tringo's hierarchy of preference toward disability groups: 30 years later. *Psychological Reports*, *86*(3), 1155–1156. https://doi.org/10.1177/003329410008600315.2

Timmons, S., McGinnity, F., & Carroll, E. (2024). Ableism differs by disability, gender and social context: Evidence from vignette experiments. *British Journal of Social Psychology*, *63*(2), 637–657. https://doi.org/10.1111/bjso.12696

Urbina-Garcia, A. (2020). What do we know about university academics' mental health? A systematic literature review. *Stress and Health*, *36*(5), 563–585. https://doi.org/10.1002/smi.2956

Van Laer, K., Jammaers, E., & Hoeven, W. (2022). Disabling organizational spaces: Exploring the processes through which spatial environments disable employees with impairments. *Organization*, *29*(6), 1018–1035. https://doi.org/10.1177/1350508419894698

Vernon, A. (1999). The dialectics of multiple identities and the disabled people's movement. *Disability & Society*, *14*(3), 385–398. https://doi.org/10.1080/09687599926217

Von Schrader, S., Malzer, V., & Bruyère, S. (2014). Perspectives on disability disclosure: The importance of employer practices and workplace climate. *Employment Rights and Responsibilities Journal*, *26*(4), 237–255. https://doi.org/10.1007/s10672-013-9227-9

Wang, K., Walker, K., Pietri, E., & Ashburn-Nardo, L. (2019). Consequences of confronting patronizing help for people with disabilities: Do target gender and disability type matter? *Journal of Social Issues*, *75*(3), 904–923. https://doi.org/10.1111/josi.12332

Waterfield, B., Beagan, B. B., & Weinberg, M. (2018). Disabled academics: A case study in Canadian universities. *Disability & Society*, *33*(3), 327–348. https://doi.org/10.1080/09687599.2017.1411251

Wilde, A., & Fish, R. (2025). *Class-based disablism in the academy*. Society for Research in Higher Education Report. Retrieved from: https://srhe.ac.uk/wp-content/uploads/2025/07/research_report_ SRHE-Wilde-and-Fish-Class-based-Disablism.pdf

Wilkinson, S., & Wilkinson, C. (2023). Pain, no gain? A joint-autoethnography of our working lives as academics with chronic illnesses. *International Journal of Changes in Education*, *1*(1), 4–10. https://doi.org/10.47852/bonviewijce32021657

Wolbring, G., & Lillywhite, A. (2021). Equity/Equality, Diversity, and Inclusion (EDI) in universities: The case of disabled people. *Societies*, *11*(2), 49. https://doi.org/10.3390/soc11020049

Chapter 5

Gender, Parenting, and Sexual Orientation

The gendered experience of academia is well established. For example, women are less likely than their male peers to be appointed professor, Head of Department, or Head of higher education institutions (Boivin et al., 2024; Treviño et al., 2015); their work is less likely to be cited (Eagly & Miller, 2016; Rotenstein et al., 2022); and they are expected to adopt a relatively high proportion of low-status service roles (Acker, Webber, & Smyth, 2016). Women are conscious of the gender inequalities which exist within academia and associated barriers to progression (Remich et al., 2016). The present chapter considers gender bias in higher education with particular emphasis on bias in research publication and funding, the hostile and sexist workplace environment, and the additional pressures placed on women through academic service and parenting. Discussion of gender identity and sexual orientation is also included. Of course, though the present chapter discusses gender, gender identity, and sexual orientation in relative isolation, intersectional experiences are important. For example, racially minoritised women report having less influence in their department than White women (Settles et al., 2006).

Gender Bias in Higher Education

There is a considerable degree of subjectivity involved in academia, and the reliance on subjectivity makes decision-making susceptible to bias (Lee et al., 2013). Indeed, Russell, Brock, and Rudisill (2019) argue that bias is "*an inherent aspect of an individual's academic leadership and decision-making processes*" (p. 291). Bias may be especially likely where clear guidelines and grading criteria are not provided. For example, in the Netherlands, female PhD students are almost two times less likely to be awarded the prestigious cum laude distinction than their male peers. Further, the awarding gap is greatest when students are evaluated by an all-male committee and decreases as evaluation committees become more equitable (Bol, 2023).

When assessing the suitability of candidates for a laboratory manager position, both male and female faculty members rate male applicants (on the basis of a CV alone) as more competent and employable than female candidates and

DOI: 10.4324/9781032639321-6

award them higher starting salaries and more mentoring (Moss-Racusin et al., 2012). Whilst some gender biases may seem minor, they have an important impact on the perception and treatment of female academics. For example, Atir and Ferguson (2018) demonstrate through both archival and experimental research that men and women are referred to differently. Compared to their female peers, men are more likely to be referred to by their surname. Importantly, those referred to by their surname are perceived to be more eminent and more deserving of a career award.

Perhaps unsurprisingly, in one study of over 140,000 tenure-track and tenured professors, Spoon et al. (2023) demonstrate that women leave academia at higher rates than men at all stages of their careers and are especially likely to report that they feel pushed out of academia. Those choosing to leave academia may experience a loss of identity (so often closely aligned to their academic research), guilt or regret at the investment (e.g., time and money) in their academic education, and stigma attached to leaving academic research (Christian et al., 2021). People may also fear a judgement that they could not "cut it" in the competitive academic environment. In many institutions, the response to such issues is, however, to "change" female researchers (e.g., intervention programmes intended to increase female assertiveness) rather than attempt to transform problematic research cultures.

Research Publication and Funding

Research indicates that female academics produce fewer journal articles and fewer high-quality journal articles than their male colleagues, even when taking factors such as discipline and experience into account (Ductor, Goyal, & Prummer, 2023). Reviewing publications in high-ranking journals and the quality of research published, Hengel (2022) concludes that female authors prepare clearer and higher-quality articles in response to the higher standards that are applied to female-authored manuscripts.

Research also suggests gendered patterns of networking and collaboration. For example, female researchers have smaller research networks than their male colleagues (Ductor, Goyal, & Prummer, 2023) and review articles led by male authors have a lower proportion of female coauthors compared to reviews led by female authors (Wheatley & Ogunlana, 2023). It is important to recognise that diversity enhances academia and the quality of work produced. For example, Campbell et al. (2013) demonstrate that gender-heterogeneous teams produce higher-quality journal articles that attract 34% more citations compared to the research produced by same-gender teams. The benefits of collaboration may, however, be less tangible for female academics. For example, Sarsons et al. (2021) indicate that male academics are tenured similarly regardless of whether they publish as a sole author or coauthor. In contrast, women are less likely to receive tenure if they coauthor, suggesting that women receive less credit for collaborative work.

Research funding is an important indicator of academic prestige and is typically referenced in academic staff appraisals, promotion criteria, and institutional targets. Funding, therefore, positively impacts academic progression and promotion. Research funding also enables researchers to devote more time to their research (with buyout of teaching responsibilities, etc.) and to plan more extensive long-term research projects with greater potential for impact. However, the funding peer review process appears to be biased against women. For example, male grant applicants receive more favourable reviewer scores than their female peers (Bol, de Vaan, & van de Rijt, 2022), and women are required to publish 2.5 times more than men (on average) in order to receive the same peer review scores (Wennerås & Wold, 1997).

Comparing over 20,000 grant funding applications from over 7,000 principal investigators, Witteman et al. (2019) conclude that gender gaps in grant funding reflect perceptions of the principal investigator rather than the perceived quality of the proposed research. Further, the gender balance of the funding review panel impacts the funding success of female applicants (Bowman & Ulm, 2009). It is of no surprise, therefore, that female academics are less likely than their male colleagues to secure research funding (Jagsi et al., 2009). This bias may impact women's willingness to engage with the funding application process. Research indicates that women are less likely to apply for research funding, and when applications are submitted, these are typically for less money covering shorter periods of time than the funding applications submitted by men (see Leberman, Eames, & Barnett, 2016, for a review). A lack of time is a clear barrier to application, and this may be especially problematic for women with additional childcare responsibilities or allocated additional pastoral support (Leberman, Eames, & Barnett, 2016).

Hostility and Sexism

Sexist behaviour in the workplace reinforces harmful gender stereotypes and creates a hostile working environment. The *Did this really happen?!* project has collected over 100 real-life examples of everyday sexism in academia (Bocher et al., 2020). The researchers identified six recurring patterns of everyday sexism: (1) behaviour that retains women in stereotypically feminine roles, (2) behaviour that retains men in stereotypically masculine roles, (3) questioning the academic skills of female researchers, (4) placing women in the outsider role in informal networking situations, (5) objectification of women, and (6) expression of neosexist views.

The most common type of everyday sexism (present in 69% of the accepted accounts) included behaviour that restricts women to stereotypically feminine roles. Examples include expecting women to take notes at a meeting or clean the laboratory and describing a female academic as the wife or girlfriend of a male academic. Also present in over half (57%) of the accepted accounts was questioning female competence. Examples included suggesting a female academic had won an award to "fill a quota" or attributing success to physical appearance. The researchers published a series of comic strips based on these real-life experiences of sexism in order to raise awareness of everyday sexism in academia. (To view these comic strips, see https://didthisreallyhappen.net).

Savigny (2014) also considers the personal experience and impact of sexism in academia. As described by one faculty member,

> The body language of my male colleagues makes it clear my voice is not worth listening too, I am made invisible in meetings. If I do get to speak, then people look out of windows, or hold their hand up to shut me up.
>
> (p. 802)

It is perhaps unsurprising then that gender discrimination, sexual harassment, and a sexist workplace environment each contribute to low job satisfaction in female academics (Settles et al., 2006; Settles et al., 2013). Workplace conflict also contributes to the burnout experienced by women in academia (Pedersen & Minnotte, 2017). In contrast, women who work in a positive environment and feel that they have a voice within their department report higher productivity and job satisfaction (Settles et al., 2006; Settles et al., 2007).

Collegiality, Service, and Academic "Housework"

In addition to more prestigious academic activities (such as leadership of a research centre), higher education relies on the successful completion of low-status routine tasks (i.e., academic "housework"). Examples include exam invigilation, attendance at open day recruitment events, and review of applications for ethical approval. In workload models, such tasks are often collectively framed as collegiality or academic service, with academics expected to complete their "fair share" of these as part of their role.

Women are more likely than their male colleagues to volunteer for or accept requests to complete service work that benefits the organisation but has little impact on promotability (Babcock, 2017; Babcock et al., 2022). Women are also more likely to be asked to complete such activities. For example, in one diary-based study, O'Meara et al. (2017) report that women received 378 new work activity requests in a four-week period, compared to the 118 new work requests disclosed by men. Indeed, academic service is perceived as less optional for women than for men, and withholding this citizenship appears to negatively impact the evaluation of women but not the evaluation of their male peers (Heilman & Chen, 2005).

There are, of course, different types of service work. For example, chairing a committee may confer status and be featured on a resume, whereas mentoring and informal support are less likely to be valued. Järvinen and Mik-Meyer (2025) consider the balance of collective vs individual interests and identify four specific types of relational work behaviour. These are compliance (completing academic service without reward), evasiveness (completing as little academic service as possible), barter (exchanging academic service work for reward), and investment (completing academic service hoping for future reward). They conclude that compliance is especially common among women, whilst evasiveness and barter are more common among men. As a consequence, men are better positioned to pursue their individual interests. Of course, attempts to achieve proportional committee representation can also be problematic and often place unrealistic demands on women in academia (Haynes & Fearfull, 2008).

Indeed, research consistently demonstrates that women are more likely to engage in academic service work and lower-status activities (Järvinen & Mik-Meyer, 2025; Mitchell & Hesli, 2013; O'Meara et al., 2017). For example, women report that they serve as "surrogate mothers", particularly for first-year students or those experiencing difficulties (Haynes & Fearfull, 2008). Women also find it more difficult to relinquish these responsibilities and secure time to devote to research and funding applications (Kjeldal, Rindfleish & Sheridan, 2005). In contrast, male academics spend more time on research, a high-status activity that is prominent in progression and promotion criteria (Misra, Lundquist, & Templer, 2012) and in professional conversations with colleagues, providing important opportunities for networking and collaboration (O'Meara et al., 2017). Whilst people may advise female academics in this position to focus on tasks with high promotability and personal gain (e.g., applications for grant funding), it is important to emphasise that the low promotability tasks *are* of value to the organisation. Rather than encouraging individual women to change their approach, we should ensure that all activities that support the institution are valued and rewarded.

Academic Conferences

Academic conferences provide important opportunities for researchers to share their work, raise their profile, and develop collaborative networks. Conferences may also signal cultural norms and expectations within academia, providing important opportunities for career advancement. Attendance at such events often requires substantial investment, both in terms of financial cost and time diverted from other activities. Indeed, many academics personally fund conference attendance, recognising the value of attendance for their academic profile. Reflecting this personal investment, access to such conferences remains unequal (Sabharwal, Henderson, & Joseph, 2020). For example, those with parenting or other caring responsibilities may be unable to attend in-person events, though a number of measures can be taken to facilitate their participation (Saccarelli et al., 2021).

For those able to attend, research indicates a gendered conference experience. For example, Blumen and Bar-Gal (2006) review the status of women at over 30 conference meetings of the Israeli Geographical Society. They report that though men continue to present most of the conference papers, the proportion of presentations delivered by female academics has increased. However, reviewing their overall contribution to the conference, women continue to be involved in less prestigious aspects of the meeting, with relatively little engagement as session chairs or keynote speakers compared to male attendees. Findings are consistent with more recent research indicating that whilst less prestigious roles (e.g., session chair) or awards (e.g., Young Investigator awards) are more gender balanced, men are more likely to be invited as keynote or plenary speakers in STEM subjects and receive prestigious Senior Investigator awards (Shishkova et al., 2017).

Speaker representation is important. For example, engagement in question-and-answer sessions (i.e., posing questions to academics presenting their work) is one way in which faculty may signal their knowledge of an area or the importance of their voice within the discipline. Traditionally, women are less comfortable participating in conference question and answer sessions than men and anticipate a backlash in response to their contribution (Jarvis et al., 2022). In conferences with greater female representation, female academics speak (when asking questions or providing comments) for longer (Kriwy, Gross, & Gottburgsen, 2013).

In addition, conferences with greater female representation are less likely to be perceived as sexist or to lead women to feel that they should behave in a masculine manner (Biggs, Hawley, & Biernat, 2018). Of course, a range of sexist behaviours may exist, including exclusion from discussions or events, a lack of acknowledgement or patronising comments, and inappropriate jokes. Sexism within academic conferences appears to have a significantly greater impact on female attendees than on their male colleagues. For example, women who perceive conferences as sexist are more likely to report intentions to leave academia. However, men perceiving a conference to be sexist are more likely to report intentions to leave the particular conference (Biggs, Hawley, & Biernat, 2018).

Family Planning and Parenting

The current academic environment and culture (see Chapters 1–3) make family planning and parenting difficult, especially for women. It is, however, important to recognise that the gendered experience of caregiving is not restricted to parenting. For example, women are often expected to care for older adults (Maximiano-Barreto et al., 2022; Zygouri et al., 2021), placing significant demands on those in this situation. Discussion of parenting responsibilities should, therefore, be regarded as one example of gender inequality, rather than the only important issue pertaining to caregiving responsibilities.

Family Planning

The decision to establish a family (impacting both personal health and time available for professional activities) may be especially problematic during early stages of the career, where precarious contracts are more likely and employment rights are less clear. Interviews with undergraduate students, PhD students, and postdoctoral researchers demonstrate the greater impact of issues, including the absence of paid parental leave, lack of clear maternity policies, and unwillingness to extend contracts, on female compared to male students and academics (Eren, 2022).

Manchester, Leslie, and Kramer (2010) also discuss the overlap between "biological clocks" and "tenure clocks", recognising that the years where academics are expected to establish their careers are also the years where academics establish a family. As a consequence, women may leave academia in favour of a more stable and secure career in another sector. Recognising this issue, some institutions adopt "stop the clock" policies whereby pre-tenure academics delay their promotion review. Manchester, Leslie, and Kramer (2010) examine the use of these "stop the clock" initiatives at one research institution. They conclude that whilst use of "stop the clock" policies did not reduce the likelihood of promotion to tenure, it did constrain pay, especially for those engaging in the scheme for family rather than non-family reasons, highlighting further inequality.

Family planning issues are not, of course, restricted to those at earlier stages of their careers. Grummell, Devine, and Lynch (2009) highlight the extent to which academia impacts the reproductive decisions made by senior management (e.g., appointments at the vice chancellor or provost level). For example, one female senior manager stated, "*I made a conscious decision that I couldn't get tenure and be pregnant and have a second child, it was just not going to happen*" (p. 199). Reflecting these pressures, tenured female faculty (26%) are more likely than their male colleagues (11%) to be single and childless, and female tenured faculty are far less likely to be married with children (44%) than their male colleagues (70%) (Mason & Goulden, 2004).

Maternity and Paternity Leave

Staff may take maternity or paternity leave following the birth of a child, though the length of this leave and proportion of time that is paid rather than unpaid vary by both country and institution. Exploring female academics' experiences of maternity leave, Maxwell, Connolly, and Laoire (2019) demonstrate that the quality of the support received also varies and may be dependent on the support of individual line managers.

In particular, workload reallocation is often problematic. For example, teaching and marking (initially scheduled for the leave period) may be brought forward, with women expected to ensure that work is completed before maternity leave is taken. As stated by one academic, "*my teaching from term 2 was moved to term 1 so I could do all my teaching duties before going on leave. This did not help my health or my pregnancy*" (Maxwell, Connolly, & Laoire, 2019, p. 147). In addition, women may be expected to engage in research and administration (e.g., preparation of teaching to be delivered on their return) during maternity leave. Workload issues are further exacerbated by a tendency to not recruit staff to cover the maternity leave period, with those on leave feeling conscious of the additional workload absorbed by their colleagues.

This issue can be especially complex for women in grant-funded research positions, where there is often a lack of clarity regarding the implications of maternity leave, with both institutions and funders uncertain how to address this. As a consequence, academics requiring maternity or paternity leave can experience substantial stress. It is important that further guidance and support are provided to those considering maternity or paternity leave, or supporting staff to do so. This should include support for staff requiring leave to prepare for and engage in fostering and adoption, and recognise the additional demands placed on parents undergoing fertility treatment, extended recovery from post-partum health issues, and supporting infants requiring extended neonatal care.

Childcare

Policies intended to support academic mothers often focus on flexibility rather than addressing more fundamental issues with the academic role and workload. As a consequence, mothers are typically expected to work long hours and continue to publish and secure research funding whilst also serving as the primary carer. Highlighting the pressures experienced by academic mothers, one female academic stated

> I can work 36 hours straight. There have been times when I've been here at the office during the day, gone home and put the children to bed, and then returned to the office. I've worked all night and then gone home and made breakfast for the children.
>
> (Thun, 2020, p. 172)

This is consistent with other research (e.g., Acker & Armenti, 2004) reporting that women often cope with their dual responsibilities by working harder and sleeping less.

Though both men and women with children experience significant conflict between the academic role and family life (Gaio Santos & Cabral-Cardoso, 2008), gendered expectations of childcare are important. Academic fathers are more likely to be praised for their parenting activities, such as collecting a child from daycare (Thun, 2020), and academic mothers are especially likely to experience guilt and shame, believing that they are unable to dedicate sufficient time to both their role as a parent and as an academic (Sutherland, 2010). Universities could support mothers by providing emergency childcare when required and ensuring that parents are not penalised when promotion and progression are considered (Mason & Goulden, 2004). Such issues are exacerbated by an academic environment that excludes and isolates women with children. For example, seminars may be held at the end of the day when childcare responsibilities prevent attendance (Savigny, 2014) and childcare responsibilities may hinder relocation to further the career (McKenzie, 2022).

The Athena SWAN Charter

Athena SWAN originally emerged from the Scientific Women's Academic Network (SWAN) and the Athena Project. The Charter was initially introduced to increase the presence of women (both staff and students) in traditionally male-dominated disciplines and to support women's careers in Science, Technology, Engineering, Maths, and Medicine (STEMM) specifically. The Charter was expanded in 2015 to non-STEMM subjects. Supporters of Athena SWAN highlight increased awareness of gender inequality within Higher Education and improved opportunities for female staff and students. For example, Athena SWAN provides the space to discuss gender inequality and areas of practice which contribute to gender inequality (Caffrey et al., 2016) and provides important examples of good practice (Tsouroufli, 2019).

Indeed, both men and women report that the Athena SWAN Charter has led to significant structural and cultural change (Ovseiko et al., 2017) and the Charter is associated with the gender diversity of managerial positions (Xiao et al., 2020). Further, female academics report that Athena SWAN has increased their visibility, leadership skills, and self-confidence (Munir et al., 2014). Concerns have, however, been expressed that the Athena SWAN programme may not make meaningful change, instead adopting a "tick box" approach to secure the award and eligibility for external funding (Caffrey et al., 2016). It can, of course, be difficult to attribute progress within a department or institution directly to the Athena SWAN Charter (Rosser et al., 2019). Further, the burden of completing Athena SWAN applications disproportionately falls on women and other marginalised groups (Tzanakou & Pearce, 2019), and it is important that those contributing to such activity are recognised and rewarded.

Gender Identity and Sexual Orientation

Relatively few studies have addressed the experience of lesbian, gay, bisexual, transgender, queer, and other sexually minoritised (LGBTQ+) staff and students compared to research addressing other protected characteristics such as gender or race and ethnicity. It is clear, however, that heterosexism is prevalent within academia, which denies, dismisses, and stigmatises non-heterosexual identities, relationships, and communities. As a consequence, LGBTQ+ academics frequently restrict conversations with peers to professional or scientific topics and are more likely to experience social isolation (Bilimoria & Stewart, 2009).

In one study involving heterosexual social work faculty, sexual prejudice (focused on sexual orientation) was endorsed by 14% of the sample as indicated by agreement with items such as "It's wrong for men to have sex with men" and "Lesbians are confused about their sexuality" (Chonody et al., 2014). This is especially concerning, as academics may be less likely to display or admit to explicit prejudice than other groups. For example, Patridge et al. (2014) explore the factors impacting the academic climate experienced by lesbian, gay, bisexual, and transgender STEM faculty. Where exclusionary behaviour was experienced, this was more commonly perpetrated by administrators or students than academics and typically took the form of derogatory remarks (40%), being deliberately ignored (40%), feeling isolated or left out (30%), and intimidation (20%). Those experiencing or observing this exclusionary behaviour were less likely to feel comfortable in the classroom, department, or on campus and were more likely to consider leaving the institution. Reflective accounts (e.g., Gregory, 2004; Liddle, 2009) documenting academics' experiences of being out in the classroom provide an important insight into this experience.

Though some academics report experiencing overt hostility, the use of more subtle discriminatory behaviour may allow employees (and the organisation) to deny that discrimination occurs and make it more difficult for the employee experiencing discrimination to report this. Recognising that much workplace discrimination may be covert rather than overt in nature, Zurbrügg and Miner (2016) consider the faculty experiences of workplace incivility. Workplace incivility refers to rude and discourteous behaviour such as repeated interruption, addressing a person inappropriately, and exclusion (Andersson & Pearson, 1999). Sexual minority women reported the greatest levels of workplace incivility, followed by heterosexual women and heterosexual and sexual minority men (Zurbrügg & Miner, 2016).

Findings demonstrate the importance of considering sexual orientation in relation to other identities, such as gender, rather than in isolation. Indeed, many organisations and programmes intended to support LGBTQ+ populations fail to address issues such as ethnicity or socioeconomic status (Misawa, 2007). It is also important to recognise that LGBTQ+ staff may encounter other difficulties. For example, gay men have reported being treated inappropriately by heterosexual women, with an assumption that they will become the "gay best friend" (Orlov & Allen, 2014). There may also be a pressure to support LGBTQ+ students or junior colleagues (Bilimoria & Stewart, 2009), placing additional pressure on these faculty.

It is important to recognise that there may be important variation in attitudes towards LGBTQ+ students and academics across disciplines and institutions (Brown et al., 2004). For example, staff at religious institutions may be especially reluctant to share their sexual orientation or gender identity, fearing reprisals and dismissal. Kirkley and Getz (2007) propose a model for sexual orientation education that, they argue, both respects the mission of the religiously affiliated university and promotes respect for the lesbian, gay, bisexual, and transgender community. They argue that the Rainbow Educator Program contributed to an increased awareness of and respect for the university's lesbian, gay, bisexual, and transgender community. For example, disclosure rates increased, and the undergraduate lesbian, gay, bisexual, and transgender organisation now openly advertises meetings and has representation on the student senate.

Recommendations

Institutions should,

- Recognise the barriers that exist for female staff, including bias in peer review of research publications and funding and in student evaluations of teaching staff. This should be acknowledged and addressed when appraising staff and reviewing applications for promotion and progression. Additional networking and leadership opportunities should be developed for female staff.
- Avoid single-gender evaluation committees, but ensure that this does not have a negative impact (e.g., unrealistic workloads) on gender minority staff. Ensure all academic work, including academic service and committee membership, is valued and rewarded. Provide clear expectations regarding collegiate tasks such as exam invigilation and open day attendance, and address persistent evasiveness when it occurs. Avoid "call outs" that rely on staff to volunteer for time-consuming but low-status tasks (e.g., additional marking).
- Monitor gender representation when organising academic conferences, especially for high-status roles such as plenary or keynote speakers. Provide clear codes of conduct in relation to inappropriate behaviour at both formal (e.g., workshops) and informal (e.g., networking) conference events and childcare facilities for both formal and informal events to ensure equity of conference experience.
- Provide appropriate maternity and paternity leave and support. This should include support for fertility treatment, neonatal care, and postnatal health issues where required. Ensure that the workload scheduled for the maternity period is not brought forward. Consider caring responsibilities when scheduling activities, and ensure that emergency leave is available.
- Address bias and discrimination relating to gender, gender identity, and sexual orientation in mandatory training delivered to all staff. Include clear guidance on being a supportive and proactive ally. Publicise the processes through which staff can report experiences of bias and discrimination (both named and anonymous).

Subject in Focus 1: Student Evaluations

Research indicates that many students hold gendered perceptions of academics, often to the detriment of female academics. For example, students are more likely to misattribute upwards (i.e., overestimate) the level of education achieved by male instructors but misattribute downwards (i.e., underestimate) for female instructors (Miller & Chamberlin, 2000). Of perhaps greater consequence, research indicates a significant bias in student evaluations such as the end of semester evaluations used to assess the quality of teaching delivered. For example, Campeggiani, Viola, and Marini (2025) report that male students (but not their female peers) rate written transcripts of lecture content as clearer, of greater learning benefit, and of more interest when apparently authored by male instructors. In a second study, using audio recordings of men and women reading the lecture transcripts, gender bias was more consistent for male and female students.

Student evaluations may have a significant impact on academic progression (Aragón, Pietri, & Powell, 2023), with positive course evaluations often included as specific promotion criteria. Indeed, this may be the only explicit measure of teaching quality considered in progression and promotion decisions, with direct observation of teaching by promotion panel members unlikely. It is, therefore, essential that institutions acknowledge this bias and attempt to minimise the impact of gender bias on academic career progression.

A range of factors (including the subject and gender composition of the department) may impact on the extent of this bias. For example, Aragón, Pietri, and Powell (2023) conducted an archival study, reviewing the teaching evaluations for over 50 courses at one North American University. For higher level courses, men and women in the gender majority (e.g., women in nursing or education, men in engineering or science) are rated more positively. In lower level courses, men and women in the gender minority (e.g., women in engineering or science, men in nursing or education) were rated more positively (though not to a significant degree). The authors argued that as over 70% of the departments were male dominated (and hence female academics were the gender minority) and courses were more likely to be delivered at higher levels, women were disproportionately affected by this bias. Specifically, they calculate that 32% of men and 52% of women would be negatively impacted by gender bias in teaching evaluations.

Subject in Focus 2: Menstrual Health

Women are presented with a range of workplace challenges. Whilst some challenges (e.g., carer responsibilities) are frequently discussed, others (e.g., menstruation, menopause, and gynaecological conditions) are rarely acknowledged. Where the impact of menstruation and dysmenorrhea (period pain) are considered, research typically focuses on the student experience (e.g., Armour et al., 2019; Suleman, 2024), with relatively few studies considering this issue from a staff perspective. It is, of course, likely that issues affecting students such as absenteeism and impaired concentration (Munro et al., 2021), also impact on the staff experience.

In one exception, Sang et al. (2021) discuss the additional labour undertaken by academic staff during menstruation including management of menstruation itself (e.g., the physical pain associated with menstruation) and accessing appropriate facilities. The stigma associated with menstruation (often manifest in shame and fear that menstruation is detected) makes it difficult to raise the subject despite often inadequate facilities. Stigma also appears to impact on those researching menstruation, impacting on academic performance (e.g., funding received) and progression (e.g., securing a permanent contract) (Owen, 2022).

In recent years, initiatives such as the provision of free period products have become more common. These initiatives both address period poverty (i.e., the financial cost of such products) and serve to reduce stigma (Gruer et al., 2021; Rawat et al., 2023). Greater consideration of menstruation within the workplace is required. In a broader (i.e., not restricted to higher education) study of menstruation and productivity, Schoep et al. (2019) reports that of the 32,748 women surveyed 4,514 disclosed absenteeism during their period and 1,108 disclosed absence every or almost every cycle. Presenteeism and decreased productivity were also evident. Managers are unlikely to appreciate the prevalence of this issue, as when women are on sickness absence due to periods, only 20.1% of women disclose to the employer or school that the absence relates to menstrual health.

References

Acker, S., & Armenti, C. (2004). Sleepless in academia. *Gender and Education*, *16*(1), 3–24. https://doi.org/10.1080/0954025032000170309

Acker, S., Webber, M., & Smyth, E. (2016). Continuity or change? Gender, family, and academic work for junior faculty in Ontario universities. *NASPA Journal about Women in Higher Education*, *9*(1), 1–20. https://doi.org/10.1080/19407882.2015.1114954

Andersson, L. M., & Pearson, C. M. (1999). Tit for tat? The spiraling effect of incivility in the workplace. *Academy of Management Review*, *24*(3), 452–471. https://doi.org/10.2307/259136

Aragón, O. R., Pietri, E. S., & Powell, B. A. (2023). Gender bias in teaching evaluations: The causal role of department gender composition. *Proceedings of the National Academy of Sciences*, *120*(4), e2118466120. https://doi.org/10.1073/pnas.2118466120

Armour, M., Parry, K., Manohar, N., Holmes, K., Ferfolja, T., Curry, C., MacMillan, F., & Smith, C. A. (2019). The prevalence and academic impact of dysmenorrhea in 21,573 young women: A systematic review and meta-analysis. *Journal of Women's Health*, *28*(8), 1161–1171. https://doi.org/10.1089/jwh.2018.7615

Atir, S., & Ferguson, M. J. (2018). How gender determines the way we speak about professionals. *Proceedings of the National Academy of Sciences*, *115*(28), 7278–7283. https://doi.org/10.1073/pnas.1805284115

Babcock, J., Peyser, B., Vesterlund, L., & Weingart, L. (2022). *The no club: Putting a stop to women's dead-end work*. Simon & Schuster.

Babcock, L., Recalde, M. P., Vesterlund, L., & Weingart, L. (2017). Gender differences in accepting and receiving requests for tasks with low promotability. *The American Economic Review*, *107*(3), 714–747.

Biggs, J., Hawley, P. H., & Biernat, M. (2018). The academic conference as a chilly climate for women: Effects of gender representation on experiences of sexism, coping responses, and career intentions. *Sex Roles*, *78*, 394–408. https://doi.org/10.1007/s11199-017-0800-9

Bilimoria, D., & Stewart, A. J. (2009). "Don't ask, don't tell": The academic climate for lesbian, gay, bisexual, and transgender faculty in science and engineering. *NWSA Journal*, *21*(2), 85–103. https://doi.org/10.1353/ff.2009.a316151

Blumen, O., & Bar-Gal, Y. (2006). The academic conference and the status of women: The Annual Meetings of the Israeli Geographical Society. *The Professional Geographer*, *58*(3), 341–355. https://doi.org/10.1111/j.1467-9272.2006.00572.x

Bocher, M., Ulvrova, M., Arnould, M., Coltice, N., Mallard, C., Gérault, M., & Adenis, A. (2020). Drawing everyday sexism in academia: Observations and analysis of a community-based initiative. *Advances in Geosciences*, *53*, 15–31. https://doi.org/10.5194/adgeo-53-15-2020

Boivin, N., Täuber, S., Beisiegel, U., Keller, U., & Hering, J. G. (2024). Sexism in academia is bad for science and a waste of public funding. *Nature Reviews Materials*, *9*. 1–3. https://doi.org/10.1038/s41578-023-00624-3

Bol, T. (2023). Gender inequality in 'cum laude' distinctions for PhD students. *Scientific Reports*, *13*, 20267. https://doi.org/10.1038/s41598-023-46375-7

Bol, T., de Vaan, M., & van de Rijt, A. (2022). Gender-equal funding rates conceal unequal evaluations. *Research Policy*, *51*(1), 104399. https://doi.org/10.1016/j.respol.2021.104399

Bowman, J., & Ulm, S. (2009). Grants, gender and glass ceilings? An analysis of ARC-funded archaeology projects. *Australian Archaeology*, *68*(1), 31–36. https://doi.org/10.1080/03122417.2009.11681887

Brown, R. D., Clarke, B., Gortmaker, V., & Robinson-Keilig, R. (2004). Assessing the campus climate for gay, lesbian, bisexual, and transgender (GLBT) students using a multiple perspective approach. *Journal of College Student Development*, *45*(1), 8–26. https://doi.org/10.1353/csd.2004.0003

Caffrey, L., Wyatt, D., Fudge, N., Mattingley, H., Williamson, C., & McKevitt, C. (2016). Gender equity programmes in academic medicine: A realist evaluation approach to Athena SWAN processes. *British Medical Journal Open*, *6*(9), e012090. https://doi.org/10.1136/bmjopen-2016-012090

Campbell, L. G., Mehtani, S., Dozier, M. E., & Rinehart, J. (2013). Gender-heterogeneous working groups produce higher quality science. *PloS ONE*, *8*(10), e79147. https://doi.org/10.1371/journal.pone.0079147

Campeggiani, P., Viola, M., & Marini, M. (2025). The boy's club: Gender biases in students' evaluations of their philosophy professors. *Philosophical Psychology*. https://doi.org/10.1080/09515089.2025.2551237

Chonody, J. M., Woodford, M. R., Brennan, D. J., Newman, B., & Wang, D. (2014). Attitudes toward gay men and lesbian women among heterosexual social work faculty. *Journal of Social Work Education*, *50*(1), 136–152. https://doi.org/10.1080/10437797.2014.856239

Christian, K., Johnstone, C., Larkins, J., & Wright, W. (2021). Why have eight researcher women in STEMM left academic research, and where did they go? *International Journal for Academic Development*, *28*(1), 31–44. https://doi.org/10.1080/1360144X.2021.1972304

Ductor, L., Goyal, S., & Prummer, A. (2023). Gender and collaboration. *Review of Economics and Statistics*, *105*(6), 1366–1378. https://doi.org/10.1162/rest_a_01113

Eagly, A. H., & Miller, D. I. (2016). Scientific eminence: Where are the women? *Perspectives on Psychological Science*, *11*(6), 899–904. https://doi.org/10.1177/1745691616663918

Eren, E. (2022). Never the right time: Maternity planning alongside a science career in academia. *Journal of Gender Studies*, *31*(1), 136–147. https://doi.org/10.1080/09589236.2020.1858765

Gaio Santos, G., & Cabral-Cardoso, C. (2008). Work-family culture in academia: A gendered view of work-family conflict and coping strategies. *Gender in Management*, *23*(6), 442–457. https://doi.org/10.1108/17542410810897553

Gregory, M. R. (2004). Being out, speaking out: Vulnerability and classroom inquiry. *Journal of Gay & Lesbian Issues in Education*, *2*(2), 53–64. https://doi.org/10.1300/J367v02n02_04

Gruer, C., Goss, T., Schmitt, M. L., & Sommer, M. (2021). Menstrual equity initiatives at USA universities: A multiple case study of common obstacles and enabling factors. *Frontiers in Reproductive Health*, *3*, 787277. https://doi.org/10.3389/frph.2021.787277

Grummell, B., Devine, D., & Lynch, K. (2009). The care-less manager: Gender, care and new managerialism in Higher Education. *Gender and Education*, *21*(2), 191–208. https://doi.org/10.1080/09540250802392273

Haynes, K., & Fearfull, A. (2008). Exploring ourselves: Exploiting and resisting gendered identities of women academics in accounting and management. *Pacific Accounting Review*, *20*(2), 185–204. https://doi.org/10.1108/01140580810892508

Heilman, M. E., & Chen, J. J. (2005). Same behavior, different consequences: Reactions to men's and women's altruistic citizenship behavior. *Journal of Applied Psychology*, *90*(3), 431–441. https://doi.org/10.1037/0021-9010.90.3.431

Hengel, E. (2022). Publishing while female: Are women held to higher standards? Evidence from peer review. *The Economic Journal*, *132*(648), 2951–2991. https://doi.org/10.1093/ej/ueac032

Jagsi, R., Motomura, A. R., Griffith, K. A., Rangarajan, S., & Ubel, P. A. (2009). Sex differences in attainment of independent funding by career development awardees. *Annals of Internal Medicine*, *151*(11), 804–811. https://doi.org/10.7326/0003-4819-151-11-200912010-00009

Järvinen, M., & Mik-Meyer, N. (2025). Giving and receiving: Gendered service work in academia. *Current Sociology*, *73*(3), 302–320. https://doi.org/10.1177/00113921231224754

Jarvis, S. N., Ebersole, C. R., Nguyen, C. Q., Zhu, M., & Kray, L. J. (2022). Stepping up to the mic: Gender gaps in participation in live question-and-answer sessions at academic conferences. *Psychological Science*, *33*(11), 1882–1893. https://doi.org/10.1177/09567976221094036

Kirkley, E. A., & Getz, C. (2007). A model for sexual orientation education at a religiously affiliated institution. *Journal of Gay & Lesbian Issues in Education*, *4*(3), 113–119. https://doi.org/10.1300/J367v04n03_07

Kjeldal, S., Rindfleish, J., & Sheridan, A. (2005). Deal-making and rule-breaking: Behind the façade of equity in academia. *Gender and Education*, *17*(4), 431–447. https://doi.org/10.1080/09540250500145130

Kriwy, P., Gross, C., & Gottburgsen, A. (2013). Look who's talking: Compositional effects of gender and status on verbal contributions at sociology conferences. *Gender, Work and Organization*, *20*(5), 545–560. https://doi.org/10.1111/j.1468-0432.2012.00603.x

Leberman, S., Eames, B., & Barnett, S. (2016). Unless you are collaborating with a big name successful professor, you are unlikely to receive funding. *Gender and Education*, *28*(5), 644–661. https://doi.org/10.1080/09540253.2015.1093102

Lee, C. J., Sugimoto, C. R., Zhang, G., & Cronin, B. (2013). Bias in peer review. *Journal of the American Society for Information Science and Technology*, *64*(1), 2–17. https://doi.org/10.1002/asi.22784

Liddle, K. (2009). Despite our differences: Coming out in conservative classrooms. *Feminism & Psychology*, *19*(2), 190–193. https://doi.org/10.1177/0959353509102196

Manchester, C. F., Leslie, L. M., & Kramer, A. (2010). Stop the clock policies and career success in academia. *American Economic Review*, *100*(2), 219–223. https://doi.org/10.1257/aer.100.2.219

Mason, M. A., & Goulden, M. (2004). Do babies matter (Part II)? Closing the baby gap. *Academe*, *90*(6), 10–15.

Maximiano-Barreto, M. A., Alves, L. C. D. S., Monteiro, D. Q., Gratão, A. C. M., Pavarini, S. C. I., Luchesi, B. M., & Chagas, M. H. N. (2022). Cultural factors associated with burden in unpaid caregivers of older adults: A systematic review. *Health & Social Care in the Community*, *30*(6), e3629–e3642. https://doi.org/10.1111/hsc.14003

Maxwell, N., Connolly, L., & Laoire, C. N. (2019). Informality, emotion and gendered career paths: The hidden toll of maternity leave on female academics and researchers. *Gender, Work, & Organization*, *26*(2), 140–157. https://doi.org/10.1111/gwao.12306

McKenzie, L. (2022). Un/making academia: Gendered precarities and personal lives in universities. *Gender and Education*, *34*(3), 262–279. https://doi.org/10.1080/09540253.2021.1902482

Miller, J., & Chamberlin, M. (2000). Women are teachers, men are professors: A study of student perceptions. *Teaching Sociology*, *28*(4), 283–298. https://doi.org/10.2307/1318580

Misawa, M. (2007). Political aspects of the intersection of sexual orientation and race in Higher Education in the United States: A queer scholar of color's perspective. *Journal of Curriculum and Pedagogy*, *4*(2), 78–83. https://doi.org/10.1080/15505170.2007.10411649

Misra, J., Lundquist, J. H., & Templer, A. (2012). Gender, work time, and care responsibilities among faculty. *Sociological Forum*, *27*(2), 300–323. https://doi.org/10.1111/j.1573-7861.2012.01319.x

Mitchell, S. M., & Hesli, V. I. (2013). Women don't ask? Women don't say no? Bargaining and service in the political science profession. *Political Science & Politics*, *46*(2), 355–369. https://doi.org/10.1017/S1049096513000073

Moss-Racusin, C. A., Dovidio, J. F., Brescoll, V. L., Graham, M. J., & Handelsman, J. (2012). Science faculty's subtle gender biases favor male students. *Proceedings of the National Academy of Sciences*, *109*(41), 16474–16479. https://doi.org/10.1073/pnas.1211286109

Munir, F., Mason, C., McDermott, H., Morris, J., Bagilhole, B., & Nevill, M. (2014). *Advancing women's careers in STEMM: Evaluating the effectiveness and impact of the Athena SWAN charter*. Equality Challenge Unit. Retrieved from: https://oxfordresearchandpolicy.co.uk/wp-content/uploads/2017/02/Evaluating-the-effectiveness-and-impact-of-the-Athena-SWAN-Charter-Full_Report.pdf

Munro, A. K., Hunter, E. C., Hossain, S. Z., & Keep, M. (2021). A systematic review of the menstrual experiences of university students and the impacts on their education: A global perspective. *PloS One*, *16*(9), e0257333. https://doi.org/10.1371/journal.pone.0257333

O'Meara, K. A., Kuvaeva, A., Nyunt, G., Waugaman, C., & Jackson, R. (2017). Asked more often: Gender differences in faculty workload in research universities and the work interactions that shape them. *American Educational Research Journal*, *54*(6), 1154–1186. https://doi.org/10.3102/0002831217716767

Orlov, J. M., & Allen, K. R. (2014). Being who I am: Effective teaching, learning, student support, and societal change through LGBQ faculty freedom. *Journal of Homosexuality*, *61*(7), 1025–1052. https://doi.org/10.1080/00918369.2014.870850

Ovseiko, P. V., Chapple, A., Edmunds, L. D., & Ziebland, S. (2017). Advancing gender equality through the Athena SWAN Charter for Women in Science: An exploratory study of women's and men's perceptions. *Health Research Policy and Systems*, *15*, 12. https://doi.org/10.1186/s12961-017-0177-9

Owen, L. (2022). Researching the researchers: The impact of menstrual stigma on the study of menstruation. *Open Library of Humanities*, *8*(1). https://doi.org/10.16995/olh.6338

Patridge, E. V., Barthelemy, R., & Rankin, S. R. (2014). Factors impacting the academic climate for LGBQ STEM faculty. *Journal of Women and Minorities in Science and Engineering*, *20*(1), 75–98. https://doi.org/10.1615/JWomenMinorScienEng.2014007429

Pedersen, D. E., & Minnotte, K. L. (2017). Workplace climate and STEM faculty women's job burnout. *Journal of Feminist Family Therapy*, *29*(1–2), 45–65. https://doi.org/10.1080/08952833.2016.1230987

Rawat, M., Novorita, A., Frank, J., Burgett, S., Cromer, R., Ruple, A., & DeMaria, A. L. (2023). "Sometimes I just forget them": Capturing experiences of women about free menstrual products in a U.S. based public university campus. *BMC Women's Health*, *23*, 351. https://doi.org/10.1186/s12905-023-02457-2

Remich, R., Jones, R., Wood, C. V., Campbell, P. B., & McGee, R. (2016). How women in biomedical PhD programs manage gender consciousness as they persist toward academic research careers. *Academic Medicine*, *91*(8), 1119–1127. https://doi.org/10.1097/ACM.0000000000001253

Rosser, S. V., Barnard, S., Carnes, M., & Munir, F. (2019). Athena SWAN and ADVANCE: Effectiveness and lessons learned. *The Lancet*, *393*(10171), 604–608. https://doi.org/10.1016/S0140-6736(18)33213-6

Rotenstein, L. S., Torre, M., Cleary, J. L., Sen, S., Guille, C., & Mata, D. A. (2022). Differences in gender representation in the altmetric top 100. *Journal of General Internal Medicine*, *37*, 590–592. https://doi.org/10.1007/s11606-021-06829-y

Russell, J., Brock, S., & Rudisill, M. E. (2019). Recognizing the impact of bias in faculty recruitment, retention, and advancement processes. *Kinesiology Review*, *8*(4), 291–295. https://doi.org/10.1123/kr.2019-0043

Sabharwal, N. S., Henderson, E. F., & Joseph, R. S. (2020). Hidden social exclusion in Indian academia: Gender, caste and conference participation. *Gender and Education, 32*(1), 27–42. https://doi.org/10.1080/09540253.2019.1685657

Saccarelli, C. R., Keenan, K. E., Shimron, E., Kasper, L., Keilholz, S. D., Wald, L. L., & Morris, E. A. (2021). The path to parent-inclusive conferences. *Journal of the American College of Radiology, 18*(2), 334–336. https://doi.org/10.1016/j.jacr.2020.06.027

Sang, K., Remnant, J., Calvard, T., & Myhill, K. (2021). Blood work: Managing menstruation, menopause and gynaecological health conditions in the workplace. *International Journal of Environmental Research and Public Health, 18*(4), 1951. https://doi.org/10.3390/ijerph18041951

Sarsons, H., Gërxhani, K., Reuben, E., & Schram, A. (2021). Gender differences in recognition for group work. *Journal of Political Economy, 129*(1), 101–147.

Savigny, H. (2014). Women, know your limits: Cultural sexism in academia. *Gender and Education, 26*(7), 794–809. https://doi.org/10.1080/09540253.2014.970977

Schoep, M. E., Adang, E. M. M., Maas, J. W., De Bie, B., Aarts, J. W. M., & Nieboer, T. E. (2019). Productivity loss due to menstruation-related symptoms: A nationwide cross-sectional survey among 32 748 women. *BMJ Open, 9*(6), e026186. https://doi.org/10.1136/bmjopen-2018-026186

Settles, I. H., Cortina, L. M., Buchanan, N. T., & Miner, K. N. (2013). Derogation, discrimination, and (dis)satisfaction with jobs in science: A gendered analysis. *Psychology of Women Quarterly, 37*(2), 179–191. https://doi.org/10.1177/0361684312468727

Settles, I. H., Cortina, L. M., Malley, J., & Stewart, A. J. (2006). The climate for women in academic science: The good, the bad, and the changeable. *Psychology of Women Quarterly, 30*(1), 47–58. https://doi.org/10.1111/j.1471-6402.2006.00261.x

Settles, I. H., Cortina, L. M., Stewart, A. J., & Malley, J. (2007). Voice matters: Buffering the impact of a negative climate for women in science. *Psychology of Women Quarterly, 31*(3), 270–281. https://doi.org/10.1111/j.1471-6402.2007.00370.x

Shishkova, E., Kwiecien, N. W., Hebert, A. S., Westphall, M. S., Prenni, J. E., & Coon, J. J. (2017). Gender diversity in a STEM subfield: Analysis of a large scientific society and its annual conferences. *Journal of the American Society for Mass Spectrometry, 28*(12), 2523–2531. https://doi.org/10.1007/s13361-017-1803-z

Spoon, K., LaBerge, N., Wapman, K. H., Zhang, S., Morgan, A. C., Galesic, M., … & Clauset, A. (2023). Gender and retention patterns among US faculty. *Science Advances, 9*(42), eadi2205. https://doi.org/10.1126/sciadv.adi2205

Suleman, A., Krishna, S., Krishnakumar, D., Nemoto, K., Nguyễn, M. L. T., & Mehta, S. D. (2024). A pilot survey of students' menstrual attitudes, experiences, and needs on an urban university campus. *Women's Health, 20*, 1–13. https://doi.org/10.1177/17455057241254713

Sutherland, J. A. (2010). Mothering, guilt and shame. *Sociology Compass, 4*(5), 310–321. https://doi.org/10.1111/j.1751-9020.2010.00283.x

Thun, C. (2020). Excellent and gender equal? Academic motherhood and 'gender blindness' in Norwegian academia. *Gender, Work & Organization, 27*(2), 166–180. https://doi.org/10.1111/gwao.12368

Treviño, L. J., Gomez-Mejia, L. R., Balkin, D. B., & Mixon, F. G. (2015). Meritocracies or masculinities? The differential allocation of named professorships by gender in the academy. *Journal of Management, 44*(3), 972–1000. https://doi.org/10.1177/0149206315599216

Tsouroufli, M. (2019). An examination of the Athena SWAN initiatives in the UK: Critical reflections. In G. Crimmins (Ed.), *Strategies for resisting sexism in the academy: Higher education, gender and intersectionality* (pp. 35–54). Springer.

Tzanakou, C., & Pearce, R. (2019). Moderate feminism within or against the neoliberal university? The example of Athena SWAN. *Gender, Work, & Organization*, *26*(8), 1191–1211. https://doi.org/10.1111/gwao.12336

Wennerås, C., & Wold, A. (1997). Nepotism and sexism in peer-review. *Nature*, *387*, 341–343.

Wheatley, R. M., & Ogunlana, L. (2023). Gender shapes the formation of review paper collaborations in microbiology. *Proceedings of the Royal Society B*, *290*, 20230965. https://doi.org/10.1098/rspb.2023.0965

Witteman, H. O., Hendricks, M., Straus, S., & Tannenbaum, C. (2019). Are gender gaps due to evaluations of the applicant or the science? A natural experiment at a national funding agency. *The Lancet*, *393*(10171), 531–540.

Xiao, Y., Pinkney, E., Au, T. K. F., & Yip, P. S. F. (2020). Athena SWAN and gender diversity: A UK-based retrospective cohort study. *British Medical Journal Open*, *10*(2), e032915. https://doi.org/10.1136/bmjopen-2019-032915

Zurbrügg, L., & Miner, K. N. (2016). Gender, sexual orientation, and workplace incivility: Who is most targeted and who is most harmed? *Frontiers in Psychology*, *7*, 565. https://doi.org/10.3389/fpsyg.2016.00565

Zygouri, I., Cowdell, F., Ploumis, A., Gouva, M., & Mantzoukas, S. (2021). Gendered experiences of providing informal care for older people: A systematic review and thematic synthesis. *BMC Health Services Research*, *21*, 730. https://doi.org/10.1186/s12913-021-06736-2

Chapter 6

Race, Ethnicity, and Culture

There is clear inequality in higher education with respect to race, ethnicity, and culture. In one survey of racially minoritised higher education staff, the University and College Union reported that 54% of respondents had often experienced barriers to progression and 36% had experienced these barriers sometimes. Only 44% of racially minoritised higher education staff reported that they had been fully informed of the process of applying for promotion, and only 29% had been supported in seeking progression and promotion by senior colleagues (UCU, 2016). Further bullying and harassment appear to be the norm rather than the exception for racially minoritised employees, with 72% of higher education staff surveyed reporting that this occurred often or sometimes from managers and 69% reporting that this occurred often or sometimes from colleagues (UCU, 2016).

The current chapter highlights the underrepresentation of racially minoritised staff in academia and significant barriers to progression and inclusion. Particular emphasis is placed on allocated responsibilities and workload, and the English language bias. The lived experience of racially minoritised staff is discussed with reference to isolation and hostility. Racism from both students and staff is considered. To highlight the extent to which racism is embedded in academia, a more detailed account of historical and contemporary issues within the medical and health professions is provided.

Racial, Ethnic, and Cultural Inequality

Significant underrepresentation exists in academia with regard to race, ethnicity, and culture that is especially evident in higher-status and leadership positions (Zhang et al., 2021). Where minoritised faculty are employed, they are less likely to be tenured and have (on average) a lower rank and status than their White colleagues (Allen et al., 2000). Racially minoritised academics are less likely to be promoted than their White peers, even when controlling for factors such as gender and tenure status (Fang et al., 2000). A range of departmental, institutional, and national factors impact the presence and experience

DOI: 10.4324/9781032639321-7

of minoritised faculty, such as undervaluation of research, biased recruitment, and isolation (Turner, González, & Wood, 2008).

Academics may find that their research is marginalised and dismissed, especially if their research is focused on equality, diversity, and inclusion issues. For example, relatively few psychology articles address race and ethnicity (Roberts et al., 2020). Indeed, academics are often required to spend additional time justifying the value or relevance of this work. Bias and exclusionary peer review contribute to such inequality (Strauss et al., 2023). In one recent study, Gatwiri, Krupka, and Abid (2025) interviewed racially and culturally minoritised early-career to senior-level academics from a range of subject disciplines and provided examples of such bias. Academics (all recruited from Australian universities) reported that challenges to the erasure of race or Western conceptualisations of race were met with defensiveness and hostility. As explained by one participant

> Reviewer 2 focused on the fact that I didn't follow the template...but the argument that I made at the beginning of that paper was like, look, this template, the status quo doesn't serve Black people particularly well. Here is an alternative.
>
> (Gatwiri, Krupka, & Abid, 2025, p. 5)

In this manner, peer review acts as a gatekeeper, serving to silence other academics and perspectives that do not conform.

The systemic and structural barriers experienced by underrepresented groups may impact both productivity (as defined by publication and funding success) and recognition of their work. Research indicates that Black and Hispanic authors receive fewer citations than their White peers (Liu et al., 2023), and minoritised applicants are less likely to receive research funding than their White peers, even after controlling for educational background, publication records, previous funding, and characteristics of the employer (Ginther, 2011). As research citations and funding are central to academic success and progression (see Chapter 1 for a discussion of the competition and monitoring that exists within higher education research culture), these academics are significantly disadvantaged.

Attempts have been made to address the inequality that exists within higher education, with particular attention to the recruitment of minoritised staff. Smith et al. (2004) report that recruitment of underrepresented academics is most likely when job descriptions include links to the study of race or ethnicity (e.g., decolonising the curriculum) or intervention strategies are used to supplement or replace traditional search processes. Further, Fraser and Hunt (2011) document the successful use of online tutorials (completed by all search committee members) focused on recruiting diverse faculty. In contrast, Gasman, Kim, and Nguyen (2011) highlight the issues that can arise when a decentralised approach to recruitment takes place, which leads to inconsistencies in the value afforded to diverse recruitment. Reflecting the advancement of research and practice in this area, a range of guides are now available to support diverse recruitment (e.g., Turner, 2002a). Of course, whilst it is important to improve the recruitment of minoritised staff, doing so without also addressing the staff experience is not sufficient and may provide a misleading impression of equality within specific institutions and the sector more broadly.

Roles, Responsibilities, and Workload

The additional responsibilities and higher workloads carried by minoritised staff represent significant barriers to progression and promotion (Allen et al., 2000). In particular, minoritised staff may be expected to take on equality, diversity, and inclusion-related roles and responsibilities, such as serving on committees and mentoring minoritised staff or students, which further reduces the time available for more prestigious activities such as research (Thompson, 2008; Turner, 2002b). Such roles require substantial time and emotional labour (Thunig & Jones, 2021). Indeed, requiring minoritised academics to engage in additional equality, diversity, and inclusion work as a representative of minoritised faculty or to promote the visibility of diversity initiatives at the institution can become exhausting (Orelus, 2013).

Despite this, academic workloads often fail to compensate for equality, diversity, and inclusion work. Further, equality, diversity, and inclusion roles may not receive the recognition or reward associated with other academic work (e.g., programme leadership). Though this issue undermines equality, diversity, and inclusion practice generally, it is likely to disproportionately affect those from minoritised and marginalised groups who most commonly undertake such work. The engagement of proactive allies (with positive attitudes towards diversity and inclusion) is essential, therefore, to ensure that the additional demands associated with equality, diversity, and inclusion work do not further disadvantage those already marginalised within academia.

The English Language Bias

English is often perceived to be the "universal language of science" (Fung, 2008), and high-status journals and conferences are typically conducted in the English language. Researchers for whom English is an additional language are, therefore, at a disadvantage. For example, Amano et al. (2023) surveyed 908 researchers, for whom English is not their first language, to assess the additional effort required to work in this "universal" language and the consequences of such language barriers. They highlight the time required to read and write papers and prepare presentations in English. These issues are especially evident at earlier stages of career development. Further, language barriers led researchers to choose not to attend academic conferences or to attend but not present their work.

The extent of this English language bias is clear. Journal submissions from Asia, South America, and Africa spend more time between submission and acceptance than those from other regions (Liu et al., 2023). Authors for whom English is not their first language are less likely to have their research accepted for publication (Smith et al., 2023), and researchers from non-Western regions are underrepresented in editorial boards (Liu et al., 2023). Those reviewing the suitability of research for publication in an academic journal may comment on the "style" in which the article is written. Indeed, frequent references to "style" within peer review for journal publication may lead some authors to pay native English speakers or offer co-authorship for correction of grammar, spelling, and style (Herrera, 1999). The impact of style may, however, extend further. In one experimental study, Politzer-Ahles et al. (2020) demonstrate that abstracts written in "non-native-like" English are more likely to be rated as having poor scientific quality than abstracts written in "native-like" English.

The language bias may be problematic (beyond the impact on individual researchers) for a number of reasons. For example, restriction to research published in the English language may effectively exclude the voices and perspectives of marginalised groups and fail to recognise the important contextual factors which influence the subject area examined (Amano et al., 2021; Wu et al., 2013). It has also been suggested that articles published in the English language appear more likely to report positive findings (Egger et al., 1997).

Language bias is further exacerbated by the common practice of conducting reviews of the literature restricted to English-language publications (Stern & Kleijnen, 2020). Some researchers have argued that the findings of meta-analyses restricted to the English language do not differ from meta-analyses that include research published in a language other than English (Morrison et al., 2012) and consider analyses based on English language research only to be sufficiently reliable (Grzybowski & Kanclerz, 2019). In contrast, other researchers suggest that the conclusions reached may differ if research published in a language other than English is included (Grégoire et al., 1995; Konno et al., 2020). Greater recognition of this issue is required.

Isolation and Exclusion

It is not uncommon for racially minoritised staff to be the only academics who are not White (or one of a few who are not White) in a department (Laden & Hagedorn, 2000). Racially minoritised faculty employed at predominantly White institutions may experience social and professional isolation and a sense of "otherness" (Arday, 2022; Tillman, 2001). For example, Tuitt et al. (2009) report, "*Feeling different, doubted, and emotionally taxed is an everyday challenge of simply existing in the world of academia as a person of color*" (p. 70).

In one study of racism in elite universities in the United States and the United Kingdom, all academics interviewed discussed the racism they had experienced, which often occurred on a daily basis (Bhopal, 2022). Racist acts included questioning the legitimacy of an appointment and dismissing the presence of minoritised faculty as "token" appointments made only to increase the diversity of the department or institution. This occurred in an environment that outwardly endorsed diversity and inclusion, making it difficult for racism to be acknowledged or taken seriously. In addition to bullying, harassment, and microaggressions, minoritised faculty may also be negatively impacted by a lack of effort (displayed by White faculty) to socialise, intellectualise, or collaborate with minoritised colleagues (West-Olatunji, 2005). Establishing safe spaces through connections with other minoritised staff who provide both emotional and academic support (including the opportunity to disclose and discuss experiences of marginalisation and isolation) can be especially important (Arday, 2022; Bhopal, 2022).

Barriers to inclusion and progression extend beyond individual institutions. Academics are expected to engage and have an impact on the sector and discipline externally. This may require serving on the committee of a professional body, securing external funding, and, of course, publishing in peer-reviewed journals. Many indicators of external esteem, for example, invitations to present at conferences and national awards, are affected by networking and academic support. Butner, Burley, and Marbley (2000) highlight the importance of collaboration, collegiality, and community for Black faculty based at predominantly White institutions, which provide important opportunities to progress professionally. Technology may be especially important in allowing minoritised staff to establish and maintain supportive networks that exist beyond departmental, disciplinary, or institutional boundaries (West-Olatunji, 2005).

It is also essential that policy and practice recognise both the variation that exists across ethnic and cultural groups (Fang et al., 2000) and the importance of intersectionality (Osho & Alormele, 2025). For example, racially minoritised women may be at risk of harassment and discrimination both because of their gender and ethnicity. In one study, Clancy et al. (2017) report that 40% and 28% of racially minoritised women in the fields of astronomy and planetary sciences feel unsafe because of their gender or ethnicity, respectively. Highlighting the impact of this on professional development, 18% of minoritised women (compared to 12% of White women) reported that they had not attended professional events because they had not felt safe attending. Specific biases are also apparent. For example, whilst Black women are more likely to report a greater need to prove themselves, Asian women are more likely to report pressure to act in a feminine way, and Latina women are more likely to be labelled as angry or emotional in response to assertive behaviour (Williams & Phillips, 2016). To explore and address the importance of intersectionality, data must be disaggregated (Leggon, 2010).

Hostility and Microaggressions

Racially minoritised staff are more likely to experience aggression and violence in a range of contexts, including the academic workplace. In Section 3, aggression and violence in higher education are examined more broadly, with a particular focus on bullying and harassment (Chapter 7) and sexual harassment and violence (Chapter 8). The term "microaggression" refers to the subtle and often commonplace hostile actions or behaviour directed at members of marginalised groups. For example, a person's presence at an event may be questioned with the implicit suggestion that they do not belong and are unwelcome.

Microaggressions may be verbal or non-verbal, intentional or unintentional, and though microaggressions are, by definition, hostile and aggressive, their "micro" nature often means that they are unchallenged or dismissed. For example, a person may claim that their behaviour was "just banter", with those distressed by it dismissed as "too sensitive" or "woke".

Sue et al. (2007) identify three categories of microaggression. These are microassaults (explicit and intentional actions that typically occur in a restricted or private environment that affords the perpetrator some degree of protection or anonymity), microinsults (typically a more subtle form of rejection or insult that can be dismissed as insensitivity and difficult to prove), and microinvalidations (verbal or non-verbal actions that invalidate the experience or feelings of a person). Microaggressions are a common experience for Black faculty based at predominantly White campuses, especially microinvalidations from colleagues and microinsults from students (Pittman, 2012).

Microaggressions can be distressing; they can also increase isolation and marginalisation (Constantine et al., 2008). Isolation is especially important given that academics are often dependent on personal and professional networks for collaborative research activity, access to resources, references, and information about academic jobs, roles, or funding opportunities. To cope with the microaggressions experienced, racially minoritised academics may create or join supportive counterspaces (e.g., university networks), respond assertively (e.g., confront those responsible for microaggressions), or engage in other forms of resistance (e.g., physical or psychological departure from the hostile environment) (Simatele, 2018). Of course, those responding to microaggression in an assertive manner may be subject to criticism (e.g., perceived as oversensitive) or stereotyping (e.g., perceived as an angry Black woman).

The microaggressions experienced by minoritised faculty may be overwhelming (West-Olatunji, 2005) and leave academics feeling that they are constantly fighting against a hostile environment. It can, however, be more difficult for those exposed to microaggressions to demonstrate the occurrence and impact of aggression than when experiencing more overt forms of racism, and microaggressions such as questioning a person's credentials or expertise are poorly accommodated by anti-discrimination law (Lukes & Bangs, 2014). As a consequence, such behaviour may be dismissed by formal sources of support (e.g., line managers, human resources), creating secondary trauma and isolation. It is essential that training highlights the prevalence and impact of microaggressions and encourages allies to ensure that microaggressions are challenged where they occur.

Student Evaluations and Behaviour

Faculty may experience racism and hostility from students (Martinez, Chang, & Welton, 2017). Black professors are more likely than their White colleagues to report that students question their competency or qualifications (76% vs. 7%) and receive inappropriate student challenges to their intellectual authority (34% vs. 7%) (Harlow, 2003). Such findings are consistent with previous research indicating that White students are more likely to challenge or disrespect racially minoritised faculty than when interacting with White professors (McGowan, 2000). As a consequence, Black academics may be anxious to appear "perfect" when preparing and delivering lectures (Harlow, 2003), conscious that they are both subject to greater scrutiny and represent their Black colleagues. As summarised by Tuitt et al. (2009), "*I have come to understand that I do not have the privilege of walking into a classroom and having students assume that I am a capable and credible teacher*" (p. 69).

Students may be more tolerant or receptive of White faculty. For example, Black professors are more likely than their White colleagues to be evaluated by their students as cold, mean, or intimidating (28% vs. 7%) or evaluated as too hard or demanding (52% vs. 28%) (Harlow, 2003). White female professors with a strict teaching style are also rated as warmer than Hispanic female professors with a strict teaching style (Anderson & Smith, 2005). Further, minority faculty appear to receive greater criticism when teaching sensitive material. For example, material on racism is rated as more controversial when taught by a Black professor compared to a White professor (Ludwig & Meacham, 1997). Of course, characteristics of the student cohort may also influence evaluations of teaching faculty. For example, male undergraduates rate a course on "Race, Gender, and Inequality" and the professor leading the course as more politically biased than female students (Anderson & Smith, 2005). Faculty are, of course, expected to prioritise the needs of their students, displaying empathy and concern. In some circumstances (e.g., where faculty have experienced microaggressions), this may involve faculty masking their emotions, requiring substantial emotional labour.

Such bias is especially important as module evaluations often contribute to recognition within the institution or promotion decisions. Further, a number of publicly accessible websites (e.g., Rate My Professor) may disseminate perceptions of academics more broadly, with important ramifications for those seeking employment elsewhere, establishing networks, etc. One faculty member explained, "*The end-of term student evaluations contribute to my racial battle fatigue as students use them as a tool to vent their racial hatred*". (Bair et al. (2010), p. 103).

This bias has been examined experimentally. In one study, Chávez and Mitchell (2020) explored student evaluations of online courses, with courses differing only in the gender and ethnicity of faculty featured in a welcome video provided at the onset of the course. Though course content, assessments, schedules, and communication did not vary, courses introduced by racially minoritised faculty or female faculty were rated lower than courses associated with White male faculty. Similarly, Bavishi, Madera, and Hebl (2010) presented students (not yet enrolled at university) with a CV of a (Black, White, or Asian) professor and asked them to rate perceived competence, legitimacy, and interpersonal skills. Black and Asian professors were rated less favourably on interpersonal skills than White professors. Further, Black professors were perceived to be less competent and legitimate than White and Asian professors. There was also a significant interaction between gender and ethnicity, such that Black women were rated lowest for competence, legitimacy, and interpersonal skills compared to other groups.

Discipline Example: Medical and Health Professions

Though it is important to highlight issues faced by minoritised staff and students across the higher education sector, it is also essential that each discipline consider the specific historical and contemporary contextual factors that may influence the experiences of minoritised students and staff. The current section highlights historical and contemporary issues associated with the medical and health professions.

Historical Abuse and the Tuskegee Syphilis Study

The Tuskegee Syphilis Study is one of the most well-known historical examples of abuse of marginalised communities by the biomedical profession. The study was initiated in 1932 by the United States Public Health Service in Alabama, aiming to document the natural course of untreated syphilis in Black men. Over 400 men contaminated by syphilis were recruited for the study and subjected to a range of invasive and painful tests. Despite the widespread availability of penicillin as a treatment for syphilis in the 1950s, men were not provided with treatment. Indeed, the researchers actively prevented men from accessing treatment. The study design and findings, including mortality rates, were published regularly in the scientific community (e.g., Rockwell et al., 1964), though the study was not terminated until 1972 following reports of the study in the national press (Jones, 1981). Further, in 2010, it was revealed that researchers had actively infected adults in Guatemala with syphilis and gonorrhoea (Tobin, 2022).

The study has shaped research practice, especially in the areas of ethical review, recruitment of marginalised populations, and informed consent (Corbie-Smith, 1999). Previous research has also explored perceptions of medical research and knowledge of the Tuskegee Syphilis Study (Freimuth et al., 2001). Findings remain inconsistent. Though some studies report that knowledge of the study predicts reluctance to engage in health promotion and research (Green et al., 1997), other studies conclude that knowledge and awareness of the study do not predict willingness to participate in biomedical research (Katz et al., 2008, 2009). Indeed, broader structural and sociocultural issues may have a greater impact on trust in the medical profession and willingness to engage with research (McCallum et al., 2006). Further research is, however, required to investigate the potential influence of such cases on willingness to become a member of the medical or health professions.

Contemporary Issues in Medical and Allied Health Professions

Though the number and percentage of racially minoritised medical faculty have increased, they remain lower than for the general population (Ogunwole et al., 2020). A lack of ethnic and cultural diversity within academia may result in inadequate attention (e.g., research and student training) paid to subjects or conditions that disproportionately impact minoritised groups, such as sickle cell disease (e.g., Pokhrel et al., 2023). Similarly, a lack of diversity may result in failure to challenge stereotypes and false beliefs across the discipline. Research demonstrates the incidence and range of false beliefs held by medical practitioners, students, and the general public with reference to ethnicity. For example, Hoffman et al. (2016) report that approximately half of White medical students and residents endorse false beliefs about biological differences (e.g., believing that Black people have thicker skin than White people). Further, those endorsing these false beliefs underestimate the pain experienced by Black patients and make less accurate treatment recommendations for those patients.

Racial, ethnic, and cultural diversity is underrepresented in teaching and learning resources such as dermatology textbooks (Adelekun, Onyekaba, & Lipoff, 2020) and ophthalmology textbooks (Cheng, Curley, & Barmettler, 2022). Of course, this issue varies across disciplines. For example, in one review of medical textbooks, Louie and Wilkes (2018) identified no images of people of colour or darker skin tones for six common cancers. Underrepresentation has a substantial impact on practice that extends beyond academia. In particular, health professionals who are not equipped to diagnose skin conditions in a range of skin types are poorly prepared to support the community. For example, in one study, Dodd et al. (2023) demonstrate that students are more likely to accurately diagnose a range of conditions (e.g., shingles, Lyme disease, meningococcal disease) in White compared to non-White skin and were more confident doing so.

To address these issues, medical student Malone Mukwende, together with senior lecturer Margot Turner and clinical lecturer Peter Tamony, created the "Mind the Gap" handbook, presenting clinical signs and symptoms in racially minoritised patients. The handbook (and additional resources) is freely available via the https://www.blackandbrownskin.co.uk website.

Recommendations

Institutions should,

- Recognise the role and importance of representation. Consider the prominence of racially minoritised staff in all materials (e.g., website images, press releases). Such representation is especially important at senior levels and in leadership positions.
- Promote opportunities for professional development. Formal training programmes, mentorship programmes, and opportunities to deputise leadership roles are each important. Development opportunities tailored for racially minoritised staff (e.g., recognising the barriers to inclusion and progression experienced by these staff) are important.
- Value the equality, diversity, and inclusion research and practice disproportionately undertaken by racially minoritised staff. For example, equality, diversity, and inclusion research should be afforded the same status as discipline-specific research.
- Recognise the barriers that exist for racially minoritised staff, including bias in peer review of research and student evaluations. This should be acknowledged and addressed when appraising staff and reviewing applications for promotion and progression. For example, some institutions include minimum teaching evaluation scores as part of their criteria.
- Provide support for staff for whom English is not their first language. In particular, additional opportunities for review of journal articles and funding applications should be provided to ensure that staff are not unduly disadvantaged when submitting to English-speaking publications or funding calls.
- Acknowledge and address the additional stressors experienced by racially minoritised staff. Where national discourse encourages racism and xenophobia, take measures to support staff. For example, allowing staff to work from home may reduce anxiety related to the use of public transport. Establish a staff support network as a forum to share social and practical support. Ensure that the network is consulted on important policy and practice developments.
- Provide mandatory training for staff and students to address both explicit and less explicit forms of racism (e.g., microaggressions). Ensure that this training includes the impact of such racism and clear guidance on being a supportive and proactive ally. Publicise the processes through which staff can report experiences of racism and discrimination (both named and anonymous).
- Recognise the importance of decolonising teaching, research, and the resources available to staff and students. Ensure that the racially minoritised staff who disproportionately undertake this work are compensated and rewarded for it. Address issues that arise in specific subject disciplines.

Subject in Focus 1: The Race Equality Charter

The Equality Challenge Unit (now Advance HE) introduced the Race Equality Charter to address the inequalities experienced by minoritised staff and students. The Charter recognises the extent to which racism and racial inequalities occur, highlights the importance of intersectionality, advocates for equal access to (and benefit from) opportunities, and encourages long-term improvement through institutional culture change. The Charter provides structure for the collection and analysis of relevant data (e.g., attainment or progression data) and reflection on the barriers experienced by minoritised staff and students. Institutions applying to the Charter also create an action plan to address these barriers.

Across the sector, there has been less engagement with the Race Equality Charter than the gender focused Charter, Athena SWAN (Bhopal & Henderson, 2019). Charters (and the information gathering and reflection required for application to the Charter) can encourage good practice and reveal previously unidentified issues, though there are concerns that this change is more superficial than substantive (Bhopal & Henderson, 2019). Indeed, the Race Equality Charter appears to have had little impact on the student attainment gap (Campion & Clark, 2022) or the proportion of staff from minoritised groups (Nwosu, 2024). Access to resources (e.g., allocation of staff time) and support from senior management each impact on institutional engagement with the Race Equality Charter (Bhopal & Pitkin, 2018) and perhaps reflects a broader commitment to this issue. Those working in the sector have, however, raised concerns that for some organisations, the Charter can be used to enhance the reputation of the institution and gain competitive advantage rather than create meaningful change (Bhopal & Pitkin, 2018).

Subject in Focus 2: The Prevent Strategy

The CONTEST strategy (introduced by the British Government) contains four central themes each designed to address extremism and radicalisation. These themes are Pursue i.e., responding to terrorism with prosecution and intelligence, Protect i.e., infrastructures including border control, Prepare i.e., risk assessment and vulnerability, and Prevent (Home Office, 2009). Prevent, aims to stop individuals supporting terrorism or engaging in terrorist activity. In 2015, implementation of the Prevent strategy became a legal duty for British universities with a legal obligation for academics to report concerns about students they believe to be at risk of radicalisation. It has, however, been argued that such monitoring of students' thoughts and behaviour casts educators as "thought police" or "agents of the state" (e.g., Miah, 2013), fundamentally changing the role of the academic and the nature of the student-academic relationship.

The Prevent strategy has attracted widespread criticism, with numerous academics recommending that Prevent be revised or withdrawn (e.g., McGlynn & McDaid, 2019; Panjwani et al., 2018). For example, the Prevent strategy problematizes an interest in social justice and a desire for radical political change though this could be considered beneficial to society (i.e., through active political engagement and citizenship). Further, it is argued that the strategy portrays British Muslims as a homogenous "suspect" community (Hickman et al., 2012), encouraging and legitimising the othering, stigmatisation, and control of Muslim students and staff. Indeed, the Communities and Local Government Select Committee described the Prevent strategy focus on Muslims as "unhelpful", "stigmatising" and "potentially alienating" (CLGC, 2010, p. 3).

An independent review of Prevent was published in February 2023 (Shawcross, 2023). Despite the positive nature of the review, it is important to emphasise that a number of human rights and community groups (e.g., Amnesty International, Liberty, and The Runnymede Trust) boycotted the review. Further, it has been argued that engagement with academic literature on radicalisation and counter-radicalisation during the review was limited and biased (see Macdonald, Whiting, & Jarvis, 2024 for a review). The review has been widely criticised (e.g., Allen, 2023; Macdonald et al., 2024), and over 200 civil society organisations, community leaders, and academics have called for the withdrawal of the review. Alternative reviews of the Prevent programme have also been published. For example, John Holmwood and Layla Aitlhadji have published both The People's Review of Prevent (2022) and a detailed response to the Shawcross review (2023).

References

Adelekun, A., Onyekaba, G., & Lipoff, J. B. (2020). Skin color in dermatology textbooks: An updated evaluation and analysis. *Journal of the American Academy of Dermatology*, *84*(1), 194–196. https://doi.org/10.1016/j.jaad.2020.04.084

Allen, C. (2023). The independent review of Prevent: Controversial, contentious and counter-productive. *Political Insight*, *14*(2), 33–35. https://doi.org/10.1177/20419058231181290

Allen, W. R., Epps, E. G., Guillory, E. A., Suh, S. A., & Bonous-Hammarth, M. (2000). The black academic: Faculty status among African Americans in U.S. higher education. *The Journal of Negro Education*, *69*(1/2), 112–127.

Amano, T., Berdejo-Espinolam, V., Christie, A. P., Willott, K., Akasaka, M., Báld, i. A., et al. (2021). Tapping into non-English-language science for the conservation of global biodiversity. *PLoS Biology*, *19*(10), e3001296. https://doi.org/10.1371/journal.pbio.3001296

Amano, T., Ramirez-Castañeda, V., Berdejo Espinola, V., Borokini, I., Chowdhury, S., Golivets, M., et al. (2023). The manifold costs of being a non-native English speaker in science. *PLoS Biology*, *21*(7), e3002184. https://doi.org/10.1371/journal.pbio.3002184

Anderson, K. J., & Smith, G. (2005). Students' preconceptions of professors: Benefits and barriers according to ethnicity and gender. *Hispanic Journal of Behavioral Sciences*, *27*(2), 184–201. https://doi.org/10.1177/0739986304273707

Arday, J. (2022). No one can see me cry: Understanding mental health issues for Black and minority ethnic staff in higher education. *Higher Education*, *83*(1), 79–102. https://doi.org/10.1007/s10734-020-00636-w

Bair, M. A., Bair, D. E., Mader, C. E., Hipp, S., & Hakim, I. (2010). Faculty emotions: A self-study of teacher educators. *Studying Teacher Education*, *6*(1), 95–111. https://doi.org/10.1080/17425961003669490

Bavishi, A., Madera, J. M., & Hebl, M. R. (2010). The effect of professor ethnicity and gender on student evaluations: Judged before met. *Journal of Diversity in Higher Education*, *3*(4), 245–256. https://doi.org/10.1037/a0020763

Bhopal, K. (2022). Academics of colour in elite universities in the UK and the USA: The 'unspoken system of exclusion'. *Studies in Higher Education*, *47*(11), 2127–2137. https://doi.org/10.1080/03075079.2021.2020746

Bhopal, K., & Henderson, H. (2019). *Advancing equality in higher education: An exploratory study of the Athena SWAN and race equality Charters.* British Academy/Leverhulme Research Report. Retrieved from: https://www.birmingham.ac.uk/Documents/college-social-sciences/education/reports/advancing-equality-and-higher-education.pdf

Bhopal, K., & Pitkin, C. (2018). *Investigating higher education institutions and their views on the race equality charter.* University and College Union. Retrieved from: https://www.ucu.org.uk/media/9526/Investigating-higher-education-institutions-and-their-views-on-the-Race-Equality-Charter/pdf/Race_Equality_Charter_Kalwant_Bhopal_Clare_Pitkin.pdf

Butner, B. K., Burley, H., & Marbley, A. F. (2000). Coping with the unexpected: Black faculty at predominately white institutions. *Journal of Black Studies*, *30*(3), 453–462. https://doi.org/10.1177/002193470003000309

Campion, K., & Clark, K. (2022). Revitalising race equality policy? Assessing the impact of the race equality charter mark for British universities. *Race Ethnicity and Education*, *25*(1), 18–37. https://doi.org/10.1080/13613324.2021.1924133

Chávez, K., & Mitchell, K. M. W. (2020). Exploring bias in student evaluations: Gender, race, and ethnicity. *Political Science & Politics*, *53*(2), 270–274. https://doi.org/10.1017/S1049096519001744

Cheng, T., Curley, M. & Barmettler, A. (2022). Skin color representation in ophthalmology textbooks. *Medical Science Educator*, 32, 1143–1147. https://doi.org/10.1007/s40670-022-01636-4

Clancy, K. B., Lee, K. M., Rodgers, E. M., & Richey, C. (2017). Double jeopardy in astronomy and planetary science: Women of color face greater risks of gendered and racial harassment. *Journal of Geophysical Research: Planets*, *122*(7), 1610–1623. https://doi.org/10.1002/2017JE005256

Communities and Local Government Committee (CLGC). (2010). *Preventing violent extremism.* HM Government. Retrieved from: http://www.publications.parliament.uk/pa/cm200910/cmselect/cmcomloc/65/65.pdf

Constantine, M. G., Smith, L., Redington, R. M., & Owens, D. (2008). Racial microaggressions against black counseling and counseling psychology faculty: A central challenge in the multicultural counseling movement. *Journal of Counseling and Development*, *86*(3), 348–355. https://doi.org/10.1002/j.1556-6678.2008.tb00519.x

Corbie-Smith, G. (1999). The continuing legacy of the Tuskegee Syphilis Study: Considerations for clinical investigation. *The American Journal of the Medical Sciences*, *317*(1), 5–8. https://doi.org/10.1016/S0002-9629(15)40464-1

Dodd, R. V., Rafi, D., Stackhouse, A. A., Brown, C. A., Westacott, R. J., Meeran, K., ... & Sam, A. H. (2023). The impact of patient skin colour on diagnostic ability and confidence of medical students. *Advances in Health Sciences Education*, 28, 1171–1189. https://doi.org/10.1007/s10459-022-10196-6

Egger, M., Zellweger-Zähner, T., Schneider, M., Junker, C., Lengeler, C., & Antes, G. (1997). Language bias in randomised controlled trials published in English and German. *The Lancet*, *350*(9074), 326–329.

Fang, D., Moy, E., Colburn, L., & Hurley, J. (2000). Racial and ethnic disparities in faculty promotion in academic medicine. *The Journal of the American Medical Association*, *284*(9), 1085–1092. https://doi.org/10.1001/jama.284.9.1085

Fraser, G. J., & Hunt, D. E. (2011). Faculty diversity and search committee training: Learning from a critical incident. *Journal of Diversity in Higher Education*, *4*(3), 185–198. https://doi.org/10.1037/a0022248

Freimuth, V. S., Quinn, S. C., Thomas, S. B., Cole, G., Zook, E., & Duncan, T. (2001). African Americans' views on research and the Tuskegee Syphilis Study. *Social Science & Medicine*, *52*(5), 797–808. https://doi.org/10.1016/S0277-9536(00)00178-7

Fung, I. C. (2008). Seek, and ye shall find: Accessing the global epidemiological literature in different languages. *Emerging Themes in Epidemiology*, *5*, 21. https://doi.org/10.1186/1742-7622-5-21

Gasman, M., Kim, J., & Nguyen, T. H. (2011). Effectively recruiting faculty of color at highly selective institutions: A school of education case study. *Journal of Diversity in Higher Education*, *4*(4), 212–222. https://doi.org/10.1037/a0025130

Gatwiri, K., Krupka, Z., & Abid, M. (2025). Maintaining standards or gatekeeping the academy? Reflections of peer review experiences by racially and culturally minoritized scholars in Australia. *Sociology Compass*, *19*(8), e70079. https://doi.org/10.1111/soc4.70079

Ginther, D. K., Schaffer, W. T., Schnell, J., Masimore, B., Liu, F., Haak, L. L., & Kington, R. (2011). Race, ethnicity, and NIH research awards. *Science*, *333*(6045), 1015–1019. https://doi.org/10.1126/science.1196783

Green, B. L., Maisiak, R., Wang, M. Q., Britt, M. F., & Ebeling, N. (1997). Participation in health education, health promotion, and health research by African Americans: Effects of the Tuskegee Syphilis Experiment. *Journal of Health Education*, *28*(4), 196–201. https://doi.org/10.1080/10556699.1997.10603270

Grégoire, G., Derderian, F., & Le Lorier, J. (1995). Selecting the language of the publications included in a meta-analysis: Is there a tower of babel bias? *Journal of Clinical Epidemiology*, *48*(1), 159–163. https://doi.org/10.1016/0895-4356(94)00098-B

Grzybowski, A., & Kanclerz, P. (2019). Language bias and methodological issues in determining reliable evidence for systematic reviews. *JAMA Ophthalmology*, *137*(1), 118–119. https://doi.org/10.1001/jamaophthalmol.2018.4945

Harlow, R. (2003). "Race doesn't matter but ..." The effect of race on professors' experiences and emotion management in the undergraduate college classroom. *Social Psychology Quarterly*, *66*(4), 348–363. https://doi.org/10.2307/1519834

Herrera, A. (1999). Language bias discredits the peer-review system. *Nature*, *397*, 467. https://doi.org/10.1038/17194

Hickman, M. J., Thomas, L., Nickels, H. C., & Silvestri, S. (2012). Social cohesion and the notion of 'suspect communities': A study of the experiences and impacts of being 'suspect' for Irish communities and Muslim communities in Britain. *Critical Studies on Terrorism*, *5*(1), 89–106. https://doi.org/10.1080/17539153.2012.659915

Hoffman, K. M., Trawalter, S., Axt, J. R., & Oliver, M. N. (2016). Racial bias in pain assessment and treatment recommendations, and false beliefs about biological differences between blacks and whites. *Proceedings of the National Academy of Sciences*, *113*(16), 4296–4301. https://doi.org/10.1073/pnas.1516047113

Holmwood, J., & Aitlhadj, L. (2022). *The people's review of prevent*. London: Prevent Watch. Retrieved from: https://peoplesreviewofprevent.org/wp-content/uploads/2022/02/mainreportlatest.pdf

Holmwood, J., & Aitlhadj, L. (2023). *A response to the Shawcross Report*. London: Prevent Watch. Retrieved from: https://peoplesreviewofprevent.org//wp-content/uploads/2023/06/response-to-shawcross-1.pdf

Home Office (2009). *Pursue prevent protect prepare: The United Kingdom's strategy for countering international terrorism*. HM Government. Retrieved from: https://assets.publishing.service.gov.uk/media/5a7ca3fae5274a38e5755d54/7547.pdf

Jones, J. (1981). *Bad blood: The Tuskegee Syphilis Experiment: A tragedy of race and medicine*. The Free Press.

Katz, R. V., Green, B. L., Kressin, N. R., James, S. A., Wang, M. Q., Claudio, C., & Russell, S. L. (2009). Exploring the "legacy" of the Tuskegee Syphilis Study: A follow-up study from the Tuskegee Legacy Project. *Journal of the National Medical Association*, *101*(2), 179–183. https://doi.org/10.1016/S0027-9684(15)30833-6

Katz, R. V., Green, B. L., Kressin, N. R., Kegeles, S. S., Wang, M. Q., James, S. A., … & McCallum, J. M. (2008). The legacy of the Tuskegee Syphilis Study: Assessing its impact on willingness to participate in biomedical studies. *Journal of Health Care for the Poor and Underserved*, *19*(4), 1168–1180. https://doi.org/10.1016/S0027-9684(15)30833-6

Konno, K., Akasaka, M., Koshida, C., Katayama, N., Osada, N., Spake, R., & Amano, T. (2020). Ignoring non-English-language studies may bias ecological meta-analyses. *Ecology and Evolution*, *10*(13), 6373–6384. https://doi.org/10.1002/ece3.6368

Laden, B. V., & Hagedorn, L. S. (2000). Job satisfaction among faculty of color in academe: Individual survivors or institutional transformers? *New Directions for Institutional Research*, *105*, 57–66.

Leggon, C. B. (2010). Diversifying science and engineering faculties: Intersections of race, ethnicity, and gender. *American Behavioral Scientist*, *53*(7), 1013–1028. https://doi.org/10.1177/0002764209356236

Liu, F., Rahwan, T., & AlShebli, B. (2023). Non-white scientists appear on fewer editorial boards, spend more time under review, and receive fewer citations. *Proceedings of the National Academy of Sciences*, *120*(13), e2215324120. https://doi.org/10.1073/pnas.2215324120

Louie, P., & Wilkes, R. (2018). Representations of race and skin tone in medical textbook imagery. *Social Science and Medicine*, *202*, 38–42. https://doi.org/10.1016/j.socscimed.2018.02.023

Ludwig, J. M., & Meacham, J. A. (1997). Teaching controversial courses: Student evaluations of instructors and content. *Educational Research Quarterly*, *21*(1), 27–38.

Lukes, R., & Bangs, J. (2014). A critical analysis of anti-discrimination law and microaggressions in academia. *Research in Higher Education Journal*, *24*, 1–15.

Macdonald, S., Whiting, A., & Jarvis. (2024). Evidence and ideology in the independent review of Prevent. *Journal for Deradicalization*, *39*, 40–76.

Martinez, M. A., Chang, A., & Welton, A. D. (2017). Assistant professors of color confront the inequitable terrain of academia: A community cultural wealth perspective. *Race Ethnicity and Education*, *20*(5), 696–710. https://doi.org/10.1080/13613324.2016.1150826

McCallum, J. M., Arekere, D. M., Green, B. L., Katz, R. V., & Rivers, B. M. (2006). Awareness and knowledge of the U.S. Public Health Service syphilis study at Tuskegee: Implications for biomedical research. *Journal of Health Care for the Poor and Underserved*, *17*(4), 716–733. https://doi.org/10.1353/hpu.2006.0130

McGlynn, C., & McDaid, S. (2019). *Radicalisation and counter-radicalisation in higher education*. Emerald Publishing.

McGowan, J. M. (2000). Multicultural teaching: African-American faculty classroom teaching experiences in predominantly white Colleges and universities. *Multicultural Education*, *8*(2), 19.

Miah, S. (2013). *'Prevent'ing education: Anti-Muslim racism and the war on terror in schools*. Palgrave Macmillan.

Morrison, A., Polisena, J., Husereau, D., Moulton, K., Clark, M., Fiander, M., ... & Rabb, D. (2012). The effect of English-language restriction on systematic review-based meta-analyses: A systematic review of empirical studies. *International Journal of Technology Assessment in Health Care*, *28*(2), 138–144. https://doi.org/10.1017/S0266462312000086

Nwosu, C. (2024). Evaluating the impact of the race equality charter on diversity staff outcomes. *Race Ethnicity and Education*, 1–11. https://doi.org/10.1080/13613324.2024.2328372

Ogunwole, S. M., Dill, M., Jones, K., & Golden, S. H. (2020). Trends in internal medicine faculty by sex and race/ethnicity, 1980–2018. *JAMA Network Open*, *3*(9), e2015205. https://doi.org/10.1001/jamanetworkopen.2020.15205

Orelus, P. W. (2013). The institutional cost of being a professor of color: Unveiling micro-aggression, racial (in)visibility, and racial profiling through the lens of Critical Race Theory. *Current Issues in Education*, *16*(2), 1–16.

Osho, Y. I., & Alormele, N. (2025). Negotiated spaces: Black women academics' experiences in UK universities. *Higher Education*, *89*, 1387–1403. https://doi.org/10.1007/s10734-024-01279-x

Panjwani, F., Revell, L., Gholami, R., & Diboll, M. (2018). *Education and extremisms: Rethinking liberal pedagogies in the contemporary world*. Routledge.

Pittman, C. T. (2012). Racial microaggressions: The narratives of African American faculty at a predominantly white university. *Journal of Negro Education*, *81*(1), 82–92.

Pokhrel, A., Olayemi, A., Ogbonda, S., Nair, K., & Wang, J. C. (2023). Racial and ethnic differences in sickle cell disease within the United States: From demographics to outcomes. *European Journal of Haematology*, *110*(5), 554–563. https://doi.org/10.1111/ejh.13936

Politzer-Ahles, S., Girolamo, T., & Ghali, S. (2020). Preliminary evidence of linguistic bias in academic reviewing. *Journal of English for Academic Purposes*, *47*, 100895. https://doi.org/10.1016/j.jeap.2020.100895

Roberts, S. O., Bareket-Shavit, C., Dollins, F. A., Goldie, P. D., & Mortenson, E. (2020). Racial inequality in psychological research: Trends of the past and recommendations for the future. *Perspectives on Psychological Science*, *15*(6), 1295–1309. https://doi.org/10.1177/1745691620927709

Rockwell, D. H., Yobs, A. R., & Moore, M. B. (1964). The Tuskegee study of untreated syphilis: The 30th year of observation. *Archives of Internal Medicine*, *114*(6), 792–798. https://doi.org/10.1001/archinte.1964.03860120104011

Shawcross, W. (2023). *Independent review of prevent*. Home Office. Retrieved from: https://assets.publishing.service.gov.uk/media/63e26a08d3bf7f172f6ce87f/Independent_Review_of_Prevent__print_.pdf

Simatele, M. (2018). A cross-cultural experience of microaggression in academia: A personal reflection. *Education as Change*, *22*(3), 1–23. https://doi.org/10.25159/1947-9417/3132

Smith, D. G., Turner, C. S., Osei-Kofi, N., & Richards, S. (2004). Interrupting the usual: Successful strategies for hiring diverse faculty. *The Journal of Higher Education*, *75*(2), 133–160. https://doi.org/10.1080/00221546.2004.11778900

Smith, O. M., Davis, K. L., Pizza, R. B., Waterman, R., Dobson, K. C., Foster, B., ... & Davis, C. L. (2023). Peer review perpetuates barriers for historically excluded groups. *Nature Ecology & Evolution*, *7*(4), 512–523. https://doi.org/10.1038/s41559-023-01999-w

Stern, C., & Kleijnen, J. (2020). Language bias in systematic reviews: You only get out what you put in. *JBI Evidence Synthesis*, *18*(9), 1818–1819. https://doi.org/10.11124/JBIES-20-00361

Strauss, D., Gran-Ruaz, S., Osman, M., Williams, M. T., & Faber, S. C. (2023). Racism and censorship in the editorial and peer review process. *Frontiers in Psychology*, *14*, 1120938. https://doi.org/10.3389/fpsyg.2023.1120938

Sue, D. W., Capodilupo, C. M., Torino, G. C., Bucceri, J. M., Holder, A. M. B. Nadal, K. L., & Esquilin, M. (2007). Racial microaggressions in everyday life: Implications for clinical practice. *American Psychologist*, *62*(4), 271–286. https://doi.org/10.1037/0003-066X.62.4.271

Thompson, C. Q. (2008). Recruitment, retention, and mentoring faculty of color: The chronicle continues. *New Directions for Higher Education*, *143*, 47–54.

Thunig, A., & Jones, T. (2021). 'Don't make me play house-n***er': Indigenous academic women treated as 'black performer' within higher education. *The Australian Educational Researcher*, *48*, 397–417. https://doi.org/10.1007/s13384-020-00405-9

Tillman, L. C. (2001). Mentoring African American faculty in predominantly white institutions. *Research in Higher Education*, *42*(3), 295–325. https://doi.org/10.1023/A:1018822006485

Tobin, M. J. (2022). Fiftieth anniversary of uncovering the Tuskegee Syphilis Study: The story and timeless lessons. *American Journal of Respiratory and Critical Care Medicine*, *205*(10), 1145–1158. https://doi.org/10.1164/rccm.202201-0136SO

Tuitt, F., Hanna, M., Martinez, L. M., Salazar, M., & Griffin, R. (2009). Teaching in the line of fire: Faculty of color in the academy. *Thought & Action*, *25*, 65–74.

Turner, C. S. V. (2002a). *Diversifying the faculty: A guidebook for search committees.* American Association of Colleges and Universities.

Turner, C. S. V. (2002b). Women of color in academe: Living with multiple marginality. *The Journal of Higher Education*, *73*(1), 74–93. https://doi.org/10.1080/00221546.2002.11777131

Turner, C. S. V., González, J. C., & Wood, J. L. (2008). Faculty of color in academe: What 20 years of literature tells us. *Journal of Diversity in Higher Education*, *1*(3), 139–168. https://doi.org/10.1037/a0012837

University and College Union (2016). *The experiences of Black and Minority Ethnic staff in further and higher education.* London. Retrieved from: https://www.ucu.org.uk/media/7861/The-experiences-of-black-and-minority-ethnic-staff-in-further-and-higher-education-Feb-16/pdf/BME_survey_report_Feb161.pdf

West-Olatunji, C. (2005). Incidents in the lives of Harriet Jacobs - a readers theatre: Disseminating the outcomes of research on the Black experience in the academy. In J. King (Ed.), *Black education: A transformative research and action agenda for the new century* (pp. 329–340). Lawrence Erlbaum.

Williams, J. C., & K. W. Phillips. (2016). Tools for change: Boosting the retention of women in the STEM pipeline. *Journal of Research in Gender Studies*, *6*(1), 11–75.

Wu, X. Y., Tang, J. L., Mao, C., Yuan, J. Q., Qin, Y., & Chung, V. C. (2013). Systematic reviews and meta-analyses of traditional Chinese medicine must search Chinese databases to reduce language bias. *Evidence-Based Complementary and Alternative Medicine*, *2013*(1), 812179. https://doi.org/10.1155/2013/812179

Zhang, Y., Silver, J. K., Tiwana, S., Verduzco-Gutierrez, M., Siddiqi, J., & Khosa, F. (2021). Physical medicine and rehabilitation faculty diversity trends by sex, race, and ethnicity, 2007 to 2018 in the United States. *Physical Medicine and Rehabilitation*, *13*(9), 994–1004. https://doi.org/10.1002/pmrj.12537

Chapter 7

Bullying and Incivility

For many employees, the workplace is unsafe and frequently associated with aggressive and abusive behaviour. The current chapter focuses on the bullying and incivility experienced by those working in the higher education sector, including the factors that increase the likelihood of such behaviour, the incidence of contrapower bullying and incivility, and the impact of bullying and incivility on targets. Numerous definitions of workplace bullying are available. For example, Einarsen et al. (2020) describe workplace bullying as

> Repeated actions and practices that are directed against one or more workers, that are unwanted by the target, that may be carried out deliberately or unconsciously, but clearly cause humiliation, offense and distress, and that may interfere with work performance and/or cause an unpleasant working environment.
>
> (p. 10)

Though available definitions vary on factors such as the inclusion of perpetrator intention, power held by the perpetrator, and repeated acts, the impact of bullying on the target remains central.

It is important to recognise that though Chapter 7 predominantly focuses on and refers to workplace bullying, such behaviour is often considered with other related and overlapping constructs, such as workplace harassment (e.g., Henning et al., 2017). To some extent, this issue is further confused by the absence of accepted definitions of each form of workplace aggression and cross-cultural variation in the terminology adopted. Incivility or inappropriate behaviour is more common than workplace bullying (Meriläinen et al., 2016) and can be conceptualised as "*low-intensity deviant behavior with ambiguous intent to harm the target, in violation of workplace norms for mutual respect. Uncivil behaviors are characteristically rude and discourteous, displaying a lack of regard for others*" (Andersson & Pearson, 1999, p. 457).

DOI: 10.4324/9781032639321-8

Bullying and Incivility Among Academics

Bullying, harassment, and incivility are especially common in education compared to other organisational sectors (Hubert & van Veldhoven, 2001). In their review of the literature, Keashly (2021) estimates that 25% of higher education faculty will identify as being the target of workplace bullying in the previous 12 months, and 50–75% will have been exposed to workplace bullying. As described by one professor, "*I have worked in both the 'real' world and academia. I have never encountered so much bullying as there is in academia. It is schoolyard bullying on steroids*". (DelliFraine et al., 2014, p. 147). It is, therefore, essential that research, policy, and practice address this issue. Indeed, a coordinated collaborative approach to workplace aggression (including action by publishers and funding bodies) may be required (Mahmoudi & Keashly, 2021), and organisations such as the Academic Parity Movement have been established to address bullying, harassment, and discrimination in higher education (https://paritymovement.org).

Investigating experiences of nursing faculty, Goldberg et al. (2013) report that specific bullying tactics employed include withholding information (e.g., providing minimal orientation and guidance), manipulation (e.g., negative feedback later found to be untrue or distorted), and providing unrealistic workloads (e.g., demanding work outside regular working hours). In the higher education sector, workplace aggression is relatively unlikely to include physical abuse or threats of physical violence, with perpetrators often taking care to ensure that they are not observed breaking official codes of conduct (Smith & Coel, 2018). Hence, incivility (such as belittling a person, interrupting, or disregarding the views of another) is likely to be more frequent than bullying (Heffernan & Bosetti, 2023).

The tactics described by Goldberg et al. (2013) are consistent with previous research demonstrating that in academia, bullying behaviour is often work-related, such as creating unmanageable workloads, excessive monitoring, excluding people from important decision-making processes, and undermining a person's reputation (Ahmad, Kalim, & Kaleem, 2017; Zabrodska & Kveton, 2013). Reputation is arguably more important in academia than in other professions, with academics dependent on their peers for important opportunities (e.g., research collaboration), favourable outputs (e.g., journal and grant review), and markers of success (e.g., invitations to present at conferences and letters of recommendation for promotion). Of course, behaviour such as denying important opportunities or socially excluding a person may be difficult to evidence. Establishing a pattern of targeted behaviour over an extended period of time may be especially helpful.

Cross-Cultural Variation

It is important to acknowledge that there is substantial variation in the incidence and nature of bullying across cultures and contexts. The 2022 Global

Inclusivity Report explored academic experiences of bullying, harassment and discrimination, noting significant variation in employee experiences.

Figures 7.1–7.3 show the percentage of academics experiencing verbal, social and cyber bullying in each global region. Data from the 2022 Global Inclusivity Report.

Significant variation also exists within continents. For example, Meriläinen et al. (2019) report variation across Europe, demonstrating a higher incidence of bullying in Estonia in the prior six months (27% of respondents) compared to Finland (18% of respondents). Further, bullying was more direct in Estonian universities (e.g., ridicule, blame) than in Finland, where indirect bullying (e.g., negative comments made when a person is not present) is more common. Factors impacting such cultural variation may include country-specific

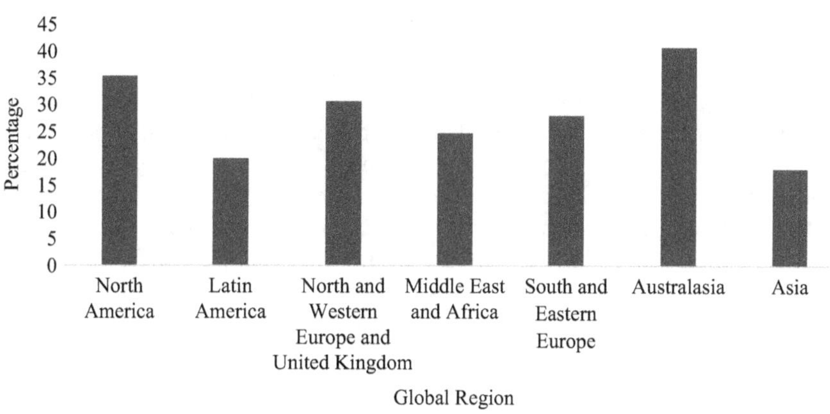

Figure 7.1 Percentage of academics with experience of verbal bullying.

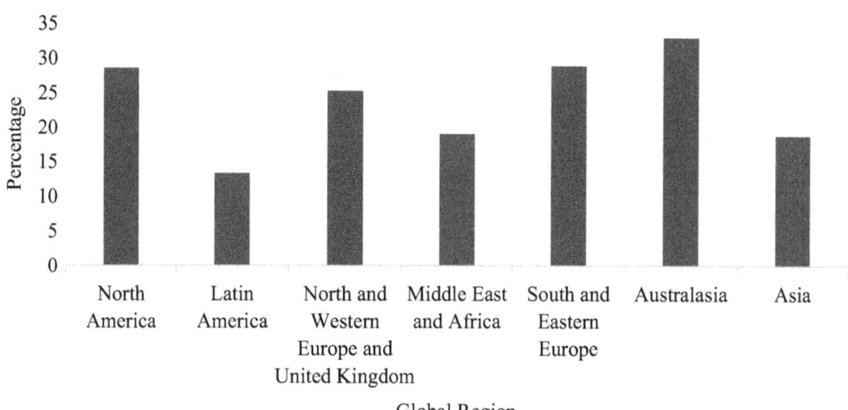

Figure 7.2 Percentage of academics with experience of social bullying.

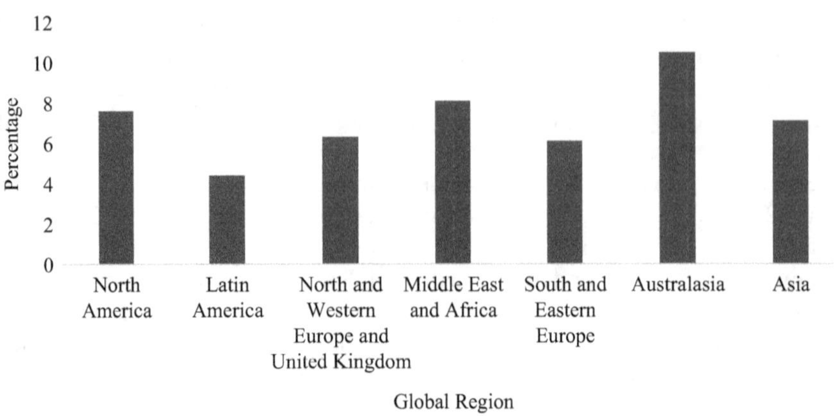

Figure 7.3 Percentage of academics with experience of cyberbullying.

external pressures (e.g., formal auditing of research outputs) and the nature of academic contracts (e.g., the prevalence of precarious contracts). The culture and context in which workplace bullying and harassment take place may also influence the impact of such behaviour (Van de Vliert, Einarsen, & Nielsen, 2013). As research investigating the incidence and form of workplace bullying is most commonly conducted in Western countries, especially Western Europe and North America (Keashly, 2021), caution is recommended when extrapolating findings to other cultures and contexts.

Professional Services

Compared to research focused on the bullying and harassment of academic staff or all staff (i.e., both academic and non-academic staff), relatively few studies have addressed the bullying and harassment of professional services staff specifically (Hodgins et al., 2024). Despite the paucity of research in this area, the bullying of professional services staff is a significant issue. For example, Hollis (2015) reports that 62% of the higher education administrators surveyed had experienced or witnessed workplace bullying in the previous 18 months. Bullies were typically at the director (40%), tenured faculty (26.3%), dean (21.1%) or vice president/provost (20.1%) level. A substantial number (28%) of respondents had witnessed vicarious bullying, and 17.5% had been the target of vicarious bullying, whereby a manager ordered an assistant or other staff member to conduct their bullying.

Common bullying strategies used against non-academic targets include inappropriate pressure to produce work, withholding necessary information, and undermining a target's ability (Thomas, 2005). In one study focusing on inappropriate behaviour directed by faculty towards nursing administrators, behaviour included rudeness, intimidation, false allegations, sabotage, and manipulation (LaSala, Wilson, & Sprunk, 2016). The consequences were both personal (e.g., harm to physical and psychological health) and professional (e.g., reputational damage). Exploring the experiences of administrative and technical staff, Hodgins and Mannix McNamara (2017) report that the informal processes used to address the bullying were ineffective. However, formal processes, including the involvement of trade unions, could escalate the situation, resulting in further isolation and segregation. Similarly, human resources were believed to be primarily concerned with protecting the institution rather than those subjected to bullying or harassment, suggesting that current procedures to support targets are inadequate. The bullying had a considerable impact on the victim's wellbeing, including the incidence of hospitalisation (Hodgins & Mannix McNamara, 2017) and greater awareness of administrator experiences is required.

Factors Impacting the Likelihood of Bullying and Incivility

The neoliberal academic environment (see Chapter 1) has contributed to the prevalence of workplace aggression. In particular, competition and precarity are associated with workplace bullying (Hodgins et al., 2024). The culture and structure of specific academic departments and institutions may also contribute to the incidence and form of bullying in higher education. For example, bullying is lower where departments are transparent about promotion policies and evaluation (Migliaccio et al., 2024). Further, research suggests that the psychological demands of academic roles contribute to the incidence of workplace bullying both directly and indirectly through increased occupational stress (Goodboy et al., 2022). Supervisor support and level of autonomy were also important. It is, of course, important to recognise that the organisational climate can be considered both a cause and a consequence of workplace bullying, and additional longitudinal research is required (Giorgi, 2012).

Further, research indicates variation in workplace incivility, bullying, and harassment across disciplines. In one study, Moss et al. (2022) examined data from 2,122 participants from 14 subject areas categorised into four main fields (applied sciences, formal sciences, natural sciences, and social sciences). Focusing on the subject areas with the highest number of respondents, the researchers revealed significant differences between the social sciences, chemistry, engineering, and neuroscience. It is, therefore, important for each subject discipline to examine the aggressive behaviour most commonly employed by perpetrators in their subject area and the practices (e.g., field work) that may contribute to this.

It is important to consider factors increasing the likelihood of workplace aggression experienced by both academic and non-academic employees separately. For example, in one longitudinal study, Björklund, Vaez, and Jensen (2021) found that a greater proportion of non-academic staff (who had not experienced bullying at time one) were being bullied at time two compared to academic staff (4.3% vs. 3.8%). Further, whilst some factors predicted the likelihood of bullying in both academic and non-academic staff (e.g., empowering leadership, support from colleagues), other factors predicted workplace aggression in academic (e.g., role conflict) or non-academic staff (e.g., support from manager) only.

Contrapower Bullying, Harassment, and Incivility

Definitions of bullying and harassment commonly include references to power and status (Baillien et al., 2017; Tight, 2023), and research often focuses on the hierarchical bullying perpetrated against lower-status targets (e.g., Smith & Fredricks-Lowman, 2020; Wieland & Beitz, 2015). Though perpetrators of bullying are most likely to be in a position of greater or similar power and status to the victim (e.g., a line manager), bullying may also be perpetrated by those of lower apparent power. For example, Heffernan and Bosetti (2023) interviewed 20 deans. Deans were more likely to be bullied by those in less senior positions than themselves and discussed an "us vs. them" culture in which management was inherently separate from those they managed. One dean stated, "*Being bullied is just part of leading. You have to put your arms up and take the punches – no one else will help you. That's how you survive as a leader*". (p. 11). To an extent, deans recognised that the bullying behaviour they experienced was a response to the situation (e.g., restructure and job uncertainty) rather than themselves personally.

In higher education, academic staff are vulnerable to workplace aggression perpetrated by students. Students' bullying and harassment of academic staff appears to have increased in recent years. In one study, 30% of academics surveyed reported being "stalked" by a student, with harassment most common during assessment periods (Williams et al., 2022). Further, though academics have greater power than students (at least to observers), almost 20% of academics surveyed felt powerless to discipline students who were harassing them and/or felt they would not be believed by management, and over 50% of academics feel powerless and helpless when attacked by students on social media (Williams et al., 2022). In part, the changing role (both in terms of hostile behaviour and increased power held by students) reflects the rise in student "consumer culture" (in response to changes to student fees and a competitive market for graduate careers) and sector focus on institutional league tables that are influenced by student satisfaction ratings (Christensen, Craft, & White, 2020).

Students can demonstrate their dislike of individual faculty with hostile behaviour that ranges from incivility to extreme bullying or harassment (May & Tenzek, 2018). White (2010) classifies such behaviour as verbal (e.g., heckling, swearing), personal (e.g., belittling comments, public humiliation), isolation (e.g., talking or using a phone during teaching sessions), and task (e.g., complaining about marking or the time taken to respond to email queries). In particular, formal student evaluations can be used to target bullied faculty (Goldberg et al., 2013), and students may threaten to make a formal complaint (May & Tenzek, 2018), both of which can have a significant impact on the target's reputation and career progression. Academics subjected to such hostile behaviour report anger, distress, and frustration and make changes to their teaching practice (Christensen, Craft, & White, 2021; May & Tenzek, 2018). Unsurprisingly, there is also a relationship between contrapower harassment and the stress and job satisfaction reported by academic staff (DeSouza, 2011).

Similar levels of incivility and bullying (perpetrated by students) are reported by male and female faculty, though women perceive these as more distressing and as having a greater impact on their professional lives and health (Lampman et al., 2009). Consistent with the greater impact of this behaviour identified by female faculty, women were more likely to take action in response to incivility or bullying than men (Lampman et al., 2009). Further, when asked to identify their "worst-ever" professors, students are more likely to use hostile and pathologising language (e.g., "psychotic", "bitch") when describing female faculty (Sprague & Massoni, 2005). It is essential that students are guided with respect to professional conduct both on campus, and online and that higher education institutions recognise the impact of contrapower harassment on academic staff.

Witness Responses and Bystander Intervention

Research, policy, and practice have, understandably, often focused on the behaviour of perpetrators and the impact of such behaviour on their targets. It is also important to consider the behaviour of those witnessing workplace bullying, especially as the proportion of employees who witness bullying often exceeds those who are targeted by it (Keashly & Neuman, 2010). Research indicates that workplace bullying has a negative impact on witnesses. For example, witnesses who are exposed to inappropriate behaviour may become fearful that they will be targeted or become detached from an organisation that they perceive to be harmful and unsupportive of its employees (Mazzone et al., 2024).

Further, whilst those who challenge workplace aggression may be subject to retaliation, those who fail to address inappropriate behaviour may feel stress, guilt, and anxiety, especially when interacting with the targeted employee. Indeed, research in non-academic contexts has documented the impact of witnessing workplace aggression on employee mental and physical health (Emdad et al., 2013; Vartia, 2001). It is, therefore, important that research investigating workplace aggression in academia considers both direct experience as a target and those witnessing such behaviour (McKay et al., 2008). Of course, as a substantial number of higher education employees witness incivility, bullying, or harassment (Keashly, 2021), there are also important opportunities for bystander intervention (e.g., reporting workplace aggression to funding bodies). Additional consideration of bystander roles and responsibilities is required (Mahmoudi, 2021) and may include consideration of the constructive or destructive and active or passive bystander response (Paull, Omari, & Standen, 2012).

Impact and Coping

Given the prevalence of bullying and incivility in higher education, it is important to consider the impact of workplace aggression. Indeed, the personal consequences of workplace bullying are well-established, especially in relation to physical and mental health. Common responses to workplace bullying experienced by faculty include stress, exhaustion (DelliFraine et al., 2014), anxiety, and helplessness (Meriläinen et al., 2016). The impact of bullying and incivility extends beyond individual physical and mental ill health to significant disruption to personal and family life (Heffernan & Bosetti, 2023). Of course, it is important to recognise that the psychological impact of workplace bullying extends far beyond the actual incidence of bullying behaviour. As described by one further education lecturer who continued to meet with other people bullied by the same individual after the bullying had ended, "*What's strange is that this stopped over 12 months ago, yet it is still very painful for all of us*". (Lewis, 2004, p. 291).

Psychological responses to workplace bullying include feelings of humiliation, alienation, self-blame, and hyper-vigilance (Goldberg et al., 2013), and those experiencing workplace bullying in higher education are more likely to report absenteeism and intentions to leave the organisation than their non-victimised colleagues (e.g., Hollis, 2017). Behaviours such as interviewing for a new position (intended to actively remove themselves from the bullying) are perceived as empowering (Wieland & Beitz, 2015). The recovery process typically begins when faculty have moved to a new institution, though long-term issues (e.g., hyper-vigilance, anger) are also apparent (Wieland & Beitz, 2015).

Workplace aggression has negative professional consequences for the individual employee. Treatment by workplace bullies (e.g., ridicule, undermining expertise) may result in academics being repeatedly overlooked for positions of responsibility or promotion (Lewis, 2004) and lower professional self-confidence and work performance (Meriläinen et al., 2016). Where academics also have a clinical or practitioner role, the impact of impaired work performance may extend to clinical ability and patient safety (Averbuch, Eliya, & Van Spall, 2021). Further, employees experiencing isolation and alienation may not have the networking opportunities or opportunities for promotion afforded to their non-victimised colleagues. As bullied academics who move to a new institution are likely to continue in the same discipline, the bullying or consequences of bullying (e.g., damaged reputation through rumour spreading) may continue even after relocation. Workplace aggression also has broader implications for the subject discipline and higher education sector, with Mahmoudi (2023a) highlighting the impact of academic bullying on the progress and evolution of science.

Autoethnographic Accounts

Bullying, harassment, and incivility can have devastating consequences for those targeted. Autoethnographic accounts provide an insight into the lived experience of workplace aggression in higher education and can support those targeted (Pheko, 2018). Both individual (e.g., Higgins, 2024, Sambrook, 2025) and collective (e.g., Zawadzki & Jensen, 2020) autoethnographies are available, which can be informed by a range of material, including journal entries and photographs (Higgins, 2024), field notes (Zawadzki & Jensen, 2020), or letters and emails (Pheko, 2018).

For example, Higgins (2024) describes her experience of workplace bullying as an administrator in higher education, reporting that she was living in fear, likening the experience to an abusive relationship to the extent that she no longer recognised herself. These are often distressing to read; for example, Sambrook (2025) refers to their "*pitiful story of how I lost my dignity, my academic identity and my self-worth*" (p. 2–3) but illustrate the personal impact of workplace bullying. Though autoethnographic accounts provide, by definition, an in-depth discussion of personal experiences informed by self-observation and reflection, they do not neglect the environmental and cultural factors that influence the likelihood or experience of bullying (Mhaka-Mutepfa & Rampa, 2024). For example, the neoliberalisation of academia and associated monitoring, insecurity, and stress (see also Chapter 1) are central to the account of bullying provided by Zawadzki and Jensen (2020).

Policy and Reporting

Universities may establish workplace bullying and harassment policies and the procedures to respond to such behaviour in order to comply with appropriate legislation or because they recognise the economic ramifications (e.g., low productivity and increased absenteeism or turnover) of workplace hostility (Rockett et al., 2017). Smith and Coel (2018) review 276 faculty codes of conduct from institutions across the United States. Policies typically focused on harassment of those with protected characteristics, with comparatively little reference (8 institutions only) to broader bullying. The requirement for individual employees to contribute to a positive organisational climate was also prominent. It is important that institutional policies targeting bullying, harassment, and incivility adopt a clear stance and define the behaviour that is not permitted. Identifying sources of support and the procedure for reporting hostile behaviour is also essential.

Even where policies are in place, those subjected to workplace aggression may be reluctant to report the behaviour or seek support, with little confidence in the institution's intent or ability to deal with the bullying appropriately (Hodgins & Mannix McNamara, 2017; McKay et al., 2008). Those witnessing workplace bullying express similar sentiments (Mazzone et al., 2024). This lack of confidence is not unfounded. In one study focusing on the experiences of graduate students and junior faculty, Hollis (2017) reports that the majority of respondents experiencing bullying (80%) reported that the organisation did not act when learning about the bullying. Further, a minority of respondents reported that the organisation had coached the bully (16%), or fired the target (8%), or moved the target to another department (3%). As outlined by one higher education employee, "*Management not only does nothing about protecting myself and others from bullying, I have also seen them protect those who bully. This enables the cycle to continue*". (McKay et al., 2008, p. 91).

Retaliation by the organisation is not uncommon, and institutions may attempt to damage the reputation of those experiencing workplace aggression in order to minimise the impact of such behaviour and potential liability (Mahmoudi, 2023b). As a consequence, Hollis (2017) reports that 32% of respondents were considering leaving higher education, and 28% had actually tried to leave their position (e.g., applied for a role elsewhere).

Non-Disclosure Agreements

Universities may use non-disclosure agreements (often colloquially referred to as "gagging orders") to silence victims of bullying or harassment and protect the reputation of the institution. Pagan (2021) describes such agreements as "*A weapon to kill the knowledge of the less powerful who have been the victim of serious misconduct to the benefit of the more powerful who perpetrate the mis conduct*". (p. 302). The formal use of non-disclosure agreements exacerbates more informal forms of silencing within higher education, such as encouraging people not to discuss misconduct or distressing issues (Fernando & Prasad, 2019).

Non-disclosure agreements both protect the identity of the perpetrator and the actions of the institution, which may include the organisational culture that enabled the bullying or harassment to take place and an inadequate response once the hostile behaviour had been reported. This process of containment and silencing makes it more difficult for others (both internal to the institution and external) to recognise, monitor, and address issues such as workplace bullying. It can, therefore, be argued that the use of non-disclosure agreements in these circumstances is immoral (Macfarlane, 2020) as they fail to protect others who may be subject to subsequent bullying or harassment. For example, a non-disclosure agreement may allow an academic who has harassed a colleague or student to move to a position at a new institution without disclosure of the harassment case. This practice is, of course, of benefit both to the individual perpetrator who is able to secure a new position and the academic institution that is able to quietly remove a "problematic" employee.

Examining oral and written evidence submitted to a parliamentary inquiry on non-disclosure agreements by the victims of misconduct (across a range of contexts) required to sign such agreements, Pagan (2021) describes the manner in which these agreements exacerbate the trauma experienced. The Speak Out Revolution is a not-for-profit organisation established in 2020 that addresses the culture of silence and silencing in response to bullying and harassment. Their site allows victims of bullying and harassment to anonymously share their experiences, creating an evidence base to inform practice and policy in the area of bullying and harassment (see https://www.speakoutrevolution.co.uk).

Recommendations

Institutions should,

- Publish clear codes of conduct addressing both staff and student behaviour. Provide definitions of important terms (e.g., bullying, harassment, and incivility) and examples. Ensure particular areas of concern for specific disciplines (e.g., laboratory work, placements) are included.
- Establish procedures for the formal reporting of workplace aggression. Recognise target and witness concerns relating to formal reporting, ensuring that such behaviour can be reported anonymously if preferred. Ensure those dealing with targets and witnesses understand the range of inappropriate behaviours that occur, including those that do not conform to stereotyped notions of bullying and incivility (e.g., mobbing and contrapower bullying and incivility).
- Recognise the impact of bullying and incivility. Provide support for those targeted and for those witnessing such behaviour. Ensure that support is not dependent on formal reporting and procedures are in place to mitigate the professional impact of workplace aggression (e.g., excluding abusive student evaluations).
- Provide mandatory education and training for all staff and students. Cover a broad range of inappropriate behaviours and highlight the impact of workplace aggression on targets and witnesses. Provide guidance for safe and effective bystander intervention. Ensure all training is evidence-based, informed by target and witness experiences, and specific to the higher education sector.
- Regularly assess the prevalence, form, and impact of workplace aggression that is not formally disclosed (e.g., through an anonymous survey). Identify important differences between disciplines and ensure separate analysis of data relating to academic and non-academic staff. Address organisational issues (e.g., levels of supervisor support) impacting the incidence of bullying and incivility. Regularly assess satisfaction with formal reporting procedures (including action taken) and the support provided.

Subject in Focus 1: Mobbing

Workplace bullying is often conceptualised as one perpetrator behaving aggressively towards one target. Leymann (1996) adopts the term mobbing when describing workplace aggression and highlights behaviour involving more than one perpetrator ganging up on one or more targets. The field is, however, complicated by use of the term mobbing to also refer to behaviour performed by a single individual. For example, Leymann (1996) states that mobbing

> Involves hostile and unethical communication, which is directed in a systematic way by one or a few individuals mainly towards one individual who, due to mobbing, is pushed into a helpless and defenceless position, being held there by means of continuing mobbing activities. (p. 168)

Indeed, as noted elsewhere in this chapter the lack of consistency (with regards to the terminology adopted and working definitions in particular) hinders progress in this field.

Leymann (1996) identified a range of mobbing activities, categorised according to their effect on the target (1) ability to communicate (e.g., silencing the target), (2) opportunity to maintain social contact (e.g., isolating targets, preventing interaction with colleagues), (3) ability to maintain personal reputation (e.g., malicious gossip, ridiculing the target's private life), (4) professional situation (e.g., denying meaningful work, allocating tasks below the target's level of expertise), and (5) physical health (e.g., physical attacks, placing targets in an unsafe working environment). Previous research demonstrates the impact of mobbing on targeted university employees (Rojas-Solís, García-Ramírez, & Hernández-Corona, 2019). For example, Hakan and Kurtbaş (2011) highlight the relationship between mobbing experiences (adopting the aforementioned five dimensions together with a sixth dimension focused on academic life) and lowered commitment to the organization, with emotional commitment to the organization especially important.

Subject in Focus 2: Measurement of Bullying

The field of workplace aggression is well-established. The wealth of literature examining bullying, harassment, and incivility in higher education is perhaps best illustrated by the number of reviews on this subject available (e.g., Henning et al., 2017; Hodgins et al., 2024; Tight, 2023).

Of course, to some degree it is difficult to compare findings across studies and reach a consensus, with substantial variation in the definition and measurement of bullying, harassment, and incivility (Crawshaw, 2009; Keashly, 2021). For example, whilst some studies ask employees to self-identify as a target of such behaviour, others ask respondents to report their experience of specific acts. Though a range of measures are used to measure the incidence, form, and impact of workplace aggression, the workplace environment shapes the type of bullying and incivility that occurs. For example, the importance of networking, collaboration, and reputation increases the effectiveness of exclusion and criticism. Bullying, harassment, and incivility measures specific to the academic workplace have, therefore, been developed.

Meriläinen and Kõiv (2019) created the Academic Bullying Inventory (ABI-10) to measure workplace bullying in universities based on the more general Negative Acts Questionnaire Revised (Einarsen, Hoel, & Notelaers, 2009). The researchers identified five related but distinct factors of academic bullying; (1) personal insults, (2) work-related blame, (3) professional understating, (4) unreasonable work-related demands, and (5) work-related malpractice. The questionnaire can be used to obtain either an overall academic bullying score or to assess each of the five bullying constructs.

In 2020, Yildiz published a mobbing scale focused on university employees. Two forms of mobbing are conceptualised, vertical mobbing (where an administrator targets an employee of a lower status or when one or more employees of a lower status targets an administrator) and horizontal mobbing (where actors are colleagues of a similar status). Additional testing of such measures and measures designed for non-academic employees based in the higher education sector is recommended. Questionnaires have also been developed to assess student experiences of bullying in higher education. For example, Harrison, Fox, and Hulme (2022) developed a measure with four subscales; (1) psychological victimisation, (2) physical act/trace victimisation, (3) social victimisation, and (4) direct verbal victimisation.

References

Ahmad, S., Kalim, R., & Kaleem, A. (2017). Academics' perceptions of bullying at work: Insights from Pakistan. *International Journal of Educational Management, 31*(2), 204–220. https://doi.org/10.1108/IJEM-10-2015-0141

Andersson, L. M., & Pearson, C. M. (1999). Tit for tat? The spiraling effect of incivility in the workplace. *Academy of Management Review, 24*(3), 452–471. https://doi.org/10.5465/amr.1999.2202131

Averbuch, T., Eliya, Y., & Van Spall, H. (2021). Systematic review of academic bullying in medical settings: Dynamics and consequences. *BMJ Open*, *11*(7), e043256. https://doi.org/10.1136/bmjopen-2020-043256

Baillien, E., Escartín, J., Gross, C., & Zapf, D. (2017). Towards a conceptual and empirical differentiation between workplace bullying and interpersonal conflict. *European Journal of Work and Organizational Psychology*, *26*(6), 870–881. https://doi.org/10.1080/1359432X.2017.1385601

Björklund, C., Vaez, M., & Jensen, I. (2021). Early work- environmental indicators of bullying in an academic setting: A longitudinal study of staff in a medical university. *Studies in Higher Education*, *46*(12), 2556–2567. https://doi.org/10.1080/03075079.2020.1729114

Christensen, M., Craft, J., & White, S. (2020). Nurse academics' experience of contra-power harassment from under-graduate nursing students in Australia. *Nurse Education Today*, *84*, 104220. https://doi.org/10.1016/j.nedt.2019.104220.

Christensen, M., Craft, J., & White, S. (2021). "I've had horrible things said about me": An inductive content analysis of nursing academic experiences of contra-power harassment from undergraduate nursing students. *Nurse Education in Practice*, *54*, 103132. https://doi.org/10.1016/j.nepr.2021.103132

Crawshaw, L. (2009). Workplace bullying? Mobbing? Harassment? Distraction by a thousand definitions. *Consulting Psychology Journal*, *61*(3), 263–267. https://doi.org/10.1037/a0016590

DelliFraine, J. L., McClelland, L. E., Erwin, C. O., & Wang, Z. (2014). Bullying in academia: Results of a survey of health administration faculty. *Journal of Health Administration Education*, *31*(2), 147–163.

DeSouza, E. R. (2011). Frequency rates and correlates of contrapower harassment in higher education. *Journal of Interpersonal Violence*, *26*(1), 158–188. http://doi.org/10.1177/0886260510362878.

Einarsen, S., Hoel, H. & Notelaers, G. (2009). Measuring exposure to bullying and harassment at work: Validity, factor structure and psychometric properties of the Negative Acts Questionnaire-Revised. *Work & Stress*, *23*(1), 24–44. https://doi.org/10.1080/02678370902815673

Einarsen, S. V., Hoel, H., Zapf, D., & Cooper, C. L. (2020). The concept of bullying and harassment at work: The European tradition. In S. V. Einarsen, H. Hoel, D. Zapf, & C. L. Cooper (Eds.), *Bullying and harassment in the workplace: Theory, research and practice* (3rd ed., pp. 3–53). CRC Press.

Emdad, R., Alipour, A., Hagberg, J., & Jensen, I. B. (2013). The impact of bystanding to workplace bullying on symptoms of depression among women and men in industry in Sweden: An empirical and theoretical longitudinal study. *International Archives of Occupational and Environmental Health*, *86*, 709–716. https://doi.org/10.1007/s00420-012-0813-1

Fernando, D., & Prasad, A. (2019). Sex-based harassment and organizational silencing: How women are led to reluctant acquiescence in academia. *Human Relations*, *72*(10), 1565–1594. https://doi.org/10.1177/0018726718809164

Giorgi, G. (2012). Workplace bullying in academia creates a negative work environment. An Italian study. *Employee Responsibilities and Rights Journal*, *24*, 261–275. https://doi.org/10.1007/s10672-012-9193-7

Global Inclusivity Report (2022). Emerald Publishing. Retrieved from: https://www.emeraldgrouppublishing.com/global-inclusivity-report-2022-download-report

Goldberg, E., Beitz, J., Wieland, D., & Levine, C. (2013). Social bullying in nursing academia. *Nurse Educator*, *38*(5), 191–197. http://doi.org/10.1097/NNE.0b013e3182a0e5a0

Goodboy, A. K., Martin, M. M., Mills, C. B., & Clark-Gordon, C. V. (2022). Workplace bullying in academia: A conditional process model. *Management Communication Quarterly*, *36*(4), 664–687. http://doi.org/10.1177/08933189221103625

Hakan, K. O. Ç., & Kurtbaş, D. (2011). The relationship between mobbing the academics are exposed to and the organizational commitment: A study in the public and private universities. *International Journal of Academic Research in Accounting, Finance and Management Sciences*, *1*(2), 17.

Harrison, E., Fox, C., & Hulme, J. (2022). Development of a measure for assessing victimisation at UK universities. *Open Scholarship of Teaching and Learning*, *2*(1), 22–47. https://doi.org/10.56230/osotl.7

Heffernan, T., & Bosetti, L. (2023). University bullying and incivility towards faculty deans. *International Journal of Leadership in Education*, *26*(4), 604–623. https://doi.org/10.1080/13603124.2020.1850870

Henning, M. A., Zhou, C., Adams, P., Moir, F., Hobson, J., Hallett, C., & Webster, C. S. (2017). Workplace harassment among staff in higher education: A systematic review. *Asia Pacific Education Review*, *18*, 521–539. https://doi.org/10.1007/s12564-017-9499-0

Higgins, P. (2024). "I don't even recognize myself anymore": An autoethnography of workplace bullying in higher education. *Power and Education*, *16*(1), 29–41. https://doi.org/10.1177/17577438231163041

Hodgins, M., Kane, R., Itzkovich, Y., & Fahie, D. (2024). Workplace bullying and harassment in higher education institutions: A scoping review. *International Journal of Environmental Research and Public Health*, *21*(9), 1173. https://doi.org/10.3390/ijerph21091173

Hodgins, M., & Mannix McNamara, P. (2017). Bullying and incivility in higher education workplaces: Micropolitics and the abuse of power. *Qualitative Research in Organizations and Management*, *12*(3), 190–206. https://doi.org/10.1108/QROM-03-2017-1508

Hollis, L. P. (2015). Bully university? The cost of workplace bullying and employee disengagement in American higher education. *SAGE Open*, *5*(2), 1–11. https://doi.org/10.1177/2158244015589997

Hollis, L. P. (2017). This is why they leave you: Workplace bullying and insight to junior faculty departure. *British Journal of Education*, *5*(10), 1–7.

Hubert, A. B., & van Veldhoven, M. (2001). Risk sectors for undesirable behaviour and mobbing. *European Journal of Work and Organizational Psychology*, *10*(4), 415–424. https://doi.org/10.1080/13594320143000799

Keashly, L. (2021). Workplace bullying, mobbing and harassment in academe: Faculty experience. In P. D'Cruz, E. Noronha, L. Keashly, S. Tye-Williams (Eds.), *Special topics and particular occupations, professions and sectors. Handbooks of workplace bullying, emotional abuse and harassment* (vol 4) (pp. 221–298). Springer

Keashly, L., & Neuman, J. H. (2010). Faculty experiences with bullying in higher education: Causes, consequences, and management. *Administrative Theory & Praxis*, *32*(1), 48–70. https://doi.org/10.2753/ATP1084-1806320103

Lampman, C., Phelps, A., Bancroft, S., & Beneke, M. (2009). Contrapower harassment in academia: A survey of faculty experience with student incivility, bullying, and sexual attention. *Sex Roles*, *60*, 331–346. https://doi.org/10.1007/s11199-008-9560-x

LaSala, K. B., & Wilson, V., & Sprunk, E. (2016). Nursing academic administrators' lived experiences with incivility and bullying from faculty: Consequences and outcomes demanding action. *Nurse Educator*, *41*(3), 120–124. https://doi.org/10.1097/NNE.0000000000000234

Lewis D. (2004). Bulling at work: The impact of shame among university and college lecturers. *British Journal of Guidance & Counselling*, *32*(3), 281–299. https://doi.org/10.1080/03069880410001723521

Leymann, H. (1996). The content and development of mobbing at work. *European Journal of Work and Organisational Psychology*, *5*(2), 165–184. https://doi.org/10.1080/13594329608414853

Macfarlane, J. (2020). How a good idea became a bad idea: Universities and the use of non-disclosure agreements in terminations for sexual misconduct. *Cardozo Journal of Conflict Resolution*, *21*(2), 361–380.

Mahmoudi, M. (2021). Academic bullying: How to be an ally. *Science*, *373*(6558), 974. https://doi.org/10.1126/science.abl7492

Mahmoudi, M. (2023a). Academic bullying slows the evolution of science. *Nature Reviews Materials*, *8*(5), 301–303. https://doi.org/10.1038/s41578-023-00549-x

Mahmoudi, M. (2023b). Tit for tat: An unacknowledged institutional response to targets of academic bullying and harassment. *Molecular Pharmaceutics*, *20*(9), 4339–4341. https://doi.org/10.1021/acs.molpharmaceut.3c00702

Mahmoudi, M., & Keashly, L. (2021). Filling the space: A framework for coordinated global actions to diminish academic bullying. *Angewandte Chemie*, *133*(7), 3378–3384. https://doi.org/10.1002/ange.202009270

May, A., & Tenzek, K. E. (2018). Bullying in the academy: Understanding the student bully and the targeted 'stupid, fat, mother fucker' professor. *Teaching in Higher Education*, *23*(3), 275–290. https://doi.org/10.1080/13562517.2017.1379482.

Mazzone, A., Karakolidis, A., Pitsia, V., Freeney, Y., & O'Higgins Norman, J. (2024). Witnessing bullying at work: Employee silence in higher education institutions. *Higher Education Quarterly*, *78*(3), 640–655. https://doi.org/10.1111/hequ.12472

McKay, R., Arnold, D. H., Fratzl, J., & Thomas, R. (2008). Workplace bullying in academia: A Canadian study. *Employee responsibilities and rights Journal*, *20*, 77–100. https://doi.org/10.1007/s10672-008-9073-3

Meriläinen, M., Käyhkö, K., Kõiv, K., & Sinkkonen, H. M. (2019). Academic bullying among faculty personnel in Estonia and Finland. *Journal of Higher Education Policy and Management*, *41*(3), 241–261. https://doi.org/10.1080/1360080X.2019.1591678

Meriläinen, M., & Kõiv, K. (2019). Theoretical dimensions of bullying and inappropriate behaviour among faculty members. *Scandinavian Journal of Educational Research*, *63*(3), 378–392. https://doi.org/10.1080/00313831.2017.1376349

Meriläinen, M., Sinkkonen, H. M., Puhakka, H., & Käyhkö, K. (2016). Bullying and inappropriate behaviour among faculty personnel. *Policy Futures in Education*, *14*(6), 617–634. https://doi.org/10.1177/1478210316639417

Mhaka-Mutepfa, M., & Rampa, S. (2024). Workplace bullying and mobbing: Autoethnography and meaning-making in the face of adversity in academia. *International Journal of Qualitative Studies in Education*, *37*(1), 1–18. https://doi.org/10.1080/09518398.2021.1991028

Migliaccio, T., Rivas, A., Rivas, B., & Stark, R. (2024). Bullying within academia: A cultural and structural analysis. *Learning, Culture and Social Interaction*, *44*, 100783. https://doi.org/10.1016/j.lcsi.2023.100783

Moss, S., Täuber, S., Sharifi, S., & Mahmoudi, M. (2022). The need for the development of discipline-specific approaches to address academic bullying. *eClinicalMedicine*, *50*, 101598. https://doi.org/10.1016/j.eclinm.2022.101598

Pagan, V. (2021). The murder of knowledge and the ghosts that remain: Non-disclosure agreements and their effects. *Culture and Organization*, *27*(4), 302–317. https://doi.org/10.1080/14759551.2021.1907389

Paull, M., Omari, M., & Standen, P. (2012). When is a bystander not a bystander? A typology of the roles of bystanders in workplace bullying. *Asia Pacific Journal of Human Resources*, *50*(3), 351–366. https://doi.org/10.1111/j.1744-7941.2012.00027.x.

Pheko, M. M. (2018). Autoethnography and cognitive adaptation: Two powerful buffers against the negative consequences of workplace bullying and academic mobbing.

International Journal of Qualitative Studies on Health and Well-being, *13*(1), 1459134. https://doi.org/10.1080/17482631.2018.1459134

Rockett, P., Fan, S. K., Dwyer, R. J., & Foy, T. (2017). A human resource management perspective of workplace bullying. *Journal of Aggression, Conflict and Peace Research*, *9*(2), 116–127. https://doi.org/10.1108/JACPR-11-2016-0262

Rojas-Solís, J. L., García-Ramírez, B. E. B., & Hernández-Corona, M. E. (2019). Mobbing on university staff: A systematic review. *Journal of Educational Psychology-Propositos y Representaciones*, *7*(3), 369–383. http://dx.doi.org/10.20511/pyr2019.v7n3.369

Sambrook, S. (2025). An organisational autoethnography of learning to manage academic workplace bullying through micro-resistance and activism. *Management Learning*, 56(4), 684–702. https://doi.org/10.1177/13505076241289174

Smith, F. L. M., & Coel, C. R. (2018). Workplace bullying policies, higher education and the First Amendment: Building bridges not walls. *First Amendment Studies*, *52*(1–2), 96–111. https://doi.org/10.1080/21689725.2018.1495094

Smith, N., & Fredricks-Lowman, I. (2020). Conflict in the workplace: A 10-year review of toxic leadership in Higher Education. *International Journal of Leadership in Education*, *23*(5), 538–551. https://doi.org/10.1080/13603124.2019.1591512

Sprague, J., & Massoni, K. (2005). Student evaluations and gendered expectations: What we can't count can hurt us. *Sex Roles*, *53*(11–12), 779–793. https://doi.org/10.1007/s11199-005-8292-4

Thomas, M. (2005). Bullying among support staff in a higher education institution. *Health Education*, *105*(4), 273–288. https://doi.org/10.1108/09654280510602499

Tight, M. (2023). Bullying in higher education: An endemic problem? *Tertiary Education and Management*, *29*(2), 123–137. https://doi.org/10.1007/s11233-023-09124-z

Van de Vliert, E., Einarsen, S., & Nielsen, M. B. (2013). Are national levels of employee harassment cultural covariations of climato-economic conditions? *Work & Stress*, *27*(1), 106–122. https://doi.org/10.1080/02678373.2013.760901

Vartia, M. A. L. (2001). Consequences of workplace bullying with respect to the well-being of its targets and the observers of bullying. *Scandinavian Journal of Work, Environment & Health*, *27*(1), 63–69. https://doi.org/10.5271/sjweh.588

White, S. J. (2010). Upward harassment: Harassment of academics in post-1992 English universities (Unpublished PhD Thesis). University of Wales, Cardiff.

Wieland, D., & Beitz, J. M. (2015). Resilience to social bullying in academia: A phenomenological study. *Nurse Educator*, *40*(6), 289–293. https://doi.org/10.1097/NNE.0000000000000169

Williams, B., King, C., Boyle, M., Clegg, L., Devenish, S., Kamphuis, C., King, J., & Reid, D. (2022). Contrapower harassment in paramedicine: Experiences of academic staff in Australian universities. *Australasian Journal of Paramedicine*, *19*, 1–15. https://doi.org/10.33151/ajp.19.1006

Yildiz, S. M. (2020). A new mobbing scale for academicians (MS-A) in higher education institutions. *African Educational Research Journal*, *8*(4), 831–840. https://doi.org/10.30918/AERJ.84.20.170

Zabrodska, K., & Kveton, P. (2013). Prevalence and forms of workplace bullying among university employees. *Employee Responsibilities and Rights Journal*, *25*, 89–108. https://doi.org/10.1007/s10672-012-9210-x

Zawadzki, M., & Jensen, T. (2020). Bullying and the neoliberal university: A co-authored autoethnography. *Management Learning*, *51*(4), 398–413. https://doi.org/10.1177/1350507620920532

Chapter 8

Sexual Harassment and Violence

In recent years, there has been greater acknowledgement of the incidence and impact of sexual harassment and sexual violence in higher education. Whilst greater recognition of such issues is important, discussion often reflects scrutiny from the media rather than proactive action from the higher education institutions themselves. For example, in one analysis of over 200 academic sexual misconduct cases naming a university employee as the alleged perpetrator, Eckert et al. (2024) revealed that almost 70% of cases were first publicly reported by local news media or student-led media. Though cases were sometimes discussed in the context of broader structural and social issues contributing to the prevalence of sexual misconduct, other cases were treated as isolated incidents, minimising the need for changes to education policy and practice. The current chapter discusses sexual harassment and violence in the context of higher education and recognises the importance of bystander behaviour and intervention. Acknowledging broader societal issues that impact the incidence and experience of sexual harassment and violence, the chapter discusses the MeToo and TimesUp movements and how these have impacted the higher education context.

The Incidence, Form, and Impact of Sexual Harassment and Violence

Sexual harassment and violence are common across the higher education sector (e.g., Agardh et al., 2022). Indeed, in their review of the literature, Bondestam and Lundqvist (2020) conclude that "*sexual harassment is an epidemic throughout global higher education systems*" (p. 397). Of course, a broad range of inappropriate sexual behaviours exists. For example, Karami et al. (2020) analysed over 2,000 personal experiences of sexual harassment in higher education, identifying five themes: Gender harassment, sex discrimination and harassment, unwanted sexual attention, sexual coercion, and retaliation. Unwanted sexual attention (e.g., unwanted touching, off-campus sexual advances, and grooming into "consensual" relationships) was especially evident, with over 50% of the topics identified assigned to this theme.

DOI: 10.4324/9781032639321-9

Gender harassment (e.g., inappropriate behaviour and sexist comments creating a hostile environment) was also prominent and featured in 14% of reports, followed by retaliation (e.g., threats against the victim-survivor for non-compliance or reporting the harassment) (7%), sexual coercion (5%), and sex discrimination (5%).

Sexual harassment can have a direct and immediate impact on academic performance. For example, in one experimental study, women participating in job interviews were asked either three sexual or non-sexual questions (e.g., "Do you have a boyfriend?" vs. "Do you have a best friend?"). Those exposed to the sexual questions were less fluent, gave lower-quality answers, and asked fewer relevant questions than those in the non-harassment condition (Woodzicka & LaFrance, 2005). In addition, harassment and violence have substantial long-term career consequences. For example, exposure to sexual harassment and gender discrimination influences medical students' choice of speciality and residency programme (Stratton et al., 2005). Of course, the impact of sexual violence and harassment is not confined to the workplace, and a substantial body of research indicates that those experiencing sexual harassment are more likely to report poor mental health and wellbeing (e.g., Chan et al., 2008; Pilgaard et al., 2025; Vargas et al., 2020). Clearly, this epidemic requires greater attention.

Discipline Example: Medical and Health Professions

Factors increasing the likelihood of sexual harassment in higher education include power dynamics, toxic academic masculinities, and a culture of silence (Bondestam & Lundqvist, 2020). There may, of course, be substantial variation in the incidence of sexual harassment and violence across subject disciplines and individual institutions. For example, harassment and violence may be especially prevalent in medicine and health-related subject disciplines for a range of reasons, including the presence of work placements which increase the range of potential perpetrators (e.g., professional colleagues, patients). For example, Vargas et al. (2020) investigated the prevalence of sexual harassment in one university medical school, reporting that 82.5% of women and 65.1% of men reported at least one incidence of sexual harassment in the previous year from staff, students, or faculty. In addition, 64.4% of women and 44.1% of men experienced harassment from patients or patients' families.

Subject content and strict hierarchical structures may also contribute to experiences of sexual harassment and willingness to formally report or disclose such behaviour. For example, Wear and Aultman (2005) report that medical students are subjected to sexualised comments directed at their own or patients' bodies. Students rarely reported the harassment, believing that no action would be taken against the perpetrator and that they could be subject to retaliation (e.g., poor references or grades). Instead, students developed other coping strategies to deal with the harassment, often accepting that it was part of the culture. Reflecting the common reluctance to report experiences of sexual harassment, the authors conclude that sexual harassment policy and practice should focus on the institutional environment rather than individual decisions to report the harassment.

Student Experiences of Sexual Harassment and Violence

Whilst this book focuses on the experiences of those employed in the higher education sector, it is important to acknowledge the sexual harassment and violence experienced by students. Indeed, there are a number of large-scale studies documenting the sexual harassment and violence experienced by student populations (e.g., Wood et al., 2021). In 2010, the National Union of Students published Hidden Marks, the first report into women's experiences of harassment, stalking, violence, and sexual assault when enrolled in further or higher education across the United Kingdom. The report was informed by an online survey completed by 2,058 women between November 2009 and January 2010. All women were enrolled in further or higher education at the time of the survey; they were typically studying at a higher education institution (93%) and enrolled full-time (94%). The findings are stark.

Whilst the vast majority of women (97%) always or mostly felt safe on campus during the day, one in ten reported that they rarely or never felt safe visiting university or college buildings during the evening, reporting that they were worried about being approached, intimidated, threatened, or attacked. Sexual harassment and violence were common. More than two-thirds of women had been victims of one or more kinds of sexual harassment, and one in seven had experienced a serious sexual or physical assault whilst enrolled as a student.

Reflecting the difficulties that arise from the campus environment, 49% of those reporting personal experience of stalking revealed that the perpetrator was a student at the same institution. This pattern is not, of course, restricted to stalking. For example, women reported that 60% of serious sexual assaults were perpetrated by a student, and of the student perpetrators, 70% were enrolled at the same institution.

The report contains detailed case studies together with quotations from students describing their experience of sexual harassment or violence. For example, "*One lecturer joked about how to cover up spiking a drink with a rape drug, then later mentioned they had been reported for misogyny and how that couldn't be true*" (p. 12). In addition to detailing the incidence of sexual harassment and violence experienced by students, the report also documented low levels of reporting, both to the institution and the police. For example, 1% and 7% of students reported less serious physical violence to the institution or police, respectively, whilst only 4% and 10% of students reported serious sexual assault to the institution or police. Stalking was the only offence category where students were more likely to report the crime to the institution (21%) than to the police (13%). The report contains a number of recommendations made in response to the survey findings.

In higher education, "lad culture", which normalises misogynistic attitudes and behaviour, contributes to the prevalence and acceptability of sexual harassment and violence. In research commissioned by the National Union of Students to investigate lad culture on campus, Phipps and Young (2013) conducted interviews and focus groups with women enrolled at university. The researchers identified a number of important issues, including the widespread objectification of women and rape-supportive attitudes. This was particularly problematic for the social aspects of university life. As revealed by one interviewee,

> The boys in my halls used to sing a drinking song about rape, which obviously was just disgusting. I think there are a lot of jokes about women and a lot of 'innocent' groping that goes on, which actually serves to make you feel very embarrassed, nervous and uncomfortable.
>
> (p. 33)

The collective nature of the activity was especially important for normalising such attitudes and behaviour. Overall, two-thirds of the women contributing to interviews or focus groups discussed sexual harassment and violence, perceiving it to be a "normal" part of university life.

Universities UK (UUK) established a task force in 2015, which focused on violence against women, harassment, and hate crime. The subsequent "Changing the Culture" report (UUK, 2016a) states that "*The Taskforce believes that tackling violence against women, harassment and hate crime is crucial to ensuring the wellbeing of students. It therefore recommends that all university leaders afford it priority status and dedicate appropriate resources to tackling it*". (p. 31). A number of specific recommendations are made, such as adopting an institution-wide approach and ensuring that interventions are evidence-based. The report also contained a discussion of the 1994 Council for Vice-Chancellors and Principals (CVCP) Final Report of the Task Force on Student Disciplinary Procedures, commonly referred to as the Zellick guidelines. Issues presented by the guidelines include the recommendation that universities should not instigate disciplinary proceedings if the victim-survivor does not report the incident to police, where law enforcement does not prosecute, or where there is an acquittal. Formal review of the guidelines led to updated guidelines published by Universities UK in 2016 (UUK, 2016b) and updated with case studies in 2024 (UUK, 2024).

Further demonstrating a shift in awareness or willingness to address the issue of sexual harassment and violence experienced by students, the Office for Students published a new condition of registration for higher education providers in 2024 (in force in 2025). The condition requires providers to take steps to protect students from harassment and sexual misconduct and establish policies and procedures to deal with harassment and sexual misconduct. Importantly, the Office for Students also recognises the abuse of power inherent in personal relationships between university staff and students and recommends a ban on intimate personal relationships between staff and students. The use of non-disclosure agreements (NDAs) is also prohibited.

Indeed, the issue of staff-student relationships has previously been highlighted as an area of concern. In 2017, the National Union of Students Women's Campaign began to work with the 1752 Group (an organisation focused on ending staff sexual misconduct in higher education) to investigate staff-student relationships. They state that 41% of students reported at least one incident of sexualised behaviour from staff. Further, 16% of women and 7% of men had been touched by a staff member in a way that made them feel uncomfortable. It is important to note that in the majority of cases, sexual misconduct is perpetrated by academic staff who may have a substantial impact on the success and reputation of students (e.g., grading of assessments, reference letters, and extenuating circumstances decisions). Further, across the sector, there appears to be a lack of internal processes to deal with staff sexual misconduct (Bull & Rye, 2018).

Academic Experiences of Sexual Harassment and Violence

In 2015, the University and College Union (UCU) surveyed members (employed in further or higher education) across the United Kingdom. Respondents were typically employed in higher education (79%), full-time (74%), and on teaching or research contracts (81%). All except three of the respondents were women. The subsequent report (Griesbach, 2016) revealed that 54% of survey respondents had experienced sexual harassment at work. Of those experiencing harassment whilst working in higher education, harassment from a colleague was most common (70%), though a substantial number of respondents (24%) reported harassment from a student. Where the type of harassment was disclosed, unwelcome or derogatory comments about appearance were the most common form of harassment (57%), followed by leering or suggestive gestures and remarks (40%), physical contact (39%), and unwelcome sexual advances/demands for sexual favours (28%).

Where staff experience sexual harassment, this typically occurs in the context of routine university operations (Agardh et al., 2022). Griesbach (2016) also documents the impact of sexual harassment on university staff. The most commonly reported effects were an impact on relationships with colleagues (50%), irritability (42%), anxiety (42%), and low confidence or self-esteem (41%), though other consequences, including fear of going to work (17%), depression (11%), and time off work (5%), were also apparent. For those who raised concerns about the harassment, action had been taken in only 40% of cases. In 2020, UCU established a task group to address sexual violence in further and higher education. They reported that 39% of those responding had directly experienced, witnessed, or been a confidant to someone else experiencing sexual violence in the previous five years (Addington et al., 2021).

Echoing findings from the Griesbach (2016) report, Addington et al. (2021) demonstrate that staff experiencing sexual violence directly were most likely to report that the perpetrator was a colleague (49%), followed by a manager (18%) and line manager (10%), though 14% reported sexual violence perpetrated by a student. Violence was more likely to occur in the context of ongoing abuse (70%) than in an isolated incident. Their report also indicates that staff who are already marginalised or minoritised (e.g., precariously employed staff, postgraduate students, disabled staff, and LGBTQ+ staff) are at greater risk of sexual violence. For example, the incidence of sexual violence in the previous five years was 16% for disabled staff compared to 8% for non-disabled staff. The majority of those experiencing sexual violence (52%) did not report or complain about the violence to their employer. Such findings highlight the importance of equality, diversity, and inclusion initiatives intended to support marginalised groups.

Harassment of Academic Staff by Students

Much of the sexual harassment literature focuses on the extent to which those with greater formal or informal power (e.g., line manager or supervisor) may subject others to harassment. It is possible, however, for those with lesser apparent power to harass an individual with greater power, a behaviour referred to as contrapower harassment (Benson, 1984). According to one survey, 16% of academics experience sexual harassment from a student (DeSouza, 2011). Harassment reported in the survey included sexist comments or jokes, sexual gestures or sexualised body language, staring, asking the academic on a date, displaying sexual material, and attempts to establish a sexual relationship. For example, "*I've noticed female students staring at my groin region while I'm teaching*" (p. 173) and "*White male student asked me out on a date twice, did not take 'no' the first time*" (p. 173).

In one powerful account, Cantrell (2018) discusses her experience of sexual harassment (as an academic) by students. The harassment included being propositioned for sex, stalking (online and offline) to the extent that she changed her phone number, inappropriate comments in course evaluations, and receiving a poem for assessment in a creative writing class describing the gang-rape of a teacher with the same name. Such findings are reinforced by data obtained from student populations. In their exploration of contrapower sexual harassment in academia, DeSouza and Fansler (2003) obtained survey data from both students and academics. A substantial number of students (31.6%) reported sexually harassing academics on at least one occasion, with such behaviour more common in male compared to female students.

Important sex differences often occur. For example, research suggests that male faculty report more sexual attention from students than their female colleagues, though female faculty perceive this attention to be more upsetting and as having a more negative impact on their health and professional lives (Lampman et al., 2009). Further, though female faculty are most likely to report harassment perpetrated by colleagues, male faculty are more likely to report harassing behaviour perpetrated by students (McKinney, 1990), suggesting that male and female victim-survivors may have different motivations for reporting their experiences of harassment. Additional research is required to explore the complex relationships between gender and the experiences of sexual harassment and violence perpetration and victimisation.

Education research, practice, and policy have traditionally focused on in-person sexual harassment and violence. It is important, however, to recognise and address the potential for online abuse, especially where comments are publicly available. In such shared or entirely public forums, even if the perpetrator posts an abusive comment on only one occasion, shares or comments from other users can perpetuate and expand the abuse. Sites such as RateMyProfessor allow students to post publicly available comments about teaching staff, and in earlier versions of the site, students were able to assign a "chilli pepper" to academics, indicating their perceived level of "hotness". Such reviews enable students to engage in bullying, mobbing, and sexual harassment (McKay et al., 2020). In addition to the personal distress this may cause to academics, this type of online abuse may have important ramifications for their academic careers, as, despite clear biases in RateMyProfessor ratings, this information may be used to inform hiring or progression decisions (Murray & Zdravkovic, 2016).

The Reporting of Sexual Harassment and Violence

Those subjected to sexual harassment are unlikely to report their experience (Foster & Fullagar, 2018). For example, Kirkner, Lorenz, and Mazar (2022) demonstrate that approximately 40% of staff and faculty recruited from North American universities did not report their harassment or disclose it informally. Perhaps, reflecting the perceived safety of the workplace environment, those who did informally disclose typically chose to do so with those outside the institution. A range of factors may contribute to the "culture of silence" that exists in academia (Östergren et al., 2025). For example, institutional norms that portray academics as honourable and beyond reproach can discourage staff from reporting sexual harassment (Mousa & Abdelgaffar, 2022). As one participant stated,

> Who will believe me if I accuse a male professor of sexually harassing me. The Egyptian society considers university professors as angels, so simply accusing a male professor of wrongdoing means facing tough action from the university and offensive reaction from the society.
>
> (p. 918)

Most discussions of sexual harassment disclosure and reporting focus on victim-survivor perspectives. In one exception, Scott and Martin (2006) identify the tactics used by perpetrators to reduce the level of "backfire" experienced (e.g., support for the victim-survivor). These tactics include (1) covering up the action (e.g., attempting to ensure information is not publicly available), (2) devaluing the target (e.g., questioning the credibility or morality of the victim-survivor), (3) reinterpreting events (e.g., providing alternative explanations for behaviour), (4) using official channels to give the appearance of justice (e.g., using grievance procedures that may focus on procedural issues or technicalities rather than the primary claim), and (5) intimidating or bribing targets, witnesses, or other relevant actors (e.g., promising promotion in return for compliance). Indeed, fear of reprisals and retaliation may be a significant barrier to reporting. To some extent, this retaliation may be covert in nature (e.g., negative comments during a grant or promotion review) (Binder et al., 2018). Therefore, victim-survivors may be unaware of the full impact of this on their careers and be unable to address this issue.

Of course, whilst it is important to address the actions of individual perpetrators (both with respect to the initial harassment and subsequent cover-up), it is also essential that actions taken by universities in response to sexual harassment and violence are reviewed. For example, as many employees are reluctant to formally report harassment, organisations may claim that victim-survivors failed to engage with appropriate policies and support in order to minimise institutional culpability. Similarly, universities may deter student engagement with law enforcement, prioritising the reputation of the institution over safeguarding (Besley, Jackson, & Peters, 2022). As a consequence, much harassment is not adequately investigated or addressed. Further, the widespread use of non-disclosure agreements or threats of expulsion may prevent victim-survivors from publicly discussing their experiences (Croxford, 2020), making these institutions complicit in the abusive behaviour. Indeed, staff are often dissatisfied or very dissatisfied with the outcome after reporting harassment or violence (Clancy et al., 2014).

Bystander Behaviour and Intervention

Bystanders (i.e., those witnessing or becoming aware of sexual harassment and violence) have an important role in supporting victim-survivors and addressing inappropriate behaviour. They may become important allies, championing awareness of harassment (e.g., awareness training workshops) and procedural change (e.g., creating codes of conduct) (Veer et al., 2021). Alternatively, they may become complicit in the violence, further silencing the voices of victim-survivors. The reluctance of many potential allies to advocate for victim-survivors or become active in this area may reflect a fear of being penalised for "bringing the university into disrepute" by publicising the existence of such behaviour. Indeed, academics engaged in this work have experienced a range of negative consequences, including marginalisation, denial of tenure, and dismissal. Other barriers to bystander intervention include the extent to which harassment or the specific incident is perceived as a serious problem (Kania & Cale, 2021; Lyons et al., 2022).

Research demonstrates the impact of failure to act. For example, Fernando and Prasad (2019) examined the role of third-party actors (such as line managers or members of the human resources department). Experiences of sexual harassment were often minimised (e.g., the behaviour did not constitute harassment) or an alternative version of events was presented (e.g., the victim-survivor encouraged inappropriate behaviour), and it was suggested that complaints could only be made if the issue was "significant and uncommon". Women were also encouraged to "move on" from the experience and "trust in the system" (e.g., encouraged to believe that if a perpetrator had been spoken to about their behaviour, there would no longer be an issue). Those continuing to raise the issue were perceived (and treated) as troublemakers and often avoided. Victim-survivors were aware of the impact that these reputational issues could have on their careers. Findings demonstrate the way in which structural and cultural factors contribute to the incidence of sexual harassment and an environment that actively discourages reporting.

Bystander-Focused Education and Intervention Programmes

Recognising the incidence and impact of sexual harassment and violence across the higher education sector, a range of education and intervention programmes have been developed. It is important to recognise, however, that the quality of sexual harassment policies and training varies (Bainbridge, Perry, & Kulik, 2018; Getgrix & Farmer, 2023), and employers may implement inadequate training (e.g., brief videos) rather than fully engage with the subject area. It is important that training includes definitions of sexual harassment and violence, highlights the (individual and organisational) consequences of such behaviour, and provides a clear overview of organisation policy, including the responsibilities of the employer and employee. Evaluation of training programmes must take place and should ensure that employees understand the training material and feel confident responding to inappropriate behaviour.

Institutions introducing education and training programmes, including those focused on bystander intervention, must ensure that these are theory- and evidence-based, informed by victim-survivor experiences, and sensitive to community and cultural norms (Crusto, Hooper, & Arora, 2024). A range of intervention strategies should be covered. For example, intervention training often includes the "5 D's": Direct intervention (e.g., challenging inappropriate comments), Distraction (e.g., interrupting the harassment), Debriefing (e.g., supporting victim-survivors after the harassment has taken place), Documentation (e.g., recording inappropriate behaviour), and Delegation (e.g., contacting a line manager). Examples of specific intervention programmes are also available, including Green Dot (Coker et al., 2015) and One Act (Alegria-Flores et al., 2017), though such training programmes often focus on student behaviour rather than the institution more broadly.

Previous research suggests that bystander intervention programmes can improve intentions to intervene and proactive bystander behaviour (Senn & Forrest, 2016), though there is the potential for unintended consequences such as reinforcement of gender stereotypes (Tinkler, 2013). Bystander training can be delivered both in person and online. Considering the relative benefits of in-person or online training, Preusser, Bartels, and Nordstrom (2011) conclude that both are received positively by participants and increase learning in university employees. It is, of course, important to recognise the impact of witnessing sexual harassment and violence on bystanders. For example, bystanders may experience distress (Witte et al., 2017), and such experiences can impact their own responses to unwanted sexual attention (Hitlan, Schneider, & Walsh, 2006). Bystanders must, therefore, themselves be provided with support.

MeToo and TimesUp in Higher Education

Broader societal discussions of sexual harassment and violence influence experiences of such behaviour in the higher education sector. In recent years, MeToo and TimesUp have arguably been the most important social movements in this area. The original Me Too campaign was founded in 2006 by Tarana Burke in order to support women and girls of colour who had experienced sexual violence. After the actress Alyssa Milano tweeted, "If all the women who have been sexually harassed or assaulted wrote 'Me Too' as a status, we might give people a sense of the magnitude of the problem", in October 2017, #MeToo began trending on social media. Within 24 hours, over 12 million #MeToo posts were written, responded to, or shared on Facebook (Lawton, 2017). The #MeToo movement highlighted the extent to which sexual harassment and violence exist in society and the extent to which victim-survivors are often silenced or mistreated. Whilst #MeToo focused on solidarity and empowerment, #TimesUp (established following the success of the #MeToo movement) sought to address systemic and structural issues that contribute to sexual harassment and violence. Research indicates that these movements have encouraged a greater understanding of harassment and violence, both generally and in specific contexts such as higher education (Prothero & Tadajewski, 2021).

Perhaps unsurprisingly, research indicates that the sexist attitudes held by university employees (e.g., denial that sexism and gender discrimination remain) predict their attitudes towards the #MeToo movement (Skewes et al., 2021). Of the open-ended comments about the movement that could be categorised as positive, ambivalent, or negative, 44% of comments were entirely positive, considering the movement to be important and necessary.

Positive comments included "*I think it is a necessary wake-up call, and hopefully it will lead to more fundamental changes in the way our society treats women*" (p. 129). Ambivalent comments (38.5% of classifiable posts) conveyed both positive and negative feelings about the movement. When negative attitudes towards the #MeToo movement were analysed (17.6% of those classifiable), two themes were identified. These were the delegitimisation of the purposes of the movement and the perception that the rights of potential sexual perpetrators were more important than the rights of potential victims. For example, "*…the movement is open to abuse by disgruntled and sometimes dishonest women who seek retaliation*" (pp. 129–130).

More controversial activism that followed the #MeToo and #TimesUp movements includes the use of social media to publicise the names and university affiliations of alleged perpetrators. For example, students at Rhodes University, Cape Town, published the names of alleged rapists (known as the RU Reference List). In response, the university principal stated that they would not expel the alleged rapists because due process had not been followed (McCall, 2019). Similarly, a crowd-sourced list of alleged sexual harassers was shared online (referred to as the List of Sexual Harassers in Academia, or LoSHA) (Bruss, 2019). The publication of such lists has been controversial. Whilst some have welcomed the naming of individuals who may pose a risk to staff and students, others highlight the need for due process and argue that focusing on individuals draws attention away from the structural issues that enable such behaviour to occur without consequence (Dey, 2020).

Recommendations

Institutions should,

- Establish clear codes of conduct covering both staff and student online and offline behaviour. Specific guidance should be provided to cover fieldwork and placements. Where events are hosted on campus (e.g., professional body conferences), ensure that organisers disseminate their own codes of professional conduct and ethics.
- Publicise procedures for the formal reporting of sexual harassment and violence. Recognise victim-survivor concerns relating to the reporting of sexual harassment and violence, ensuring that such behaviour can be reported anonymously if preferred. Ensure those dealing with victim-survivors understand the range of inappropriate behaviours that occur, including those that do not conform to stereotyped notions of sexual harassment and violence (e.g., contrapower harassment).
- Provide support for victim-survivors of sexual harassment and violence, and ensure that such support is not dependent on formal reporting. Ensure support is sensitive to the context in which harassment and violence occur.
- Provide mandatory education and training specific to sexual harassment and violence for all staff and students. Sessions should include the range of

behaviours that constitute sexual harassment and violence, and the impact of these on victim-survivors. Training should also provide guidance for safe and effective bystander intervention. Ensure all training is evidence-based, informed by victim-survivor experiences, and specific to the higher education sector.

- Regularly assess the prevalence, form, and impact of sexual harassment and violence that occurs without formal disclosure (e.g., through an anonymous survey). Identify members of the university community (e.g., doctoral students) most at risk. Regularly assess satisfaction with formal reporting procedures (including action taken) and the support provided.

Subject in Focus 1: The Importance of Intersectionality

As discussed throughout this book, staff and students with protected characteristics are at greater risk of mistreatment. It is also important to acknowledge the impact of intersectionality. For example, the specific experience of being a racially minoritised woman that is not captured when considering the impact of gender or ethnicity in isolation. Bailey (2021) uses the term "misogynoir" to refer to the violence experienced by women as a consequence of both racial and gender marginalization and argues that this misogynoir both increases the likelihood that Black women will experience sexual violence and legitimizes the actions of the perpetrator. Further exacerbating these issues, Black women have often been excluded from discussions of sexual harassment and violence (Brown, 2019; Crenshaw, 1991).

The importance of intersectionality extends to impact of sexual harassment and violence (Klein & Martin, 2021; Woods, Buchanan, & Settles, 2009) and the treatment of victim-survivors (Kelley, 2023). For example, Wallace et al. (2024) uses the concept of the "(un)victim" to explore the way in which the experiences of Black women are delegitimized; arguing that they are denied the status and legitimacy of victimhood. In part this reflects stereotypes of hypersexualized Black women and racial injustice/systemic barriers to formal reporting and help-seeking (Zounlome et al., 2019). Despite the importance of intersectionality in understanding and addressing experiences of sexual harassment and violence, academic practice and policy often fail to address intersectionality (Calafell, 2014). Guidance has, however, been created to support an intersectional approach to training on sexual harassment and violence. For example, Page et al. (2019) provides support for training facilitators wishing to develop an intersectional approach, with particular emphasis on bystander intervention and responses to disclosure of violence.

Subject in Focus 2: The EmilyTest

The EmilyTest (EmilyTest, 2021a) is a gender-based violence Charter for colleges and universities, originally founded in Scotland. The Charter was developed by Fiona Drouet, in honour of her daughter Emily who died by suicide following a campaign of physical, psychological, and sexual violence perpetrated by her boyfriend, a fellow student (see Drouet & Gerrard-Abbott, 2022 for a detailed account of the case). It is based on the principle that there were a range of missed opportunities to save Emily and aims to ensure no other student has the same experience, asking "Would your institution have saved Emily's life?"

The Charter was developed between 2020 and 2021, following research and collaboration with students, higher education staff, gender-based violence professionals, and organisations focused on minoritised or marginalised groups (e.g., disabled students) (EmilyTest, 2021b). The Charter recognises the aspects of gender-based violence specific to education and the manner in which these issues impact on victim-survivors. For example, where students study, live, and socialise with the same network of people, opportunities for surveillance and bullying increase as there be may few opportunities for victim-survivors to distance themselves from a perpetrator (Drouet & Gerrard-Abbott, 2023). The Charter, initially introduced in Scotland and since expanded to England and Wales, sets minimum standards for prevention, intervention, and support in relation to gender-based violence in higher education. EmilyTest also provides a range of training. These include the (1) L.I.S.T.E.N. Risk Assessment Training, (2) Aware and Empowered Educational Programme, and (3) Tailored Training Sessions. For example, the L.I.S.T.E.N. programme has been created to support those working in universities, especially in front line positions, to respond to students disclosing gender-based violence.

Indeed, sexual harassment and violence have received greater attention across the higher education sector in recent years, with a range of guidance now available. In January 2021 only 9 of 133 universities in the United Kingdom had a specific domestic abuse policy. An International Expert Advisory Committee, funded by Research England, produced the first domestic abuse policy guidance for UK Universities. The policy guidance (Khan, 2021) was endorsed by a range of national organisations, including the Office for Students, Universities UK, Women's Aid and SafeLives, and the Domestic Abuse Commissioner for England and Wales. A subsequent review (Khan et al., 2023) indicated that 58% of universities in the United Kingdom were aware of and had read the guidance. Of these 37% had used the guidance to create new or update existing policy, 29% had used the guidance to create new training, 39% had used the guidance to issue domestic abuse communication.

References

Addington, C., Sundari, A., Baars, V., Day, K., Domoney-Lyttle, Z., Downes, J., … & Grady, J. (2021). Eradicating sexual violence in tertiary education: A report from UCU's sexual violence task group. Retrieved from: https://eprints.whiterose.ac.uk/id/eprint/219414/1/UCU_sexual_violence_task_group_report_20211220.pdf

Agardh, A., Priebe, G., Emmelin, M., Palmieri, J., Andersson, U., & Östergren, P. O. (2022). Sexual harassment among employees and students at a large Swedish university: Who are exposed, to what, by whom and where: A cross-sectional prevalence study. *BMC Public Health*, *22*, 2240. https://doi.org/10.1186/s12889-022-14502-0

Alegría-Flores, K., Raker, K., Pleasants, R. K., Weaver, M. A., & Weinberger, M. (2017). Preventing interpersonal violence on college campuses: The effect of one act training on bystander intervention. *Journal of Interpersonal Violence*, *32*(7), 1103–1126. https://doi.org/10.1177/0886260515587666

Bailey, M. (2021). *Misogynoir transformed: Black women's digital resistance*. New York University Press.

Bainbridge, H. T. J., Perry, E. L., & Kulik, C. T. (2018). Sexual harassment training: Explaining differences in Australian and US approaches. *Asia Pacific Journal of Human Resources*, *56*(1), 124–147. https://doi.org/10.1111/1744-7941.12169

Benson, K. A. (1984). Comments on Crocker's "An analysis of university definitions of sexual harassment". *Signs*, *9*(3), 516–519.

Besley, T., Jackson, L., & Peters, M. A. (2022) Named or nameless: University ethics, confidentiality and sexual harassment. *Educational Philosophy and Theory*, *54*(14), 2422–2433. https://doi.org/10.1080/00131857.2021.1952865

Binder, R., Garcia, P., Johnson, B., & Fuentes-Afflick, E. (2018). Sexual harassment in medical schools: The challenge of covert retaliation as a barrier to reporting. *Academic Medicine*, *93*(12), 1770–1773. https://doi.org/10.1097/ACM.0000000000002302

Bondestam, F., & Lundqvist, M. (2020). Sexual harassment in higher education: A systematic review. *European Journal of Higher Education*, *10*(4), 397–419. https://doi.org/10.1080/21568235.2020.1729833

Brown, N. E. (2019). Mentoring, sexual harassment, and black women academics. *Journal of Women, Politics & Policy*, *40*(1), 166–173. https://doi.org/10.1080/1554477X.2019.1565455.

Bruss, S. M. D. (2019). Naming and shaming or 'speaking truth to power'? On the ambivalences of the Indian 'list of sexual harassers in academia' (LoSHA). *Ephemera*, *19*(4), 721–743.

Bull, A., & Rye, R. (2018). *Institutional responses to staff sexual misconduct in UK higher education*. The 1752 Group & University of Portsmouth.

Calafell, B. M. (2014). "Did it happen because of your race or sex?": University sexual harassment policies and the move against intersectionality. *Frontiers: A Journal of Women Studies*, *35*(3), 75–95. https://doi.org/10.5250/fronjwomestud.35.3.0075

Cantrell, K. (August 23rd, 2018). #MeToo: Sexual harassment by students can no longer be ignored. *Times Higher Education*. Retrieved from: https://www.timeshighereducation.com/features/metoo-sexual-harassment-students-can-no-longer-be-ignored

Chan, D. K., Chow, S. Y., Lam, C. B., & Cheung, S. F. (2008). Examining the job-related, psychological, and physical outcomes of workplace sexual harassment: A meta-analytic review. *Psychology of Women*, *32*(4), 362–376. https://doi.org/10.1111/j.1471-6402.2008.00451.x

Clancy, K. B. H., Nelson, R. G., Rutherford, J. N., & Hinde, K. (2014). Survey of Academic Field Experiences (SAFE): Trainees report harassment and assault. *PLoS One*, *9*(7), e102172. https://doi.org/10.1371/journal.pone.0102172

Coker, A. L., Fisher, B. S., Bush, H. M., Swan, S. C., Williams, C. M., Clear, E. R., & DeGue, S. (2015). Evaluation of the Green Dot bystander intervention to reduce interpersonal violence among college students across three campuses. *Violence Against Women*, *21*(12), 1507–1527. https://doi.org/10.1177/1077801214545284

Crenshaw, K. (1991). Mapping the margins: Intersectionality, identity politics, and violence against women of color. *Stanford Law Review*, *43*(6), 1241–1299. https://doi.org/10.2307/1229039

Croxford, R. (February 12th, 2020). Sexual assault claims 'gagged' by UK universities. *BBC News*. Retrieved from: https://www.bbc.com/news/uk-51447615

Crusto, C. A., Hooper, L. M., & Arora, I. S. (2024). Preventing sexual harassment in higher education: A framework for prevention science program development. *Journal of Prevention*, *45*(4), 501–520. https://doi.org/10.1007/s10935-024-00780-4

DeSouza, E. (2011). Frequency rates and correlates of contrapower harassment in higher education. *Journal of Interpersonal Violence*, *26*(1), 158–188. https://doi.org/10.1177/0886260510362878

DeSouza, E., & Fansler, A. G. (2003). Contrapower sexual harassment: A survey of students and faculty members. *Sex Roles*, *48*(11–12), 529–542. https://doi.org/10.1023/A:1023527329364

Dey, A. (2020). 'Me Too' and the 'list': Power dynamics, shame, and accountability in Indian academia. *IDS Bulletin*, *51*(2), 63–79.

Drouet, F., & Gerrard-Abbott, P. (2022). EmilyTest: From tragedy to change. In C. J. Humphreys and G. J. Towl (Eds.). *Stopping gender-based violence in higher education* (pp. 151–170). Routledge.

Drouet, F., & Gerrard-Abbott, P. (2023). The EmilyTest: The education sector in crisis. In M. Mellins, R. Wheatley, and C. Flowers (Eds.). *Young people, stalking awareness and domestic abuse* (pp. 225–251). Springer.

Eckert, S., Metzger-Riftkin, J., Albrehi, F., Akhther, N., Aniapam, Z., & Steiner, L. (2024). #MeToo academia: News coverage of sexual misconduct at U.S. Universities. *Journalism Practice*, *18*(5), 1329–1348. https://doi.org/10.1080/17512786.2022.2077807

EmilyTest (2021a). *Gender-based violence (GBV) Charter for universities and colleges*. Retrieved from: https://emilytest.co.uk/

EmilyTest (2021b). *Gender-based violence (GBV) charter research report*. Retrieved from: https://emilytest.co.uk/

Fernando, D., & Prasad, A. (2019). Sex-based harassment and organizational silencing: How women are led to reluctant acquiescence in academia. *Human Relations*, *72*(10), 1565–1594. https://doi.org/10.1177/0018726718809164

Foster, P. J., & Fullagar, C. J. (2018). Why don't we report sexual harassment? An application of the Theory of Planned Behaviour. *Basic and Applied Social Psychology*, *40*(3), 148–160. https://doi.org/10.1080/01973533.2018.1449747

Getgrix, E., & Farmer, C. (2023). Heteronormative assumptions and expectations of sexual violence: Language and inclusivity within sexual violence policy in Australian universities. *Sexuality Research and Social Policy*, *20*, 725–750. https://doi.org/10.1007/s13178-022-00718-7

Griesbach, D. (2016). *Findings from a survey of University and College Union female members on the subject of sexual harassment in the workplace*. University and College Union. Retrieved from: https://policycommons.net/artifacts/2675441/findings-from-a-survey-of-university-and-college-union-female-members-on-the/3698554/

Hitlan, R. T., Schneider, K. T., & Walsh, B. M. (2006). Upsetting behavior: Reactions to personal and bystander sexual harassment experiences. *Sex Roles*, *55*, 187–195. https://doi.org/10.1007/s11199-006-9072-5

Kania, R., & Cale, J. (2021). Preventing sexual violence through bystander intervention: Attitudes, behaviors, missed opportunities, and barriers to intervention among Australian university students. *Journal of Interpersonal Violence*, *36*(5-6), 2816–2840. https://doi.org/10.1177/0886260518764395

Karami, A., White, C. N., Ford, K., Swan, S., & Spinel, M. Y. (2020). Unwanted advances in higher education: Uncovering sexual harassment experiences in academia with text mining. *Information Processing and Management*, *57*(2), 102167. https://doi.org/10.1016/j.ipm.2019.102167

Kelley, S. M. (2023). Post-sexual assault decision making: Centering Black women's experiences. *Feminist Criminology*, *18*(2), 133–155. https://doi.org/10.1177/15570851221150912

Khan, R. (2021). *Domestic abuse policy guidance for UK universities.* Honour Abuse Research Matrix (HARM). University of Central Lancashire. Retrieved from: https://clok.uclan.ac.uk/id/eprint/37526/1/Domestic%20Abuse%20Policy%20Guidance%20for%20UK%20Universities%202021.pdf

Khan, R., Morris, P., Hall, B., & Alam, A. (2023). *Evaluation of domestic abuse policy guidance for UK universities.* University of Central Lancashire. Retrieved from: https://clok.uclan.ac.uk/id/eprint/48902/1/HARM%20Evaluation%20-%20Domestic%20Abuse%20Policy%20Guidance%20for%20UK%20Universities%20%28Sept%202023%29.pdf

Kirkner, A. C., Lorenz, K., & Mazar, L. (2022). Faculty and staff reporting & disclosure of sexual harassment in higher education. *Gender and Education*, *34*(2), 199–215. https://doi.org/10.1080/09540253.2020.1763923

Klein, L. B., & Martin, S. L. (2021). Sexual harassment of college and university students: A systematic review. *Trauma, Violence, and Abuse*, *22*(4), 777–792. https://doi.org/10.1177/1524838019881731

Lampman, C., Phelps, A., Bancroft, S., & Beneke, M. (2009). Contrapower harassment in academia: A survey of faculty experience with student incivility, bullying, and sexual attention. *Sex Roles*, *60*, 331–346. https://doi.org/10.1007/s11199-008-9560-x

Lawton, G. (28th October, 2017). *#MeToo is here to stay.* The Guardian.

Lyons, M., Brewer, G., Caicedo, J. C., Andrade, M., Morales, M., & Centifanti, L. (2022). Barriers to sexual harassment bystander intervention in Ecuadorian universities. *Global Public Health*, *17*(6), 1029–1040. https://doi.org/10.1080/17441692.2021.1884278

McCall, B. (2019). Taking the battle against sexual harassment in global academia online. *The Lancet*, *393*(10171), 512–514. https://doi.org/10.1016/S0140-6736(19)30314-9

McKay, R., Irwin, B., & Appel, R. (2020). When RateMyProfessor meets the #MeToo movement: Bottom-up bullying in academia. *International Journal of Digital Society*, *11*(2), 1591–1598.

McKinney, K. (1990). Sexual harassment of university faculty by colleagues and students. *Sex Roles*, *23*(7–8), 421–438. https://doi.org/10.1007/BF00289230

Mousa, M., & Abdelgaffar, H. A. A. (2022). Coping with sexual harassment in the Egyptian context: A study on female academics. *Equality, Diversity, and Inclusion*, *41*(6), 907–926. https://doi.org/10.1108/EDI-10-2021-0281

Murray, K. B., & Zdravkovic, S. (2016). Does MTV really do a good job of evaluating professors? An empirical test of the internet site RateMyProfessor.Com. *Journal of Education for Business*, *91*(3), 138–147. https://doi.org/10.1080/08832323.2016.1140115

National Union of Students. (2010). Hidden marks: A study of women students' experiences of harassment, stalking, violence and sexual assault. London. Retrieved from:

https://assets.prod.unioncloud-internal.com/document/documents/60237/aa3daeedd93a84cbc2aabc654f463f40/Hidden_Marks_report.pdf

National Union of Students (2017). *Power in the academy: Staff sexual misconduct in UK Higher Education.* Retrieved from: https://1752group.com/wp-content/uploads/2021/09/4f9f6-nus_staff-student_misconduct_report.pdf

OfS (2024). *Annex A: Condition E6: Harassment and sexual misconduct. General ongoing condition of registration.* Retrieved from: https://www.officeforstudents.org.uk/media/bpfhauth/hsm-condition-and-guidance.pdf

Östergren, P. O., Canivet, C., Andersson, U., & Agardh, A. (2025). What determines the 'culture of silence'? Disclosing and reporting sexual harassment among university employees and students at a large Swedish public university. *PloS One*, *20*(3), e0319407. https://doi.org/10.1371/journal.pone.0319407

Page, T., Sundaram, V., Phipps, A., & Shannon, E. (2019). *Developing an intersectional approach to training on sexual harassment, violence and hate crimes: Guide for training facilitators.* University of York. https://doi.org/10.17863/CAM.40706

Phipps, A., & Young, I. (2013). *That's what she said: women students' experiences of 'lad culture' in higher education.* University of Sussex. Retrieved from: https://hdl.handle.net/10779/uos.23405024.v1

Pilgaard, F., Östergren, P. O., Priebe, G., & Agardh, A. (2025). Workplace sexual harassment is associated with poor mental well-being among employees at a large Swedish university. *Global Health Action*, *18*(1), 2465050. https://doi.org/10.1080/16549716.2025.2465050

Preusser, M. K., Bartels, L. K., & Nordstrom, C. R. (2011). Sexual harassment training: Person versus machine. *Public Personnel Management*, *40*(1), 47–62. https://doi.org/10.1177/009102601104000104

Prothero, A., & Tadajewski, M. (2021). #MeToo and beyond: Inequality and injustice in marketing practice and academia. *Journal of Marketing Management*, *37*(1–2), 1–20. https://doi.org/10.1080/0267257X.2021.1889140

Scott, G., & Martin, B. (2006). Tactics against sexual harassment: The role of backfire. *Journal of International Women's Studies*, *7*(4), 111–125.

Senn, C. Y., & Forrest, A. (2016). "And then one night when I went to class...": The impact of sexual assault bystander intervention workshops incorporated in academic courses. *Psychology of Violence*, *6*(4), 607–618. https://doi.org/10.1037/a0039660

Skewes, L., Skewes, J. C., & Ryan, M. K. (2021). Attitudes to sexism and the #MeToo movement at a Danish University. *Nordic Journal of Feminist and Gender Research*, *29*(2), 124–139. https://doi.org/10.1080/08038740.2021.1884598

Stratton, T. D., McLaughlin, M. A., Witte, F. M., Fosson, S. E., & Nora, L. M. (2005). Does students' exposure to gender discrimination and sexual harassment in Medical School affect specialty choice and residency program selection. *Academic Medicine*, *80*(4), 400–408.

Tinkler, J. E. (2013). How do sexual harassment policies shape gender beliefs? An exploration of the moderating effects of norm adherence and gender. *Social Science Research*, *42*(5), 1269–1283. https://doi.org/10.1016/j.ssresearch.2013.05.002

UUK. (2016a). *Changing the culture: Report of the Universities UK taskforce examining violence against women, harassment and hate crime affecting university students.* Universities UK & Pincent Masons. Retrieved from: https://www.universitiesuk.ac.uk/sites/default/files/field/downloads/2021-07/changing-the-culture.pdf

UUK. (2016b). *Guidance for higher education institutions: How to handle alleged student misconduct which may also constitute a criminal offence.* Universities UK. Retrieved from: https://www.universitiesuk.ac.uk/sites/default/files/field/downloads/2021-07/guidance-for-higher-education-institutions.pdf.

UUK. (2024). *How to handle alleged student misconduct: Case studies. Supplemental note to UUK-Pincent Masons guidance.* Retrieved from: https://www.universitiesuk.ac.uk/sites/default/files/field/downloads/2024-03/alleged-student-misconduct-2024-case-studies.pdf

Vargas, E. A., Brassel, S. T., Cortina, L. M., Settles, I. H., Johnson, T. R. B., & Jagsi, R. (2020). #MedToo: A large-scale examination of the incidence and impact of sexual harassment of physicians and other faculty at an academic medical center. *Journal of Women's Health, 29*(1) 13–20.

Veer, E., Zahrai, K., & Stevens, S. (2021). I stood by: The role of allies in developing an inclusive and supportive academic environment post #MeToo. *Journal of Marketing Management, 37*(1–2), 162–179. https://doi.org/10.1080/0267257X.2020.1772344

Wallace, P. S., Miller, K., Myers, K., Ingram, C., & Civilus, T. (2024). Framed as (un) victims of sexual violence: An intersectional model. *Feminist Criminology, 19*(3), 243–268. https://doi.org/10.1177/15570851241227937

Wear, D., & Aultman, J. (2005). Sexual harassment in academic medicine: Persistence, non-reporting, and institutional response. *Medical Education Online, 10*(1), 4377. https://doi.org/10.3402/meo.v10i.4377

Witte, T. H., Casper, D. M., Hackman, C. L., & Mulla, M. M. (2017). Bystander interventions for sexual assault and dating violence on college campuses: Are we putting bysstanders in harm's way? *Journal of American College Health, 65*(3), 149–157. https://doi.org/10.1080/07448481.2016.1264407

Wood, L., Hoefer, S., Kammer-Kerwick, M., Parra-Cardona, J. R., & Busch-Armendariz, N. (2021). Sexual harassment at institutions of higher education: Prevalence, risk, and extent. *Journal of Interpersonal Violence, 36*(9–10), 4520–4544. https://doi.org/10.1177/0886260518791228

Woods, K. C., Buchanan, N. T., & Settles, I. H. (2009). Sexual harassment across the color line: Experiences and outcomes of cross-versus intraracial sexual harassment among Black women. *Cultural Diversity & Ethnic Minority Psychology, 15*(1), 67.

Woodzicka, J. A., & LaFrance, M. (2005). The effects of subtle sexual harassment on women's performance in a job interview. *Sex Roles, 53*, 67–77. https://doi.org/10.1007/s11199-005-4279-4

Chapter 9

Conclusion and Additional Resources

This book has provided a bleak picture of higher education, highlighting the competition, inequality, and violence that exist across the sector.

There are, however, reasons to be hopeful. Academics typically report that inclusivity is important, both for the academic workplace and for research methodology and practice (see Figure 9.1). Perceived benefits of an inclusive approach include promoting different ways of thinking (90.1%), enriching the quality of research outputs (79.8%), improving the relevance of research to those outside academia (78.2%), and improving the wellbeing and performance of those in academia (78.2%) (Global Inclusivity Report, 2022). The appetite for an equitable and inclusive academy is further evidenced by an increase in equality, diversity, and inclusion research focused on the higher education sector and the range of initiatives and interventions that have been developed (Zhao et al., 2024). Of course, the extent to which initiatives to promote workplace inclusivity are embedded in higher education varies by discipline, institution, and country (Global Inclusivity Report, 2022), as shown in Figure 9.2, and greater sharing of good practice would be beneficial.

Though the volume of equality, diversity, and inclusion work conducted suggests positive change, it is important that work to improve the safety, accessibility, and inclusivity of higher education institutions is meaningful rather than tokenistic. Indeed, employees are more responsive to equality, diversity, and inclusion organisational cues that are evidence-based (e.g., with data demonstrating improved diversity) rather than values-based (e.g., a mission statement) (De Cock, Celik, & Toma, 2025). It is also important that equality, diversity, and inclusion policy and practice are authentic (Pizarro Milian & Wijesingha, 2023) and extend beyond superficial issues to address more foundational social justice subjects (Bea & Recio-Saucedo, 2025). In essence, it is the equity of access and experience rather than equal representation alone that is important.

It is essential that employees are provided with the time necessary to conduct this work and receive appropriate recognition for it. All too often, employees conduct equality, diversity, and inclusion work on a voluntary basis, and such work does not contribute to (or is perceived to be detrimental to) career

DOI: 10.4324/9781032639321-10

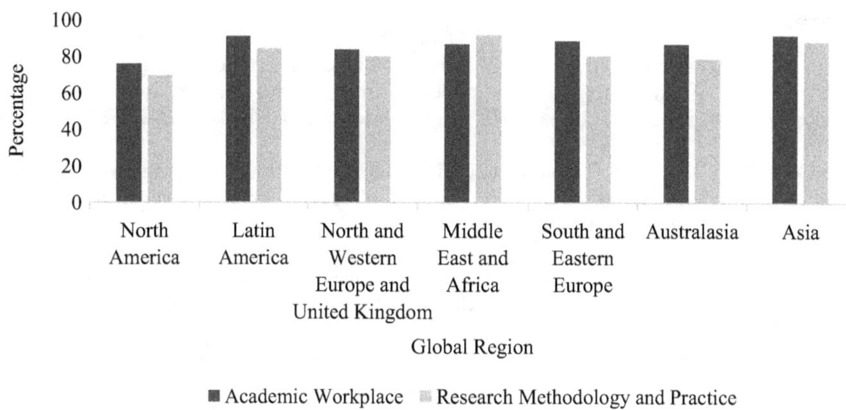

Figure 9.1 Percentage of academics in each global region rating inclusivity as important (i.e., those scoring 8–10 on a 10-point scale). Data from the Global Inclusivity Report (2022).

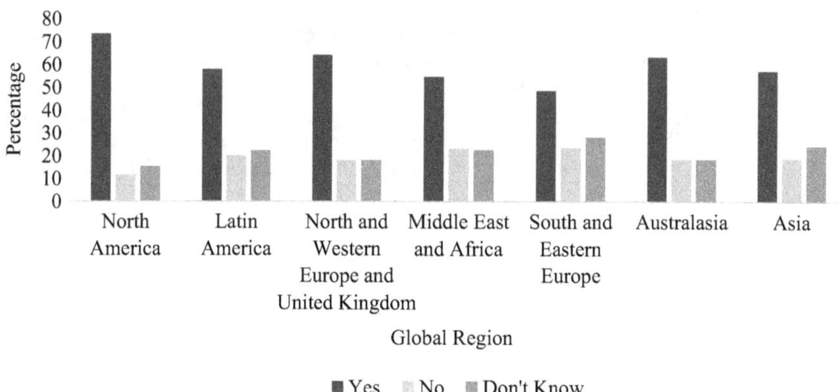

Figure 9.2 Percentage of academics in each global region reporting inclusivity initiatives taking place in their workplace. Data from the Global Inclusivity Report (2022).

progression. It is also important to recognise that activism can be challenging and exhausting (Eckert & Broadhurst, 2025) and supportive spaces, especially for those from marginalised groups, are essential (Margherio et al., 2025). Such spaces should provide both social and practical support, creating opportunities for shared resources and activism. Senior leaders have an important role and must communicate the value of equality, diversity, and inclusion work for the individual institution and broader sector, with employees often more supportive of diversity initiatives when considering the "bigger picture" than the specific organisation (Toma, Carter, & Phillips, 2025). Their commitment to such work (both verbally and in action) is essential to counter the dominant competition-based narratives that negatively impact employee wellbeing.

References

Bea, L., & Recio-Saucedo, A. (2025). EDI in academic policy engagement: Lived experience of university based knowledge brokers and marginalised academics. *Evidence & Policy*, *21*(1), 46–70. https://doi.org/10.1332/17442648Y2024D000000030

De Cock, V., Celik, P., & Toma, C. (2025). The proof is in the pudding: Workers care about evidence-based diversity cues. *Journal of Applied Social Psychology*, *55*, 52–70. https://doi.org/10.1111/jasp.13076

Eckert, E., & Broadhurst, C. (2025). "We were just so shattered": Identity and the emotional impact of supporting student activism. *Journal of Diversity in Higher Education*, *18*(1), S1–S11. https://doi.org/10.1037/dhe0000535

Global Inclusivity Report (2022). Emerald Publishing. Retrieved from: https://www.emeraldgrouppublishing.com/global-inclusivity-report-2022-download-report

Margherio, C., Swan, A. L., Horner-Devine, M. C., Mizumori, S. J. Y., & Yen, J. W. (2025). Counterspaces as a site of network formation within academia. *Journal of Diversity in Higher Education*, *18*(1), 89–99. https://doi.org/10.1037/dhe0000549

Pizarro Milian, R., & Wijesingha, R. (2023). Why do EDI policies fail? An inhabited institutions perspective. *Equality, Diversity and Inclusion*, *42*(3), 449–464. https://doi.org/10.1108/EDI-02-2022-0048

Toma, C., Carter, A. B., & Phillips, K. W. (2025). Diversity? Great for most just less so for me: How cognitive abstraction affects diversity attitudes and choices. *Behavioral Sciences*, *15*(5), 585. https://doi.org/10.3390/bs15050585

Zhao, X., Wider, W., Jiang, L., Fauzi, M. A., Tanucan, J. C. M., Lin, J., & Udang, L. N. (2024). Transforming higher education institutions through EDI leadership: A bibliometric exploration. *Heliyon*, *10*(4). https://doi.org/10.1016/j.heliyon.2024.e26241

Additional Resources

Numerous books have been published focusing on the academic environment and the impact of this on higher education employees. Increasingly, academic journals also recognise the importance of this issue (e.g., *Journal of Diversity in Higher Education*). Below, books relating to each book section are listed to support those pursuing work in this area.

The Academic Role and Environment

Addison, M., Breeze, M., & Taylor, Y. (2022). *The Palgrave handbook of imposter syndrome in higher education*. Palgrave Macmillan.

Ahmed, S. (2021). *Complaint!* Duke University Press.

Ayres, Z. J. (2022). *Managing your mental health during your PhD: A survival guide*. Springer.

Badiozaman, I. F. A., Ling, V. M., & Sandhu, K. D. (2023). *Women practicing resilience, self-care and wellbeing in academia: International stories from lived experience*. Routledge.

Boynton, P. (2020). *Being well in academia: Ways to feel stronger, safer and more connected*. Routledge.

Dobele, A. R., & Farrell, L. (2024). *Supporting and promoting wellbeing in the higher education sector: Practices in action*. Routledge.

Giroux, H. A. (2014). *Neoliberalism's war on higher education.* Haymarket Books.
Giroux, H. A. (2016). *The university in chains: Confronting the military-industrial-academic complex.* Routledge.
Gonzalez, S. (2010). *Burnout in academia: The impact of academic workload on burnout levels and the need for sustainable workloads.* VDM Verlag.
Smyth, J. (2017). *The toxic university: Zombie leadership, academic rock stars, and neoliberal ideology.* Palgrave Macmillan.

Representation and Inequality

Ahmed, S. (2012). *On being included: Racism and diversity in institutional life.* Duke University Press.
Bhambra, G. K., Gebrial, D., & Nişancıoğlu, K. (2018). *Decolonising the university.* Pluto Press.
Brewer, G. (2022). *Disability in higher education: Investigating identity, stigma and disclosure amongst academics.* Open University Press.
Brown, N. (2021). *Lived experiences of ableism in academia: Strategies for inclusion in higher education.* Policy Press.
Brown, N., & Leigh, J. (2020). *Ableism in academia: Theorising experiences of disabilities and chronic illnesses in higher education.* UCL Press.
Crew, T. (2020). *Higher education and working-class academics: Precarity and diversity in academia.* Palgrave Macmillan.
Khadka, S., Davis-McElligatt, J., & Dorwick, K. (2019). *Narratives of marginalized identities in higher education: Inside and outside the academy.* Routledge.
Mintz, B., & Rothblum, E. D. (1997). *Lesbians in academia: Degrees of freedom.* Routledge.
Mosley, P., & Hargrove, S. K. (2014). *Navigating academia: A guide for women and minority STEM faculty.* Academic Press.
Stewart, A. J., & Valian, V. (2022). *An inclusive academy: Achieving diversity and excellence.* MIT Press.
Taylor, Y., Brim, M., & Mahn, C. (2023). *Queer precarities in and out of higher education: Challenging institutional structures.* Bloomsbury Academic.
Thomson, A., & Gooberman-Hill, R. (2024). *Nurturing equality, diversity and inclusion: Support for research careers in health and biomedicine.* Policy Press.
Thwaites, R., & Pressland, A. (2017). *Being an early career feminist academic: Global perspectives, experiences, and challenges.* Palgrave.

Violence and Aggression

Chalmers, C. (2022). *They don't want her there: Fighting sexual and racial harassment in the American University.* University of Iowa Press.
Gray-Rosendale, L. A. (2020). *Me too, feminist theory, and surviving sexual violence in the academy.* Lexington Books.
Hollis, L. P. (2021). *Human resource perspectives on workplace bullying in higher education: Understanding vulnerable employees' experiences.* Routledge.
Humphreys, C. J., & Towl, G. J. (2023). *Stopping gender-based violence in higher education: Policy, practice, and partnerships.* Routledge.
Johnson, P. A., Widnall, S. E., & Benya, F. F. (2018). *Sexual harassment of women: Climate, culture, and consequences in academic sciences, engineering, and medicine.* The National Academies Press.
Lester, J. (2013). *Workplace bullying in Higher Education.* Routledge.

Patel, F. (2021). *Power imbalance, bullying and harassment in academia and the glocal (local and global) workplace*. Nova Science.
Pritchard, E., & Edwards, D. (2023). *Sexual misconduct in academia: Informing an ethics of care in the University*. Routledge.
Twale, D. J. (2018). *Understanding and preventing faculty-on-faculty bullying: A psycho-social-organizational approach*. Routledge.
Twale, D. J., & De Luca, B. M. (2008). *Faculty incivility: The rise of the academic bully culture and what to do about it*. Jossey-Bass.

Index

Pages in **bold**/*italics* refer to boxes.

www.ingramcontent.com/pod-product-compliance
Lightning Source LLC
LaVergne TN
LVHW010903110826
845149LV00005B/1453

* 9 7 8 1 0 3 2 6 3 9 3 0 7 *